Global Civil Society and Transversal Hegemony

There has been clear recognition of tendencies towards uncritically celebrating resistance and the need for critical appraisal within the literature on globalization and contestation.

This book provides a conceptual history of global civil society and a critical examination of the global political economy of resistance. Using a dialectical method of analysis, the book illustrates the conceptual stasis of mainstream approaches to questions of globalization and contestation, while demonstrating the potential of a Gramscian approach to reconstitute civil society and hegemony as key analytical and explanatory tools. The author offers insight to the movements of transversal hegemony and existent and anticipated modes of social relation through the case studies of the World Social Forum and the World People's Conference on Climate Change.

Offering a more comprehensive understanding of change in the global political economy, *Global Civil Society and Transversal Hegemony* will be of interest to students and scholars of international political economy, international politics, globalization, global civil society, sociology and social movements.

Karen M. Buckley is a lecturer in International Politics at the University of Manchester, UK.

Rethinking Globalizations

Edited by Barry K. Gills, *University of Newcastle, UK*

This series is designed to break new ground in the literature on globalization and its academic and popular understanding. Rather than perpetuating or simply reacting to the economic understanding of globalization, this series seeks to capture the term and broaden its meaning to encompass a wide range of issues and disciplines and convey a sense of alternative possibilities for the future.

Global Civil Society and Transversal Hegemony

The globalization-contestation nexus

Karen M. Buckley

Routledge
Taylor & Francis Group

LONDON AND NEW YORK

First published 2013
by Routledge
2 Park Square, Milton Park, Abingdon, Oxfordshire OX14 4RN

Simultaneously published in the USA and Canada
by Routledge
711 Third Avenue, New York, NY 10017

First issued in paperback 2014

Routledge is an imprint of the Taylor and Francis Group, an informa business

British Library Cataloguing in Publication Data
A catalogue record for this book is available from the British Library

Library of Congress Cataloging in Publication Data
Buckley, Karen M.
  Global civil society and transversal hegemony : the globalization-contestation nexus / Karen M. Buckley.
    p. cm. – (Rethinking globalizations)
  Summary: 'There has been clear recognition of tendencies towards uncritically celebrating resistance and the need for critical appraisal within the literature on globalization and contestation'– Provided by publisher.
  Includes bibliographical references and index.
  1. Anti-globalization movement. 2. Globalization–Social aspects. 3. Civil society. 4. Protest movements. I. Title.
  JZ1318.B785 2013
  303.48'2–dc23
                    2012047349

ISBN 978-0-415-69862-7 (hbk)
ISBN 978-1-138-90940-3 (pbk)
ISBN 978-0-203-62658-0 (ebk)

Typeset in Times New Roman
by Taylor & Francis Books

To Xavi

Contents

Acknowledgements

First, thanks to Owen Worth and the department of politics and public administration at the University of Limerick for providing an intellectual home for the supervision, initial funding, and development of my PhD. Thanks to Owen for inspiring my initial interest in Gramsci and for his insight and advice along the way. Many thanks to UL faculty and co-researchers who made my time at the university so worthwhile; to the many contributors to staff–student seminars, to those who offered comments and advice particularly Lucian Ashworth, Neil Robinson and Alex Warleigh; and to the many students in the University of Limerick and Trinity College Dublin for being a constant source of encouragement. The financial doctoral support from the Irish Research Council for the Humanities and Social Sciences and John and Pauline Ryan bursary allowed much of this research to take place.

The University of Manchester provided a lively and intellectually stimulating environment to work on completion of this book. This was enhanced by the many faculty and students in Politics who have been welcoming, friendly and, particularly my mentor, Maja Zehfuss, on hand with advice. Contributors to the Gramsci reading group and GPE research cluster have been especially helpful and I would particularly like to thank Phil Cerny, Inderjeet Parmar, Kevin Morgan, anonymous reviewers, and contributors at the various venues where I have presented research papers for their comments on my work.

In particular, a sincere thank you to the Routledge 'Rethinking Globalization' series editor Barry Gills for his support in helping this book reach completion and for his invaluable advice. Thank you to Hannah Shakespeare, Heidi Bagtazo, Alexander Quayle, Dominic Corti and others at Routledge for their further support in seeing the book through to publication. Anonymous reviewers gave invaluable comments to which I hope I have given justice.

Lastly, this book would not have been written but for Xavi, my parents, family and friends, who have each given me tremendous support and encouragement along the way. I am indebted to each of you; thank you.

Abbreviations

AACC	All Africa Council of Churches
ABONG	Brazilian Association of Non-governmental Organizations
AFL/CIO	American Federation of Labor and Congress of Industrial Organizations
AFM	Articulación Feminista Marcosur
AIDOH	Art in Defence of Humanism
ALBA	Alianza Bolivariana para los Pueblos de Nuestra América/ Bolivarian Alliance for the Peoples of the Americas
ASM	Assembly of Social Movements
ATTAC	Association pour la Taxation des Transactions Financière pour l'Aide aux Citoyens
AWG-LCA	Ad hoc Working Group on Long-term Cooperative Action
CACIM	India Institute for Critical Action: Centre in Movement
CADTM	Committee for the Abolition of Third World Debt
CBJP	Brazilian Justice and Peace Commission
CBO	Community-Based Organization
CCFD	Comité Catholique Contre la Faim et Pour le Développement/ Catholic Committee against Hunger and for Development
CCS	Centre for Civil Society (Durban)
CETRI	Centre Tricontinental
CFSC	Civil Society Facilitating Committee
CIPE	Critical International Political Economy
CIVES	Brazilian Association of Entrepreneurs for Citizenship
CJA	Climate Justice Action
CONGO	Co-ordinating bodies of Non-Governmental Organizations
CONSEU	Conferencia de Naciones sin Estado de Europa
CUT	Central Única dos Trabalhadores/United Workers Confederation
DAWN	Development Alternatives with Women for a New Era
DONGO	Donor-Organized Non-Governmental Organization
EAOC	Eastern Africa Organizing Committee
ECOSOC	Economic and Social Council (UN)
EED	German Church Development Service

EESC	European Economic and Social Committee
ENDA	Environmental Development Action in the Third World
ESF	European Social Forum
ESM	Environmental Social Movement
EU	European Union
EZLN	Zapatista Army of National Liberation
G8	Group of Eight
GATS	General Agreement on Trade in Services
GCS	Global Civil Society
GDA	Global Day of Action
GDP	Gross Domestic Product
GJ(S)M	Global Justice (and Solidarity) Movement
GNP	Gross National Product
GPE	Global Political Economy
GRAP	Group for Reflection and Support for the WSF Process
GSM	Global Social Movements
IBASE	Brazilian Institute of Social and Economic Analysis
IC	International Council (of the WSF)
ICCO	Inter-Church Organisation for Development Cooperation
ICFTU	International Confederation of Free Trade Unions
IMF	International Monetary Fund
ILO	International Labour Organization
IPE	International Political Economy
IPS	Inter-Press Service
IR	International Relations
IS	International Situationniste
LGBT	Lesbian, gay, bisexual and transgender
MAI	Multilateral Agreement on Investment
MAS	Movimiento al Socialismo/Movement Toward Socialism
MEI	Multilateral Economic Institution
MST	Movimento dos Sem Terra/Landless Rural Workers Movement (Brazil)
NAFTA	North American Free Trade Association
NGO	non-governmental organization
NIGD	Network Institute for Global Democratization
NIPE	New International Political Economy
NOVIB	Netherlands Organization for International Assistance (Oxfam NOVIB)
OC	Organizing Committee (of the WSF)
OECD	Organisation for Economic Co-operation and Development
PT	Partido dos Trabalhadores/Brazilian Workers Party
REDD	Reducing Emissions from Deforestation and forest Degradation
REMTE	Red Latinoamericana de Mujeres Transformando la Economía/Latin American Network of Women Changing the Economy
SODNET	Social Development Network

TIPNIS	Isiboro-Sécure Indigenous Territory and National Park
UN	United Nations
UNASUR	Unión de Naciones Sudamericanas/Union of South American Nations
UNCED	United Nations Conference on Environment and Development
UNCSD	United Nations Conference on Sustainable Development
UNFCCC	United Nations Framework Convention on Climate Change
UNRISD	United Nations Research Institute for Social Development
US	United States
USSF	United States Social Forum
WEF	World Economic Forum
WMW	World March of Women
WPCCC	World People's Conference on Climate Change and the Rights of Mother Earth
WSSD	World Summit on Sustainable Development
WSF	World Social Forum
WTO	World Trade Organization

1 Introduction: globalization and contestation

For just over a decade, the World Social Forum (WSF) has functioned as a focal meeting point for movements, groups and individuals to discuss and develop alternatives to neoliberal globalization. Partly emergent from the optimism and strength of anti-globalization demonstrations and social movement formations of the late 1990s, early assessments centred on the 'globalization of solidarity' and the World Social Forum as a concrete expression of 'counter-hegemonic globalization' headed by an 'emancipatory global civil society' (Santos 2006a: 42–43). This was carried forward by the momentum of its annual event and support by organizers and participants. During the early years, there was a consistent increase in attendance at annual gatherings such as Mumbai, India in 2004 and Porto Alegre, Brazil in 2005. The annual forum was extended to Nairobi, Kenya in 2007, Dakar, Senegal in 2011, and Tunis, Tunisia in 2013.[1] The momentum of the World Social Forum has been reinforced by descriptions of it as a novel 'open space' (Whitaker 2004) or 'new Bandung' (Hardt 2002) in which the disparate groups that make up an 'emancipatory' global civil society are able to converge and synthesize their common points of opposition to neoliberal globalization and work towards the creation of another possible world (Worth and Buckley 2009).

However, expressions of global civil society in relation to global contestation and global governance more broadly tend uncritically to celebrate resistance rather than engage in critical conceptualization to understand more fully the position of global civil society on the terrain of the global political economy. This takes places alongside recognition of the conceptual shortcomings of global civil society. It is described as 'to a large extent an analytical mirage' that lacks sufficient accuracy in providing clear accounts of changing forms of globalization and contestation (Cerny 2006: 97). It is also argued that global civil society retains illusory and phantasmal qualities that 'may actually stunt rather than stimulate political thinking about what might be born in the world economy' (Drainville 2004: 6). Indeed, global civil society has been considered 'an analytical and political milestone around postmarxist necks'— for its analysis of globalization, reification of boundaries and spheres, and failure to deal with the political implications of the differences between global movements (Eschle 2001: 62).

There is much evident interest in global civil society and a corresponding proliferation of literature, theories and empirical accounts on contesting globalization and global governance. Within critical and Gramscian frameworks, there has been a recent shift in attention towards resistance and counter-hegemony in the global political economy (Marchand 2005: 216; Marchand 2003: 147). Additionally, a number of key discussions and frameworks to conceptualize the 'politics of resistance' assess interrelations between neoliberal economic globalization and social forces (Gills 2000). However, when drawing on global civil society in particular, accounts on contesting globalization and global governance converge towards similar delimited understandings of processes of change and contestation. Considerable scope remains for the further development and articulation of modes of social relation engaged in by global civil society in and towards the global political economy (cf. Drainville 2004, 2012). In this book, I draw explicit attention to the potential insights and new ways of seeing and understanding that Gramscian civil society and hegemony offer. Global civil society and transversal hegemony are used throughout as key analytical and explanatory tools towards understanding change in the global political economy.

The global political economy of resistance

The relatively recent disciplinary call for a 'new International Political Economy' (NIPE) and subsequent periodic reminders seeking to retain its continued relevance (Murphy and Tooze 1991; Gills 2001; Shields *et al.* 2011), in addition to emerging areas such as critical globalization studies (Mittelman 2005), are considered in this book to provide an initial point of theoretical clarity in their potential applications to the global political economy of resistance. Intending to offer more adequate explanations of the changing global political economy, the call for a NIPE, for example, proposes to:

- Move beyond a narrow view of the most important questions in the field;
- Update and broaden our view of scholarly 'rigor'; and
- Integrate developments in the philosophy of social science (Murphy and Tooze 1991).

A broad range of 'world order' approaches drawing on Cox (1981, 1983, 1987), in particular, reinforce many of these proposals. Among them, a volume on theoretical innovation and historical transformations in international studies, edited by Gill and Mittelman (1997), seeks to extend the world order approach to focus on the changing contours of world order, the remaking of global theory, globalization and structural change, and social movements. This is followed by a forum in *New Political Economy* on re-orienting the new (International) Political Economy (Gills 2001). This piece takes stock of the potential of a new political economy that is simultaneously rooted in the traditions of political economy and in its capacity to engage in holistic multidisciplinary knowledge construction on the important issues affecting the world political economy. More recently, in a volume on 'Critical International Political Economy' (CIPE), Shields *et al.* (2011) issue similar reminders to critical scholars to engage in intellectual candour and scholarly innovation, rather than assume critical attributes to be self-evident in their own work. Adopting a tripartite structure, this volume emphasizes critical dialogue to encourage conceptual reflexivity and an enriched understanding of the world, critical debate to unsettle unwarranted silences, and critical dissensus to assert a transformed means of understanding the world in which we live.

While the path towards a critical global political economy of resistance can be traced back through periodic reminders, the works mentioned here are not exclusive to this trajectory but are in themselves indicative of the objective of critical thinking to encourage reflexivity and the translation of reflexivity into concrete analysis. The reminder, then, that critical attributes can be portrayed as increasingly self-evident in critical work, is taken seriously in this book and extended to my concern with global civil society and the global political economy of resistance. The political economy concerns with which I engage are located close to those of the politics of resistance. An edited collection on *Globalization and the Politics of Resistance* (Gills 2000), initially published as a special issue of *New Political Economy* at the same time as Gill and Mittelman's intervention, sought to intervene in the debate on globalization and alter its intellectual and political direction. In particular, the politics of resistance picked up on an essential critique of Cox's 'patient' support for a new polity to emerge from the gradual, almost passive, elongation of a war of position (cf. Drainville 1994). The politics of resistance, in contrast, would 'reclaim the terrain of the political' and 'make concrete strategies and concepts of "resistance" central' to analyses of globalization (Gills 2000). The rationale for this approach retains contemporary relevance; sustained market and financial volatility, for example, continues to push people to find more innovative ways to safeguard their futures, to which emerging social movements, alter-globalization movements, movements for social justice—Occupy Wall Street, the Spanish *Indignados* and Arab uprisings, amongst many others—attest (cf. Boyer and Drache 1996, cited in Gills 2000). From a disciplinary perspective the continued technical and definitional emphasis of argumentation also reaffirms the meaning of the politics of resistance in the current context. Furthermore, the integration of resistance into the study on *Power and Resistance in the New World Order* (Gill 2008) underlines the need for a more critical approach to resistance. Paying more attention to these reminders in the contemporary context builds on the aims of earlier research to generate:

> a perspective which needs to be understood as *a part of* the historical process, that is, its form of engagement involves human knowledge, consciousness and action in the *making* of history and shaping our collective futures.
>
> (Gill 1993: 17)

The politics of resistance, nonetheless, continues to jostle for a place in International Political Economy and the contemporary context of globalization and contestation places particular demands on critical political economy perspectives to pay more attention to accumulated periodic reminders.

The components of 'critical globalization studies' (Mittelman 2005; Appelbaum and Robinson 2005)[2] potentially contribute to a critical framework from which globalization and contestation can be analysed and strengthened conceptualizations of civil society and hegemony applied. The first component of critical globalization studies centres on reflexivity and emphasizes the relationship between knowledge and material and political conditions. Reflexivity, like critical theory (Cox 1986), investigates the historical background of theories and perspectives and the nature of interests underpinning them. It highlights the post-positivist challenge to distinguish between facts and values and is applied, for example, to textual analysis on studies considering the position of civil society in contesting global governance in this book. Further to this, critical globalization studies introduces a temporal dimension and builds on reflexivity through proposing 'rigorous historical thinking' (Mittelman 2005: 24). Globalization, therefore, is not inevitable but is open-ended and encompasses its own social relations (see also Thompson 1963). In this book the inevitable nature of globalization and contestation is critiqued and focus is placed on various modes of social relation in the global political economy. 'Historicism', meanwhile, connects with advice to put in place an open-ended and multi-directional form of research which critically considers the meaning and history of ideas (cf. Germain and Kenny 1998). Decentring, in addition, points to the significance of a variety of perspectives on globalization that emerge not just from the centre but also from the margins. There are challenges associated with decentring hegemonic perspectives on globalization, even within more 'marginal' forums in the global political economy such as the World Social Forum and World People's Conference on Climate Change and the Rights of Mother Earth (WPCCC), held in Cochabamba, Bolivia, in 2010. Additionally, what many consider to be marginal civil society in Southern Africa is particularly demonstrative of the patterns of inclusion and exclusion, internal paradoxes and conflicts within civil society (cf. Söderbaum 2007), and also has a bearing on conceptualizations of global civil society.

A further component of critical globalization studies emphasizes the importance of crossovers 'between the social sciences and complementary branches of knowledge' (Mittelman 2005: 25). A combination of many research avenues that may bridge, for example, medical, social, cultural, economic and political research, contributes to holistic understandings. Interdisciplinary learning is a vital aspect of research on globalization and contestation as it embraces wide cross-fertilization and processes of knowledge construction. While interdisciplinary learning or multidisciplinarity may complicate the character and content of a given discipline, and presents considerable difficulties in terms of intellectual control, rigour and focus (Gills 2001: 236), it nonetheless offers more potential to address global, more complex, themes (Schuurman 2009: 832). Internal crossovers or intra-perspective analyses are particularly emphasized towards the end of this book. The advantage of intra-perspective analysis is to encourage a comprehensive evolution of Gramscian approaches from critique of other International Relations (IR) and Global Political Economy (GPE) approaches to constructive engagement with them. Lastly, critical globalization studies also offers a productive focus on strategic transformations: 'Strategic transformations are about establishing counter-hegemony: how to engage hegemonic power, upend it, and offer an emancipatory vision' (Mittelman 2005: 25). This component, while significant, is most neglected in studies on contestation. Gramscian studies, for example, can do much more to deepen their analyses of hegemony and counter-hegemony, more concretely locate civil society within hegemony, and consider modes of relation in the global political economy.

There is a clear rationale then for articulating the following study on contestation alongside the theoretical precepts of calls for an NIPE, CIPE and critical globalization studies. These calls point acutely to the evolving and contested nature of conceptualizing power and resistance in the global political economy. Taking them seriously intimates that contestation is placed on broad theoretical foundations which are open to crossovers from a range of perspectives. Notably, there has been a recent shift in attention towards resistance in the global political economy, albeit alongside more extensive interdisciplinary interest in global civil society, social movements and activism. Less evident, however, in studies on global contestation is 'an empathic understanding of societal phenomena' and recognition of 'the historical dimension of human behaviour and the subjective aspects of the human experience' (Frankfort-Nachmias and Nachmias 1996: 280). The approach that is extended in this book remains attentive to the continuing analytical and methodological contributions of Thompson (1963, 1978), in addition to the more recent innovations by Drainville (2004, 2012) towards understanding and explaining the 'making' and 'unmaking' of transnational subjects with the explicit aim of uncovering more radical possibilities (ibid.). There is some sense, then, that resistance to neoliberal economic globalization is indeed a 'central theme of praxis' in the contemporary time (cf. Gills 2000). However, much more remains to be done to achieve a global political economy of resistance that takes conceptual innovation seriously and considers new ways of seeing, doing and understanding. In particular, the global political economy of resistance can be more carefully developed through close attention to the contributions of Gramsci (1971).

Gramscian civil society and hegemony

Through this book, I aim to contribute to the analysis of globalization and contestation from a Gramscian critical perspective with global civil society and hegemony as key conceptual tools.[3] This draws on Gramsci's legacy as 'a series of powerful analytical tools through which social orders and social transformations may be understood' (Wyn Jones 2001: 6). However, this legacy as told through analytical tools such as hegemony, historical blocs and common sense and applied to social orders and social transformations, is essentially contested and requires further development if civil society and hegemony are to contribute meaningfully to further understanding on the nexus between globalization and contestation. The Gramscian conceptualization of *global* civil society that I put forward redraws attention to the 'dialectics of concept and reality', which has been largely overlooked in more mechanical reappraisals of the dual nature of civil society to stabilize and contest hegemonic power (cf. Cox 1999). Re-attending to this notion of the dialectics between concept and reality is an attempt to initiate a dialogue between on the one hand, conceptual formulations or processes of knowledge construction and constitution, and on the other hand, the material location of tangible activities carried out in their name on the terrain of the global political economy. Interrogating the dialectical interaction between conceptualizations of global civil society and its material realities has the potential to uncover strategies through which primarily rational and instrumental analytical instruments are disrupted to emphasize, instead, processes of engagement between human knowledge, consciousness and action (Gill 1993) and the possibilities for human struggles in the global political economy. Global civil society is therefore considered as a philosophy of praxis; reaching the equation between or equality of philosophy and politics, thought and action (Gramsci 1971: 356–57).

Many representations of global civil society, as examined in Chapters 2 and 3, have been developed within the normative sphere of the ideal in the form of a Polanyian counter-movement or Habermasian public sphere. Meanwhile, many critiques derive from apparently separate epistemological orientations which, for example, when starting from an empirical prioritization, establish an uneasy correspondence to normative delineations. Dialectics, in this case, initiate and facilitate a dialogue between contending views. From this, it might be shown that it is not a stretch of the imagination concretely to locate global civil society in thought and action. It is, nonetheless, challenging for a philosophy of praxis to establish its location in the global political economy. From this point of view it is not the World Social Forum or global governance that is the primary point of focus—it is not one or the other that makes an alternative global civil society or global governance possible—but global civil society in thought and action that is the focus of this book. This re-orientates the point of focus to historical subjects of contestation and their modes of social relation in and towards the global political economy.

A Gramscian conceptualization of global civil society, in turn, has much to offer towards achieving greater conceptual clarity on hegemony. A focus on 'transversal hegemony', enabled through global civil society and developed more fully in Chapter 7, is suggestive of further possibilities which have not generally been achieved in accounts of 'counter-hegemonic resistance'. This reflects the view that 'the really hard work on counter-hegemonic theorization remains to be done' (Peet 2007: 194). Highlighting the transversal nature of hegemony challenges the spatial and temporal assumptions of orthodox theory (Walker 1993) and coheres with the following extract:

> If we are to gain an adequate understanding of contemporary dissent, and of global life in general, we must look beyond the lines that have been arbitrarily drawn into the sand of international politics. We must think past the current framing of the level of analysis problem. It is the steady breeze, the gusty bursts of energy, the transversal forms of agency, that are gradually transforming the lines and shapes of contemporary life. Expressed in more prosaic words, a multitude of actors, actions, spheres and issues must be recognised and discussed as legitimate parts of international relations debates.
>
> (Bleiker 2000: 7)

Bleiker uses Gramsci's concept of hegemony in fusion with Foucault (in an attempt to counter pessimistic readings of the latter) to examine the transformation of values that led to the collapse of the Berlin Wall (Bleiker 2000: 173–84). In this way, he explains social change through discursive understandings of power and practices of transversal dissent, whereby discourse is defined as 'frameworks of knowledge and power through which we comprehend (and constitute) the world around us' (ibid.: 11). 'Transversal' is also used to denote theoretical separation from transnational, international or national 'sovereign-centred' understandings of struggles in world politics.[4] A transversal understanding of hegemony moves from studies based on the concrete opposition of hegemony and counter-hegemony and draws attention to processes involved in its construction, maintenance and extension, and thus to inherent interactions, negotiations and interstices. This is applied particularly in Chapter 7 through attention to the interaction between structural and post-structural approaches in order to reach a conceptualization of both hegemony and civil society which elucidates processes of continuity and change in the global political economy.

This discussion has broad consequences for developing a critical Global Political Economy perspective on globalization and contestation. Much Gramscian work focuses on the hegemonic project of neoliberal globalization as it is conveyed, extended, maintained and intensified by an amalgam of social forces. Essentially, this entails an intensification of commodification or the shaping of social relations by the new right, elites and emerging middle classes in the Third World as labour and nature are turned into exchangeable commodities (Gill 2003: 125). There is, however, a tendency on the part of activists and academics alike to equate globalization with neoliberal economic developments in a way that reduces *both* globalization and contestation to singular but contrasting economic and social logics. More recently, the association of globalization with a singular logic has been rejected by some critical commentators and there has been increased recognition of globalization in its

multiple forms. Mittelman (1996), for example, while viewing economic liberalism as implicit in globalization, suggests two competing models of globalization:
neoliberal globalization and democratic globalization with the latter, a 'far
less coherent counterforce' connected to the emergence of global civil society.
It has elsewhere been suggested that we may be witnessing the emergence of
'social neoliberalism' which combines the embedded liberal consensus with 'a
political imperative to reinvent the social dimensions of politics in a complex,
multi-level world' (Cerny 2004). The World Social Forum is identified as one
such social dimension through its efforts to shift the focus from anti-globalization
to alternative approaches to globalization. These examples of 'democratic
globalization' and 'social neoliberalism' are suggestive of a more varied
range of interpretations of globalization. Further insight into the plurality of
globalizations, moving from binary presentations, is to be found in allusions
to the 'clash of globalizations' between disciplinary neoliberalism and the
post-modern prince, even as the present conjuncture calls for further development
of the latter (Gill 2002a). Further insight into the 'clash of globalizations' is
expressed through the historically open and undetermined Empire and Cosmopolis in a collision that is 'certainly occurring, and the historical tension
between these forms, which express radically different visions of humanity
and global governance, is intensifying moment by moment' (Gills 2005: 7).

A dialectical Gramscian reading of the pluralities of globalization and
contestation is predominantly used in this book. 'Contesting globalization', a
phrase which I frequently use, encompasses the broad terms of globalization
and contestation and applies a dialectical mode of analysis towards understanding continuity, change and transformation. This mode of analysis is not
based on linear progression, evolutionary stages, or cyclical, law-like patterns
(Gills 2003: 89). Rather, a critical historical method understands change and
continuity in a '*dialectical* manner, where forms and principles of regulation
exist in a high state of historical tension' (ibid.). Gramscian approaches
('Open Marxism') have been taken to task for failing to acknowledge historical
tensions, exaggerating the coherence of neoliberalism, and offering little analysis
on modes of contestation (Drainville 1994). Neoliberalism, thus understood,
represents an instance of Althusserian over-determination in neglecting to
show the possibilities inherent in its negotiated, hesitant, partial and contradictory
composition (ibid.). I refer to the globalization-contestation nexus to initiate
conceptual dialogue while also examining meeting points of convergence and
divergence within global social relations. These are explained further through
the case of the World Social Forum.[5]

The politics of knowledge construction

The critical globalization studies proposal to 'generate new common sense'
and 'produce alternative knowledge and powerful counterrepresentations'
(Mittelman 2004: 98) is applied in this book through critical literature evaluation, historicism and a focus on the role of perceptions, experience and

observation (cf. Frankfort-Nachmias and Nachmias 1996: 6). Thus, critical literature evaluation and historical, observational and participatory methods are utilized in this book to scrutinize how: language and concepts such as global civil society and hegemony are used to frame processes within studies of contestation to globalization; knowledge is constructed through academic processes; and how both knowledge/concept and context condition possibilities of thought and action. Each of these areas of scrutiny is relevant in re-conceptualizing global civil society. These core concerns are integrated into a dialectical framework of analysis, further discussed in Chapter 2, which highlights the interaction between the concept of global civil society and its explicit realities.

Corresponding objectives in this book flow from a specific conceptual concern with global civil society to a wider, and to a large degree overlapping, concern with developing clearer forms of analysis with which to conceptualize the global political economy of resistance. I am initially concerned with the conceptual neglect of Gramscian civil society in studies of contestation to neo-liberal globalization and global governance and the contemporary relevance of a reformulated conceptualization. This requires, first, consideration of the significance of the conceptual history of civil society and the impact of its accumulated and contested meanings. Varying representations of civil society are considered in this book from activist to governance representations (Hall and Trentmann 2005; Kaviraj and Khilnani 2001; Keane 2003; Putnam 2000; Scholte 2007b; Skidmore 2001; Wagner 2006). In addition, the emergent (Anheier *et al.* 2001; Colás 2002; Cox 1999; Falk 1998; Lipschutz 1992, 2008; Taylor 2004) and provoking (Amoore and Langley 2004; Baker 2002a; Baker and Chandler 2005; Bartelson 2006; Chandler 2004a, 2004b; Germain and Kenny 2005; Söderbaum 2007) properties of 'global civil society' are considered in a conceptual overview to demonstrate historical continuity with understandings, conceptualizations and practices of civil society. A more coherent attempt can be made towards understanding global civil society and practices of contestation through understanding problematic conceptualizations of civil society and the dialectical relationship between the concept and reality of global civil society.

As suggested in the opening section of this chapter, a further core objective of this book is to contribute to conceptualizing the 'politics of resistance' (Gills 2000), which I tend to counter-pose as globalization and contestation. A clear temptation to uncritically celebrate resistance and the consequent need for critical appraisal within the literature on globalization and contestation has been elsewhere noted (Kiely 2000: 1060–61). In addition, it has been suggested that insufficient attention has been paid to conceptual and empirical studies on 'anti-globalization' (Eschle and Maiguashca 2005), while key criticisms of critical approaches in their assessments of contesting globalization have been put forward (Drainville 2004). For these reasons, which are aligned with the objective of achieving an improved conceptualization of global civil society, a critical review of the literature on globalization and contestation that emerged before and after the 'anti-globalization' demonstrations in Seattle 1999 is undertaken in this book. This literature includes, for example, the edited volumes by Abbott and Worth (2002), Amoore (2005), Appelbaum and Robinson (2005), Bieler and Morton (2001), Eschle and Maiguashca (2005), Fisher and Ponniah (2003), Gill and Mittelman (1997), Gills (2000), Hamel *et al.* (2001), Hettne (1995), Mittelman (1996), Murphy (2002), Sen *et al.* (2004), Sen *et al.* (2007), and Wilkinson and Hughes (2002). In this book their key contributions are drawn out and built upon. Areas of conceptual neglect in explaining modes of relation between globalization and contestation in the global political economy are identified, while possible avenues through which critical theory can address these conceptual shortcomings are suggested. The purpose of focusing on critical readings of this literature in this book is not solely to delineate the content of the literature on globalization and contestation, but, more crucially, to show how greater conceptual clarity can be reached and a dialectical understanding of change and contestation in the global political economy formulated. This approach is narrowed in the next chapter to focus on the post-modern prince (Gill 2000) and multitude (Hardt and Negri 2000, 2005). It will be shown how a more adequate conceptualization of contestation can be achieved through an assessment of the attributes of global civil society at the World Social Forum and World People's Conference on Climate Change which was held in Cochabamba in 2010.

A related objective of this book is to demonstrate that approaches which rely solely on an analysis of social movements, anti-globalization movements, or indeed on multitude or the post-modern prince, insufficiently account for the conceptual dynamics of change and contestation in the global political economy. This reflects and takes seriously the view that the complex and multifaceted domain of global civil society 'has so far been barely grasped by social scientific inquiry' and 'if anything, research has tended to constrain understanding and served to hinder full interpretations of global civil society' (cf. Taylor 2002: 341). A broader framework for analysing contestation in the global political economy, which is based on the multifaceted concept of global civil society, is proposed to draw on anti-globalization and related approaches centring on social movements and collective action (van Apeldoorn 2000; Hamel *et al.* 2001; Imig and Tarrow 2001; Murphy 2002; van der Pijl 1998; Sklair 2002; Walker 1994), while also allowing for a more comprehensive understanding of change in the global political economy than more restricted or singularly focused analyses permit. This framework is particularly significant in its application to the World Social Forum, wherein many, although by no means all, of the broad constituents of global civil society are represented. It also brings further insight into the integration of climate change into the sphere of 'global contestation'.

Throughout this book, Gramscian approaches to Global Political Economy and their relation to modes of contestation to globalization are depicted and analysed with the objective of engaging with and critically reassessing Gramscian approaches in addition to articulating an alternative conceptualization of global civil society and understanding of hegemony. I seek to integrate more prominently critical theoretical precepts to produce a reflexive form of conceptualization through an examination of the constitution and formulation of the concept of global civil society, not only through examining modes of relation to global governing institutions, but also through authorial processes of knowledge construction. Reflexive conceptualization is further illustrated through integrating, towards the end of this book in particular, poststructuralist insights such as the primacy of power relations with a refocused perspective on global civil society (cf. Amoore and Langley 2004, 2005; de Goede 2006; Jessop and Sum 2006). The critical political economy perspective on resistance that is developed is also influenced by the contributions of new IPE and related approaches (Murphy and Tooze 1991; Gills 2001; Shields *et al.* 2011), critical globalization studies (Mittelman 2005), and International Relations/Global Political Economy critical theory broadly (Cox 1981, 1983, 1987; Gill 1993; Gill and Mittelman 1997; Hoffman 1987; Linklater 1996; Neufeld 1995; Smith *et al.* 1996).

The case study of the World Social Forum (WSF, or simple 'the forum') presented in this book exemplifies the tendency to celebrate uncritically resistance to globalization. Gramscian studies suggest it is a counter-hegemonic alternative to the World Economic Forum (Carroll 2007), while as mentioned in the introduction to this chapter, it is also considered to represent an emancipatory civil society (Santos 2006a). The objective, therefore, is to demonstrate the need for a critical appraisal of the forum, which overcomes the shortcomings of contemporary conceptualizations of global civil society and hegemony, and forwards the necessity of a new concept of global civil society that draws on a critical Global Political Economy of resistance approach. While, therefore, attention to the question of contestation through the forum has notably neglected to recognize the potential conceptual contributions of global civil society, it is the aim of this book to elucidate these contributions through demonstrating the complexities of hegemony, through 'transversal' hegemony, the persistence of power relations, the politics of place, and inclusive and exclusive features of agency.

More broadly, a philosophy of praxis seeks to contribute to further theoretical development through sustaining discussion on theory and practice, philosophy and politics, scholasticism and lived experience. Broader social science preoccupations with regard to conceptual development and identification of adequate tools of analysis are reflected throughout here. The approach used in the following chapters aims to extend the state-centred characteristics of traditional Global Political Economy approaches while also challenging— and examining the effects of—assumptions that contributions resting on non-state actors automatically transcend the boundaries of traditional social sciences. Through openness to a transdisciplinary approach (cf. Gills 2001; Mittelman 2005; Schuurman 2009), the analytical framework of global civil society is used to acknowledge the contributions of other disciplines and move towards a more critical assessment of contestation.

Chapter outline

In Chapter 2 the limitations of hegemony and counter-hegemony are shown increasingly to converge with broader examinations of power and counter-power. Examples of the post-modern prince (Gill 2000) and multitude (Hardt and Negri 2005) are expanded upon to give some initial insight into the failure of converging accounts—in a neo-Polanyian mode of analysis—to clarify the transversal, rather than binary, nature of Gramscian hegemony and the broader contributions that can be derived from consideration of the dialectical nexus between concept and reality. Focusing on the dialectical or dialogic interaction between normative conceptual promise and complex empirical realities, such as proposed in this chapter, aims to recover the substantive meanings of a dialectical form of Gramscian Marxism. It also involves a commitment to recognizing the evolving and approximate nature of knowledge formation which can capture the potential of the global political imagination alongside clear attention to the material dimensions of change (Jameson 1990; Gramsci 1971; Thompson 1978). The capacity of critical perspectives to adapt continually to changing realities is underlined as an essential strategy towards achieving greater and much-needed clarity on the conceptual position and historical context of civil society and hegemony.

In Chapter 3, a method of conceptual and contextual historicism is used to chart the production of knowledge on global civil society in an era of apparent global complexity. The differing and at times incommensurable conceptual histories of global civil society are shown significantly to neglect to demonstrate their intersection and points of (re)articulation with hegemony in the global political economy. The literature on global civil society proliferates alongside literature on 'new social movements', 'critical social movements' and 'the alter-globalization movement', with each revealing similar conceptual and empirical shortcomings. These limitations are particularly manifest through distinct 'non-political economy' conceptualizations of civil society (Cerny 2006). There is, therefore, a need to re-orientate key understandings to explain more fully and further the range of 'hopeful and critical voices' on the concept (cf. Baker and Chandler 2005). Without doing so, a sustained analysis of contestation on the terrain of the global political economy that considers the strategies undertaken by global civil society, including alter-globalization movements, non-governmental organizations (NGOs), indigenous peoples and other varied constituents, cannot be carried out.

This theme is extended and applied to assessments of studies on contesting global governance in Chapter 4. The benefits of a sustained and critical interrogation of the construction, elaboration and dialectical interaction of modes of social relation to the global political economy are considered in this chapter (cf. Drainville 2004, 2012). A number of key texts are critically assessed to demonstrate the conflicting and ideologically diverse meanings that are attributed to global civil society. This also helps to articulate how narratives of meaning are constructed not only through contextual political, social and economic conditions, but also through authorial and institutional practices of defining global civil society and asserting its instrumental or normative uses. Gramscian categories of research ranging from instrumentalism to voluntarism draw attention to the constitution of global civil society which is further related to the dialectical nexus between concept and reality (Gramsci 1971). This confirms how contemporary conceptualizations of global civil society are less effective at explaining changes in the global political economy (Amoore and Langley 2004)—especially as they relate to globalization and its contestation—and are more indicative of a normative desire to contribute to the 'making' of a virtuous global civil society or to highlight its instrumental and functional roles. In contrast, a focus on concrete modes of social relation locates global civil society within the fluctuating material and political realities of the global political economy. Meanwhile, attention to the dialectical nexus highlights how the privileging of normative and/or instrumental conceptualizations delimits and decontextualizes the concrete range of possibilities for change and transformation in the global political economy. The dialectical nexus therefore draws attention to how practices of definition and usage affect the concept of global civil society and, in turn, condition possibilities of action, thought and political imagination.

In Chapter 5, the dialectics of presence at the World Social Forum is considered in relation to civic-consensual modes of social relation and demarcation of space. Representations of the World Social Forum as a new form of 'open' space for the empowerment of global civil society and as an opportunity for the reinvention of the Left are assessed alongside manifest experiences of contestation at the forum. Incongruence between predominant conceptual representations of global civil society and the complex realities of representation, elitism, funding, convergence, power and strategy at World Social Forums is clearly demonstrated. The WSF strategy of convergence is highlighted to illustrate movements of *trasformismo* and conformation towards a civic-consensual middle ground of contestation. This strategy, it is argued, has resulted in a reluctance to confront competing ideologies at the WSF and a consequent inherently contradictory convergence of conservative, progressive Right and traditional Left ideologies towards new civic-consensual modes of relation. The highly uneven 'making' of civic-consensual global civil society and the exclusion and marginalization of divergent ideologies is also reflected in the further 'levelling' and gridding of social spaces at the forum—each of which add up to an ambiguous, although not settled, dialectics of presence at the World Social Forum. The possibilities for transformative modes of contestation through the forum are thus not precluded.

The following chapter, Chapter 6, moves beyond the terrain of the World Social Forum to consider wider assessments of global convergence and specificities at the World People's Conference on Climate Change and the Rights of Mother Earth (WPCCC) in Cochabamba in 2010. The production of the People's Agreement and associated working group documents during the Cochabamba process are assessed in terms of deepening a debate on the global political economy of resistance which moves from and outside of the World Social Forum and rests on articulations of 'climate justice' and 'environmental debt' at sites of resistance. The WPCCC is also part of the wider assessment of the formation of and tensions within the 'dialectical relationship between consciousness and being' that are raised in other chapters (Neufeld 2002: 3; cf. Thompson 1978: 225). This dialectical relationship considers experiences of contestation at the centre of academic discourse in the case of alter-globalization and the World Social Forum, but also charts an accessible approach to contestation from the margins and a broader multi-disciplinary take on social theory of the periphery and articulations of contestation.

These chapters demonstrate how current conceptualizations of global civil society are constituted, used and apply to an examination of mutually constitutive relations of globalization and contestation at work in the global political economy. The principal focus of enquiry in Chapter 7 rests on the explanatory uses of current conceptualizations of global civil society and also on their key limitations. It is the objective of this chapter to demonstrate how a reformulated study of contestation in the global political economy which draws on global civil society and key Gramscian insights while also integrating some contributions from post-structural interpretations of resistance, can work to overcome the delimiting 'neo-Polanyian' tendency (which has become increasingly inherent to conceptualizing resistance movements), and instead move towards a conceptual grounding in transversal hegemony. Broad contributions to studies of globalization and its contestation are elucidated and consolidated in the final conclusions. The, at best, anomalous integration of conceptual envisioning such as global civil society in studies on global contestation and counter-hegemony is thus disrupted or unsettled in this book. The potential of the dialectical nexus to elucidate the nature of global contestation in the global political economy—its sites of power, inequalities, hierarchies, exclusions, and relationship between the market, state and society—and for integrating conceptual reflexivity on how knowledge is produced is further underlined.

Notes

1 Estimations of WSF attendance vary but figures suggest attendance of approximately 15,000–20,000 in 2001 in Porto Alegre; 50,000 in 2002 in Porto Alegre; 100,000 in 2003 in Porto Alegre; 115,000 in 2004 in Mumbai; 155,000 in 2005 in Porto Alegre; 125,00 including the three poly-centric locations in Bamako, Caracas and Karachi in 2006; 57,000 in 2007 in Nairobi; 113,000 in 2009 in Belem, Brazil; and 75,000 in 2011 in Dakar (WSF 2007, 2009, 2011; Karumba 2007).

2 While Mittelman outlined the main components of 'critical globalization studies', this is part of a broader trend to acknowledge the contested, problematic and political nature of globalization through instigating a new *Critical Globalization Studies* edited by Richard Appelbaum and William Robinson (2005).

3 See, for example, Gills (2000), Eschle and Maiguashca (2005), Marchand and Runyan (2000). On another note the reference to 'Gramscian' approaches instead

of the more usual term 'neo-Gramscian' is used here to indicate that approaches that use Gramsci or refer to his work range in degree of adherence to his writings.

4 Bleiker (2000) uses the collapse of the Berlin Wall to illustrate the slow transformation of societal values and how everyday forms of discursive transversal resistance such as mail exchange between East Germany and the rest of the world and the presence of the outside media in East Germany precede acts of overt rebellion.

5 The nature of this research implied that a significant proportion of my research was web-based requiring consultation with online discussion forums, alternative media websites and social movement, activist and anti-globalization websites. Online discussions through forums such as WSFDiscuss and Critical Engagement with Open Space (CEOS) were monitored, for example, and WSF process was researched before I attended the World Social Forum in Nairobi, Kenya on 20–25 January 2007. Meanwhile, primary documentation such as official reports of World Social Forum International Council meetings was an important source of information. Field research involved the first-hand collection of information through observation to achieve a detailed picture of the WSF in this setting; its location, the organization of space, management of the event, the actors involved and activities carried out. My role at the WSF was principally observational although I also participated in seminars such as that organized by the 'WSF 7 years' group composed of the Alternative Information Center Jerusalem-Bethlehem, Centre for Civil Society (Durban), Center of Indian Trade Unions (Cetri), the International Press Service, Paolo Freire Institute, and the Program on Democracy and Global Transformation.

2 The dialectics of concept and reality

> At the level of the global economy ... the phenomenon of transformation
> not only strains the available vocabulary but on some accounts, its very
> occurrence remains in doubt.
>
> (Ruggie 1993: 141)[1]

Increasing recognition of the possibilities of continuity and change in the
global political economy has translated into a burgeoning of inter-disciplinary
vocabulary and concepts. The vocabulary of power, domination and
hegemony is used in ever-more creative and explanatory ways and frequently
strained to take in counter-power, resistance and counter-hegemony.
'Disciplinary neoliberalism', for example, encompasses the structural power
of capital—its capacity to shape expectations, material constraints and
incentives—and behavioural power—shaped to develop a panoptic system of
control over individuals, rendering them obedient and manipulatable to
modernity (Gill 2003: 130–35). 'Empire', in addition, includes abundant new
structures of power in a quasi-global arrangement—it is a network and
biopower that creatively self-sustains through permanent warfare (Hardt and
Negri 2005). In a contemporary period of interregnum, the search for a
vocabulary to absorb alternatives to disciplinary neoliberalism and Empire
has resulted in consideration of the post-modern prince (Gill 2000, 2003,
2008) and multitude (Hardt and Negri 2000, 2005). These are placed in this
chapter within diverse and dispersed answers, asides and critiques which
characterize the disciplinary response of critical Global Political Economy—
that part of the discipline most concerned with counter-hegemony—to
explaining continuity and change. Discussion in the second part of this
chapter is formulated in response to dissatisfaction with Gramscian responses
to the possibilities of interregnum that, it is argued, derives from a persistent
neo-Polanyian influence. It is said, for example, that Gramscian approaches
give inadequate attention to the logic and nature of counter-hegemony
(Eschle and Maiguashca 2005), more usually address counter-hegemony as a
residual matter for future research (Morton 2003), and have yet to do any
really hard work on counter-hegemonic theorization (Peet 2007: 194). Poor
attention to counter-hegemony is argued in this chapter to derive from an

over-reliance on neo-Polanyian versions of change in the global political economy. In moving towards 'a concept of something we cannot imagine' the dialectical nexus between concept and reality is evoked in this and subsequent chapters of this book through conceptualizations of civil society and hegemony (Jameson 1990; Gramsci 1971; Cox 1999; Thompson 1963). The nexus points to the approximate and provisional nature of concept-formation and proposes global civil society and transversal hegemony as central to strengthening critical GPE responses to the possibilities of interregnum.

The politics of power and resistance

First, the key aspects of a Gramscian account of power and resistance in the new world order are considered in this section through focusing on disciplinary neoliberalism and the post-modern prince (Gill 2008). This critical, historical materialist perspective on political economy and international relations offers a conceptual lens which, through the work of Fernand Braudel, Karl Marx, Antonio Gramsci, Michel Foucault and others, views the development of social structures and social relations as constituted by collective action through and over time. This method captures at once the temporal and people-centred nature of power and resistance from which an historical period of 'organic crisis' is posited to signify the exhaustion of old politics and processes of struggle for the consolidation of a new order and form of political and civil society (Gill 2003: 48).

The consideration of power through disciplinary neoliberalism details the intensification of the discipline of capital in social relations while re-engaging and applying commodification and alienation to the contemporary context. The structural power of capital is further imposed through new and quasi-constitutional political and legal frameworks. New constitutionalism combines the dominant power of the propertied and globalizing elites and relatively legitimately perceived processes of policy making and implementation. Hegemony, thus conceptualized, is enormously persuasive and effective in intensifying, imposing and extending its remit through a form of 'market civilization' which encompasses not only ideas, institutions and material things but 'a whole way of life' (Gill 2003: 13; Gill 2000). Building on this, the character of a particular social structure comprises ideas, ideologies and theories, social institutions, a prevailing socio-economic system and set of power relations (ibid.: 17). Social change, therefore, cannot be the simple product of the preponderance of state power since 'human beings have consciousness and a degree of free will or agency within the limits of the possible' (ibid.: 37).

Growing contradictions within the global rule of capital indicate a 'clash of globalizations' and an intensifying economic, social and ecological 'global organic crisis' (Gill 2002a, 2012a). Opposition to the prevailing political order of disciplinary neoliberalism entails a complex and persistent amalgamation of social and political forces—'a constellation of democratic and progressive social forces' (Gill 1997a)—which can persuasively argue for an alternative order. Presently, for example, radical potential is found to be developing through the World Social Forum, Left forums and numerous worldwide revolts, resistances and uprisings (Gill 2012a). These, it is argued, need to connect to other more long-standing forms of regional and global politics such as carried forward by landless workers, peasants and indigenous peoples. Cautiously moving away from the sectarianism associated with the old Left, this approach instead appropriates a distinctively forward-looking progressive vision (Chase-Dunn and Gills 2005). The Landless Rural Workers Movement/ Movimento dos Sem Terra (MST) in Brazil and Rigoberta Menchú, respectively representative of agrarian interests and feminist indigenous voices, are highlighted for their assertion of a sense of dignity and political identity, re-making the material basis of their lives and contributing much to advanced political thinking (Gill 2012b: 517–18). Each form of agency is located within the limits of the possible which allow them potentially to transform the social structures that constitute and constrain them (cf. Gill 2003: 17, 37). This is the role of the 'post-modern prince'—or myth-prince in Gramscian terms—a new form of collective political identity and agent that aims to transform prevailing social structures and, potentially, create new, ethical and democratic political institutions and practices (Gill 2000):

> The modern prince, the myth-prince, cannot be a real person, a concrete individual. It can only be an organism, a complex element of society in which a collective will, which has already been recognised and has to some extent asserted itself in action, begins to take concrete form.
>
> (Gramsci 1971: 129, cited in Gill 1997b)

The concrete form of this new constellation of forces was especially tentative at the time of the initial articulation of the post-modern prince but it was nonetheless seen to constitute the mobilizing myth of a new historical bloc. It concerns 'the possibility of a world-wide political association or imagined community of the progressive counter-movements' which more recently draws on a philosophy of praxis and organic intellectuals (Gill 1997b, 2012a). The neo-Gramscian post-modern prince, in contrast to the vocabulary of disciplinary neoliberalism, claims to assert a 'realistic political optimism that is creative and forward-looking' (Gill 1997b: 3).

Disciplinary neoliberalism and the post-modern prince have a particular influence in critical GPE to which they offer a newly articulated vocabulary to describe and explain continuities and changes. From a radical inter-disciplinary perspective Michael Hardt and Antonio Negri (2000, 2005) offer a diffuse account of power and counter-power claiming the influence of Niccolò Machiavelli, Thomas Hobbes, Karl Marx, Michel Foucault, Gilles Deleuze, Félix Guattari and Baruch Spinoza. Broadly addressed in a separate volume to the earlier published *Empire*, *Multitude* is a response by the authors to give further background to 'the living alternative that grows within', and works through Empire 'to create an alternative global society' in a language and form that has resonance with anti-globalization activists disillusioned with the old Left (Hardt and Negri 2005: xiii, xvii; Choonara 2005).

Empire is a new global form of sovereignty; a 'network power' including dominant nation-states, supra-national institutions, major capitalist corporations and other powers (Hardt and Negri 2005: xii). The new global form of sovereignty rules over a fractured and hierarchical global order that, based on a permanent state of warfare, has come to use war in a creative and self-sustaining way (ibid.: xiii, 21). It converges various forms of power, economics, war, politics and culture to become a biopower or 'mode of producing social life in its entirety' (ibid.: 334). Empire is historically situated in the current period of transition or interregnum wherein the national paradigm of political bodies passes towards a global form and abundance of new structures of power (ibid.: 163). During the interregnum, the authors propose that while nation-states retain many of their traditional functions, they are nonetheless transformed 'by the emerging global power they tend increasingly to serve' (ibid.). The new structures of power constitute a form of quasi-global government or three-tiered array of governance mechanisms consisting of private regimes of global law working to maximize profits, complex forms of global sovereignty which construct trade agreements, and global regulatory institutions such as the World Bank and International Monetary Fund (IMF) (ibid.: 171, 175).

During the interregnum Empire constitutes one face of globalization and multitude the other, one destructive and the other constructive: 'In the face of the destructive state of exception of biopower, then, there is also a constituent state of exception of democratic biopolitics' (ibid.: 357). Multitude, the other face of globalization, is an open and expansive network, a place for encounters, cooperation and collaboration where the commonalities between humanity and the means to achieve a democratic society are discovered. The project of multitude, Hardt and Negri propose, will create an open and inclusive democratic global society which will bring with it equality and freedom and, thus, a way out of conflict and war (ibid.: xi). To fulfil this project, multitude organizes as an alternative to 'the global political body of capital' (ibid.: 189) and links with the new international and nodal cycle of struggles that emerged to resist globalization during the 1990s:

> The global cycle of struggles develops in the form of a distributed network. Each local struggle functions as a node that communicates with all the other nodes without any hub or center of intelligence. Each struggle remains singular and tied to its local conditions but at the same time is immersed in the common web. This form of organization is the most fully realised political example we have of the concept of multitude. The global extension of the common does not negate the singularity of each of those who participates in the network. The new global cycle of struggles organizes and mobilizes the multitude.
>
> (Hardt and Negri 2005: 217)

The creation of an alternative world entails exodus and flight from sovereignty and anarchy: 'Not only must the multitude configure its exodus as resistance, it must also transform that resistance into a form of constituent power, creating the social relations and institutions of a new society' (Hardt and Negri 2005: 348). From the decline of the socialist and communist organized Left, multitude configures a new political agency which reinvents the Left 'by naming a form of political organization and a political project' that is already an 'existing social and political tendency' (ibid.: 220). It is nonetheless a class concept—although not exclusive to the working class—and directly related to the Marxist project of class struggle and concern with conditions of possibility, i.e. with what the multitude can become (ibid.: 105).

Hardt and Negri are concerned with the global crisis of democracy and representation which, they argue, requires a 'new science of the multitude' or theoretical paradigm (Hardt and Negri 2005: 355, 353). Symptoms of the crisis of democracy such as protests and demands for democracy from below can be relieved through changing how democracy is practiced and conceived: 'we will once again have to reinvent the concept of democracy and create new institutional forms and practices appropriate to our global age' (ibid.: 236–38). The authors want to go back to the untarnished eighteenth-century concept of democracy which would allow us to see how, just as Athenian democracy could not be transferred to the national level, national models of democracy and representative institutions cannot be transposed to a global scale (ibid.: 307). It is, for example, considered 'ridiculous' to demand that multitude form a party or fixed organizational structure (Brown and Szeman 2005: 378).

Philosophy and praxis

Both the post-modern prince and multitude offer conceptual discussions on power, governance, and conditions of continuity and change in the global political economy. They are broadly concerned to offer conceptual clarity and a vocabulary to engage with the potential of change, to assert the potential of new political Left-oriented movements, and to look towards more ethical and democratic ways of governance, doing politics and participating in society. Their commonalities mirror key concerns on the part of social scientists to conceptualize contemporary institutional, structural and behavioural preponderances of power and counter-power. Each account posits a contemporary position of interregnum. The post-modern prince alludes to a transitional process from collective will to concrete form so that the more recent sketching of the World Social Forum, protest movements, indigenous and Leftist movements might be seen to affirm the merging of political realities and progressive aspirations. Multitude, placed more firmly in the shadow of Empire, configures the historical trajectory of varied movements and demands for change and places them within contemporary dispersed, nodal patterns of interaction. The former is formulated close to disciplinary concerns to configure a new politics of resistance in International Political Economy (IPE). The latter collaborates with a host of studies on new social movements and international organization, while more successfully engaging with activist concerns on new imperialism and biopower.

Through their work, both Gill and Hardt and Negri mirror cross-disciplinary trends in situating counter-power and resistance in relation to power and changing patterns of governance. Early focus tends to be placed on relations of power, as confirmed by the earlier publication of *Empire* and supplementary writing of *Multitude*. Similarly, accounts of disciplinary neoliberalism and market civilization are markedly detailed and developed especially when compared alongside the more tentatively sketched evolution of the postmodern prince. This confirms the view that more effort is placed on 'mapping structural relations of power and domination than on theorising the logic and nature of resistance or counter-hegemony' (Eschle and Maiguashca 2005: 3–4). The structural characteristics of power may be theoretically tempered by behavioural patterns and thus understood to provide some opening towards resistance but the nature, substance and conceptualization of resistance is not the main contribution of the study on *Power and Resistance in the New World Order* (Gill 2008). Indeed, analysis of the emerging counter-hegemonic postmodern prince does not result in a reassessment of the hegemony of 'market civilization' (Eschle and Maiguashca 2005), a concept that is considerably more developed than its counterpart. It is particularly a feature of Gramscian analyses on the breakdown of the post-World War II settlement and the theorization of a transnational hegemonic capitalist class (e.g. Gill 1993; van der Pijl 1984, 1997, 1998). From the global restructuring of state and social relations a transnational capitalist class faction led by 'organic policy intellectuals' or leaders of transnational financial corporations and key financial institutions such as the IMF was the focus of research (Gill 1993: 266). This led to the postulation of the 'G-7 Nexus', a recent phase of a process of transnational class formation, which is defined as 'the constellation of social and political forces which regulate, police and protect a disciplinary neo-liberal world order', which comprises 'a set of institutional arrangements, material capacities and discursive practices which have taken their contemporary form since the onset of the global economic crisis in the early 1970s' (Gill 1999: 113). This imbalance is also echoed in *Empire* and *Multitude* even though counter-power is understood through an alternative Foucauldian explanation of power.

Taken further and placed in the contemporary context, the imbalance in focus may be related to the perception that further to the notion of vocabulary explained above, the analytical tools with which to conceptualize counter-power are simply not accessible. This feature of inaccessibility is heightened through perceptions of the greater complexity of 'global' processes and will be examined further in relation to the making of civil society in Chapter 3. Responses to inaccessibility centre on calls for new forms of social consciousness, a new ontology and even the creation of new institutional forms—loosely linked to multitude and the post-modern prince. The diffuse nature of multitude (as singularities that act in common) and nebulous nature of early formulations of the post-modern prince (as a new form of global consciousness) heightens the perceived inaccessibility of global trans-formation which calls at once for more local, specified and individualized forms of resistance alongside the philosophical status of achieving a more global social consciousness and transformation in how we understand the world. The stated philosophical basis of *Multitude* reflects on the need to rethink concepts such as power and resistance and most evidently to work out the conceptual basis of a new project for democracy (Hardt and Negri 2005: xvi, 328). The philosophical basis is contrasted by the authors to proposals for a concrete programme of action, evaluations of the timing of a 'revolutionary political decision', answers to the question 'what is to be done?' which, in an anomalous contrast to the focus on singularities that act in common, are not considered to be the subject of *Multitude* (ibid.: xvi, 357). Intonations of a philosophy of praxis in contrast, come nearer to the goal of 'realistic political optimism' (Gill 1997b: 3) or the 'realistic development of imagined alternatives' (Gill 2012a: 253), but the nebulous form of resistance risks cohering better with the notion of a philosophy which resides in the thought process.

In turn, the tendency to focus on hegemonic power and disposition towards conceptual inaccessibility both reinforce a further caveat that can be summed up as the 'domination-resistance' motif (Urry 2005). The 'simple dichotomy and decision' presented in *Multitude* has been critiqued for positing a stark choice between imperial biopolitical control or a new possibility for democracy (Rayner 2005: 28). This leads to what Rayner describes as a 'simplistic discussion of the struggle between the multitude and Empire' with each presented in absolute. For example, 'the 'absolute' democracy of the multitude' gives scant insight into struggles within multitude itself (ibid.). The post-modern prince, by virtue of its positioning as an ethical and democratic impulse for resistance appears to also evade accounting for internal core, marginal and opposing struggles.

Nonetheless, the authors of the post-modern prince and multitude are acutely aware that expressions of solidarity risk masking areas of fragmentation and inequality (Walker 1994). Multitude, for example, is described as 'an active social subject' or 'singularities that act in common', which means that its 'constitution and action is based not on identity or unity … but on what it has in common' (Hardt and Negri 2005: 100, 105). Local struggles retain their singularity within multitude while, at the same time, acting as a node or part of a common 'web' or network (ibid.: 217). This opens towards a further caveat in terms of conceptualizing counter-power or counter-hegemony which underlies the interstices of resistance and links to the transverse optimum of hegemony. On the one hand, the absence of a coherent subject of resistance might be considered to constitute an obstacle towards conceptualization.

However, adding up singularities or particularisms with little or no hegemonic mediation between them is as ineffectual as plucking from thin air the correct counter-hegemonic form. The dispersed Foucauldian-influenced nature of power in *Empire* and *Multitude* risks power taking on a mystical all-pervading form, resists any concrete localization of its paths and structures (Thompson 2003), and makes it difficult to theorize resistance because its portrayal as a network extinguishes any notion of agency (Davies 2006), and moreover, denotation of a location or position in the global political economy (Drainville 2004). These deficiencies occur to a lesser extent in *Power and Resistance in the New World Order*, where the 'post-modern' of the post-modern prince and Foucauldian influences are more tightly circumscribed within a Gramscian approach, but as discussed later in more detail, some further issues arise in relation to finding the dialectical nexus between concept and reality.

Both accounts of power and resistance told through the media of the post-modern prince and multitude are significant for the eclectic Marxist, critical and post-structural political economy perspectives they employ. These accounts bear out alternative assessments of movement in the global political economy from an organic crisis out of which a new social consciousness is struggling to emerge (Gill 2003), or from an interregnum or period of transition to reveal another face to Empire (Hardt and Negri 2005). They encourage us to rethink categories such as neoliberalism, sovereignty, imperialism and, to some degree, class. The authors suggest, to varying extents, that a change in ontology or paradigm shift is necessary. However, from the present assessment, a number of caveats arise which have consequences for how resistance is conceptualized and articulated in relation to the global political economy. First, while inequality and powerlessness might be better understood in relation to power, the hegemonic and pervasive nature of power can result in less conceptual attention to resistance. This is heightened by a perception that the analytical tools with which to further explanations of counter-hegemony are neither available nor accessible. Already indicated by proponents of the post-modern prince and multitude, the philosophy of resistance is interpreted in alternating ways. This gives some indication that any consideration of a 'new ontology' or new theoretical paradigm cannot fail to engage with the apparently 'settled boundaries and concepts' that characterize the 'old' (de Goede 2006: 5). It is not clear that multitude succeeds in resolving the conflict between Marxism and post-structuralism from which it is derived. Hardt and Negri do not see any conflict between these two discourses and streams of thought, simply believing them to be enriched by contact (Brown and Szeman 2005: 187). Meanwhile, multitude succumbs to the critique of traditional accounts of global civil society for meaning all things to all people (Axford 2005: 187) and the search continues for the post-modern prince. Each responds to calls for a new vocabulary but what results must be strained to convince entirely that new ways of 'seeing' are being envisaged (cf. Marchand 2003).

Box 2.1 Gramscian selections

Many of the concepts elaborated in *Selections from the Prison Notebooks* (Gramsci 1971) are particularly relevant to the question of continuity and fundamental social change. Moments or relations of force through revealing 'the points of least resistance, at which the force of will can be most fruitfully applied' offer a particular understanding of movement, change and historical development (ibid.: 185). The first moment or 'relation of social forces' is 'closely linked to the structure, objective, independent of human will, and … measured with the systems of the exact or physical sciences' (ibid.: 180). Studying 'fundamental data' such as the level of economic development allows for an assessment of contradictions that may suggest ideal conditions for the transformation of a particular society. The second moment refers to the 'relation of political forces'. This allows for 'an evaluation of the degree of homogeneity, self-awareness, and organisation attained by the various social classes' (ibid.: 181). Historically, the achievement of hegemony through the second relation of social forces has been achieved through movement from the economic-corporate level to the unison of economic and political aims combined with intellectual and moral unity. Practically, or 'in real history', these movements 'imply each other reciprocally' both horizontally across activities and vertically across countries (ibid.: 182). The third 'relation of military forces' exists in technical-military and politico-military senses while the three moments of force work in continual and pliant movement with each other:

> The third moment is that of the relation of military forces, which from time to time is directly decisive. (Historical development oscillates continually between the first and the third moment, with the mediation of the second.) But this is not undifferentiated, nor is it susceptible to immediate schematic definition.
>
> (Gramsci 1971: 183)

The three moments of social forces, political forces and military forces can be applied to the occurrence of fundamental historical crises. The observation that 'it may be ruled out that immediate economic crises of themselves produce fundamental historical events' (Gramsci 1971: 184) when read in conjunction with relations of force, is illustrative of oscillation between moments. Any rupturing of the 'equilibrium of forces … occurred in the context of conflicts on a higher plane than the immediate world of the economy; conflicts related to class "prestige" (future economic interests), and to an inflammation of sentiments of independence, autonomy and power' (ibid.).

The reciprocal oscillation between relations of forces relies on a dialectical, historicist understanding that in a further illustration from the Gramscian selections, considers the past to be 'one of the elements of the present and one of the premises of the future' (ibid.: 147). The historical bloc (*blocco storico*), for example, reflects the reciprocal dialectical interaction of structures and superstructures (ibid.: 366). Elsewhere, it is briefly jotted: '"historical bloc", i.e. unity between nature and spirit (structure and superstructure), unity of opposites and distincts' (ibid.: 137), but it is not difficult to find further evidence of Gramscian historicism and ontological basis:

> The discovery that the relations between the social and natural orders are mediated by work [education], by man's theoretical and practical activity ... provides a basis for the subsequent development of an historical, dialectical conception of the world, which understands movement and change, which appreciates the sum of effort and sacrifice which the present has cost the past and which the future is costing the present, and which conceives the contemporary world as a synthesis of the past, of all past generations, which projects itself into the future.
>
> (Gramsci 1971: 34–35)

This particular ontology is supplemented in the Gramscian selections through a number of conceptual tools. Consent and coercion, for example, understood through the Machiavellian image of the centaur as 'half-animal and half-human', are significant attributes of hegemony as the following demonstrates: 'Man must respect this legal order through spontaneous assent, and not merely as an external imposition—it must be a necessity recognised and proposed to themselves as freedom, and not simply the result of coercion' (Gramsci 1971: 170, 26–43). However, further understanding of movement and change in an historical context may be derived from the concept of 'passive revolution' to which may be applied 'the interpretative criterion of molecular changes which in fact progressively modify the pre-existing composition of forces, and hence become the matrix of new changes' (ibid.: 109). Alongside passive revolution the importance of *trasformismo*, or assimilation of alternative ideas, as a form of historical development that has been inadequately emphasized is underlined. *Trasformismo* was the term used from the 1880s onwards to describe the process whereby the Left and Right parties that emerged from the *Risorgimento* (the period of and movement for the political unification of Italy in the nineteenth century) tended towards convergence (ibid.: 58, note 8).

The above, however, is more fully understood within what is referred to as the 'dialectical nexus' between 'categories of research' and 'categories of movement' (Gramsci 1971: 58). The dialectical nexus permeates the *Prison Notebooks* and works through a constantly overlapping didactic concern with the relation between the concrete on the one hand and the theoretical and abstract on the other. Organic movements are composed of wide social groupings and, reflecting their long-lasting historical significance, give rise to 'socio-historical criticism' (ibid.: 178). More immediate conjunctural movements are incessant and persistent in emphasizing that the necessary conditions already exist to accomplish 'certain historical tasks' (ibid.). Despite appearances, however, 'the dialectical nexus between the two categories of movement, and therefore of research, is hard to establish precisely' and a 'common error in historico-political analysis consists in an inability to find the correct relation between what is organic and what is conjunctural' (ibid.: 178). The didactic and at times moralistic nature of writing in the Gramscian selections can be seen to emit from this concern which presents, for example, the distinction between political and civil society as 'merely methodological ... since in actual reality civil society and the State are the one and the same' (ibid.: 160). The nexus concerns the relation between practical or 'concrete' activity and scholarly intent. The distinction between structure and superstructure has been elsewhere described as 'merely didactic', a process that is important in clarifying concepts and putting forward essential starting points of enquiry (Augelli and Murphy 1988: 32). Meanwhile, any 'concrete analysis' of the relations of forces should recognize that the relations of force are not ends in themselves '(unless the intention is to write a chapter of past history), but acquire significance only if they serve to justify a particular practical activity, or initiative of will' (Gramsci 1971: 185).

Neo-Polanyian optimism of the will

The vocabulary of change and continuity in Global Political Economy such as it is expressed through disciplinary neoliberalism/post-modern prince and Empire/multitude does not yet convince of new ontological positioning but does offer an initial entry point of insight into the discipline. Despite the urgency with which the authors conceive of the need for new paradigms and ontologies of change, their respective accounts are together illustrative of the challenges involved in bearing out these conceptions. These challenges are brought in the second part of this chapter to critical GPE, here understood as that part of the discipline most pronouncedly concerned with counter-hegemony and within which a recognizable and endurable 'neo-Polanyian' influence will be shown to have particular consequence for conceptualizing civil society and hegemony.

   In 1944, Karl Polanyi (1886–1964) first published *The Great Transformation: The Political and Economic Origins of Our Time*, an account of the political and economic origins of nineteenth-century civilizational collapse and ushering in of a great transformation (Polanyi 2001: 3). He was fiercely critical of the socially polarizing tendencies of the rise of the market economy, the portrayal of *laissez-faire* as non-state interference, the transformation of the 'natural and human substance of society into commodities', and the creation of the 'fictitious commodities' of land, labour and capital (Polanyi 2001: 44, 71–80). Labelled 'economic liberalism', these processes form the first organizing principle in society and part of the double movement. The second organizing principle of 'social protection' relies on 'the varying support of those most immediately affected by the deleterious action of the market— primarily, but not exclusively, the working and the landed classes— ... using protective legislation, restrictive associations, and other instruments of intervention as its methods' (ibid.: 138–39). These counter-measures are in constant tension with the self-regulated market as society and the state step in to mitigate the worst effects of the ever-expanding, self-regulating market through, for example, the Gold Standard, laws to protect child labour, controls to improve factory safety, limitations to working hours, social insurance and, eventually, the welfare state. This 'toing-and-froing', or constant tension between the dynamics of the market and counter-measures, constitutes the double movement (Harvey *et al.* 2007: 8).

Polanyi is moulded to a variety of uses by critical GPE and productive engagement can be found between the 'Gramscian selections' detailed in Box 2.1 and the Polanyian deconstruction of the neoliberal myth of natural and inevitable progress. Primarily, the insight that the transition to capitalism constituted a 'great transformation' rather than a natural, inevitable process is applied to the transition from embedded liberalism to disciplinary neoliberalism. If, therefore, globalization or neoliberalism is not a natural, self-regulating process, then the imagination to envision alternatives is facilitated (Bernard 1997: 79–89). This affirms globalization as the political project of a constellation of dominant social forces rather than a spontaneous, inevitable and incontestable process and gives further substance to the transnational hegemonic capitalist class (Rupert 2000: 42; Gill 1993, 1999; van der Pijl 1984, 1997, 1998). In ideological format, neoliberalism has not emerged from an historical or political vacuum but has sustained an identifiable process of development. This confirms its promotion as a specific project by an array of actors in particular, differing, historical contexts rather than a natural or inevitable rise to dominance (Williams and Taylor 2000: 22). Such contributions demonstrate how the neoliberal myth has been used to sustain hegemony through denying the existence of alternatives to the prevailing order (Gill 2002b).

These applications of Polanyi's work significantly contribute to critical GPE understandings on neoliberal myths and are accepted in the perspective on hegemony and civil society with which this book deals. However, accounts of contemporary neoliberal and resistance movements in critical GPE problematically mirror Polanyi's account of the great transformation producing a delimiting tendency towards 'neo-Polanyian optimism' (cf. Evans 2008). They tend to explain the retraction of state involvement in the economy, expansion of market activities, consequent deleterious effects inspiring a movement by society to re-embed the economy and instil principles of democracy without considering the implications of fusing Gramscian and Polanyian concepts. For example, Cox considers that the contemporary initiation of another double movement follows the past patterns of the failure of the self-regulating market; the current project of neoliberalism is leading to greater polarization between the rich and poor, the disintegration of social bonds and further alienation (Cox 1995: 39). According to another account, society is now in the midst of a second double movement as renewed liberal economic structures associated with contemporary globalization generate both large-scale disruptions and sustained pressure for self-protection through new social movements (Mittelman 1996: 3, 10). In this way, the 'globalization of capitalism seems to be replicating globally the sequence of historic development identified by Polanyi' (Robinson 2002: 52–54). Similarly, in the contemporary sequence of development global capitalism, through neoliberalism, succeeds in removing protective mechanisms against capital accumulation, breaking up and commodifying public and private spheres, and making 'every layer of the social fabric' accessible to transnational capital (ibid.). Meanwhile, even as 'the state defers to the market as the sole organizing power in the economic and social sphere', mass pressure for change is emanating from popular disaffected majorities organizing into diverse egalitarian social movements for social change (ibid.). This account, however, is not without a certain caution towards the capacity for movements for social change to mount a full hegemonic challenge or to contest transnational capital. The irony of the proliferation of social movements alongside deepening inequalities and polarization is noted and criticism of Gramscian approaches broached (Robinson 2002: 72; Robinson 1996, see below).

The failings of the neoliberal discourse on democratization are the focus of another study which builds on the metaphorical potential of the double movement (Gill 1996, 1995). It is suggested that a second socio-political double movement encompasses 'a broad process of human empowerment that can promote a more substantive democratization of both state structures and civil society' (Gill 1996: 213–18). The double movement, thus, poses a challenge to the spread of formal, attenuated, democracy that gives unequal weight to the enlightened and/or propertied. This 'Schumpeterian elitist' theory of democracy is even more indirect and selective at the global level and usually combines with neoliberal economic prescripts that contribute to the growing gap between rich and poor (ibid.). It is suggested that a new type of politics or multilateralism is emerging, especially among the poor and marginalized in the Third World, which uses local political organization to challenge indifference and reverse disillusionment and alienation. The task of the Left, in this case, lies in linking local and transnational initiatives and relating them to labour organizations and other 'progressive elements of global civil society' (ibid.: 222):

We may, then, be in the midst of a 1990s version of Polanyi's double movement as social movements are remobilized and new coalitions are formed. Some of these will seek to protect society from the unencumbered logic of neoliberal globalizing forces and to contest the restricted idea that human possibility and worth is defined primarily through the process of consumption ... For [this type of development] to prevail would require not only ideas and networks but also institutional and material capabilities, access to resources, and the capacity to demonstrate in practical ways the ability to meet the broad needs of the people ... It would provide minimum criteria for new models of global governance and for new principles and processes of political participation and accountability.

(Gill 1996: 226)

The double movement frames broad critical GPE discourses on continuity and change. This appears to nurture productive engagement between Polanyi and Gramsci consistent with the asserted potential of Polanyi to contribute to underdeveloped aspects of Gramsci's work (Burawoy 2003). Accordingly, Polanyi is considered to provide a theory of the originating birth of civil society as a reaction to the market. Polanyi also helps to broaden Gramsci's focus on the national to the operation of markets at a variety of local, national and global levels. Lastly, cautionary reference to Polanyian active society can enhance the poor development of counter-hegemony by Gramsci through locating civil society in the realm of the private and, thus, not just in the public economic sphere (ibid.).

The Polanyian 'counter-movement' has been used in a related sense, and often interchangeably with the double movement, to explain the emergence of movements such as the Association for the Taxation of Financial Transactions for the Aid of Citizens (Association pour la Taxation des Transactions Financière pour l'Aide aux Citoyens, or ATTAC).[2] The counter-movement is considered to be spontaneous, containing no agreed upon societal or political alternative, or in other words it is a 'generalized social reaction ... largely a defensive movement' (Munck 2006a: 180). An analysis of ATTAC, however, disputes its emergence as a spontaneous counter-movement and instead locates its opposition to globalization as 'the result of a political and cultural process conditioned by previous contentious episodes and struggles' (Ancelovici 2002: 429). This view finds agreement in a further study in which a Polanyian analysis of ATTAC is rejected in the context of current state-society relations (Birchfield and Freyberg-Inan 2004). The 'protectionist collective reaction' of Polanyi's active society is not considered to be directly comparable to the current 'premeditated, ideologically driven response' (ibid: 280–81).[3] Despite this source of agreement, however, the former analysis is constrained by an almost exclusive emphasis on state-society relations within national institutional configurations. In contrast, the latter characterizes ATTAC as a global social movement that signals the emergence of global civil society (Birchfield and Freyberg-Inan 2005).[4] This association with an 'embryonic' global civil society or transnational counter-hegemonic societal force, however, remains tentative.

While these accounts do not share this book's focus on the conceptual potential of global civil society, their critiques of the presentation of ATTAC as a counter-movement are more mindful of possible tension and contradiction between Polanyian and Gramscian perspectives than other critical GPE studies. Meanwhile, as I will examine further in the next chapter, a conceptual, agency-centred focus on global civil society contributes to a critical political economy perspective on resistance in a way that questions a seamless integration of Polanyi into critical GPE. It facilitates a revision of our understandings on hegemony that breaks down the increasingly binary reference to its counterpart as counter-hegemony. Telling stories of 'great folly and gradual redress' (cf. Lacher 1999a: 322),[5] critical IPE has not yet engaged fully with the contradictions between counter-hegemony and double/.counter-movements. The fusion of Polanyi and Gramsci gives 'a certain automatic and inevitable quality to resistance, as though it emerges naturally from subordination' (Amoore 2005: 14). It tends to reduce opposition to globalization to 'a structural side effect' or 'a spontaneous countermovement' (Ancelovici 2002: 429). From a categorical research perspective, while the starting point of Gramscian approaches is not in question, further engagement between conceptual interaction and substantive social conditions would make it plausibly more surprising if counter-movements were not to emerge than if they were to do so (cf. Thompson 1963: 647).

These representations of contestation are especially problematic in relation to political agency and here lies the essential contradiction that emanates from their fusion (Neufeld 2002). This contradiction is present in the neo-Gramscian use of the notion of the 'double movement' to conceptualize the automatic reactionary rise of resistance to the globalization of capital, despite theorizing, at the same time, a self-conscious agency in the making of history (ibid.). The myth of the double movement and reluctance to extend analyses beyond the structural power of capital stymies neo-Gramscian efforts to consider active resistance (ibid.: 12). Implicit recognition of this contradiction and continued reluctance to address it may also explain the characteristic caution that can be found in Gramscian approaches to resistance. In response, in this book I draw on E.P. Thompson (1963, 1978), among other critical scholars, to emphasize the role of a self-conscious agency in the making of history.[6] This aims to move beyond the more superficial development of 'metaphors', which has led to a noticeable failure of more tangible accounts of resistance to emerge (cf. Birchfield 1999). Thus, the focus in this book turns from using Polanyi's double movement as a 'metaphor' for the 'socio-political forces which wish to assert more democratic control over political life' (Gill 1995: 67, cited in Birchfield 1999: 39). While social scientific conventions might agree that 'analogies, metaphors, images are not the same thing as concepts' (Thompson 1978: 296), the main issue on which I wish to focus concerns the nature of association to more tangible realities. I focus on a conceptualization of global civil society which more readily admits me to suggest a method of translation through the dialectics of concept and reality.[7]

The dialectics of concept and reality

The empirical attributes of the changing realities of global restructuring and related changes in production and consumption patterns are intensely negotiated in IPE through an expanding array of concepts, metaphors, analogies and images. There are, nonetheless, remaining challenges in using counter-hegemony and civil society to conceptualize resistance in the global political economy. In confronting them, it is useful first to recall a central tenet of critical thought which considers that '[b]ecause it deals with a changing reality, critical theory must continually adjust its concepts to the changing object it seeks to understand and explain' (Cox 1981: 209). The evolution of concepts to fit their object of understanding and explanation is not without contention. A recent interpretation of Gramscian hegemony, for example, considers that it is no longer relevant to contemporary radical social movements (Day 2005). In considering how hegemony might productively be used today it is to Gramsci's method itself to which I return. Introduced in Box 2.1, Gramscian concepts are not exempt from many of the 'general problems of meaning and understanding in the history of ideas' (Germain and Kenny 1998: 13), as I discuss in the next chapter in relation to civil society. The prison notebooks convey a form of 'absolute historicism' or 'approach to philosophy and concrete political activity that conceived the historical process as a synthesis of past and present' (Morton 2003: 126). This approach situates Gramscian concepts in their specific contextual background, and enunciates absolute historicism as a way through which Gramsci may be read in order to appreciate his ideas in and beyond their context. Meanwhile, it is recognized that an extreme emphasis on contextual issues can result in an austere historicism 'that stymies any attempt to appreciate the contemporary resonance of Gramsci's work' and 'reduces past forms of thought to their precise historical context and tends to regulate Gramsci to history' (Morton 2003: 120, 127). Thus, it has been contended that *Gramsci is Dead* (Day 2005).

Care might still be taken to distinguish between concepts that are relevant to current circumstances and those that remain limited to their specific historical context (Morton 2003). An absolute historicist reading of Gramsci appreciates the contemporary significance of his writings without automatically assuming that they are relevant for all contexts. Gramsci himself notes that Machiavelli is considered to be 'relevant in every period' and advises that he 'should be considered more as a necessary expression of his time, and as closely tied to the conditions and exigencies of his time' (Gramsci 1971: 140–43). This is not to deny the possibility of contemporary applications of Machiavelli but, rather, to encourage critical engagement with the exigencies of past and present concepts. Even so, neo-Gramscians have been criticized for failing to develop a theoretical specification of the principal structures of the international system: 'for no amount of discussion of such themes as 'hegemony', 'historic blocs' and 'transnational capital' adds up to a theory of the modern states system or of the world market' (Bromley 1995: 232). They have been further challenged for failing to raise a host of questions concerning resistance to global forces and for not analysing concrete alternatives to neoliberalism (Robinson 1996: 382 cited in Morton 2000: 255; and above). Partly, these shortcomings may be attributed to rigid adherence to Gramsci's text which produces a form of austere historicism and prevents the generation of new meanings within contemporary contexts (Morton 2003, 2007a).

In this book, Gramscian concepts are applied to the contemporary political economy in a manner that while remaining sensitive to the exigencies of Gramsci's time, extends and builds on the initial conceptual and contextual conditions within which they were founded. This approach remains cognisant that ideas, concepts and theories can be adjusted to changing realities to produce more effective understandings and explanations of change and contestation. It is understood as implicitly sharing broad post-positivist precepts so that 'all theoretical efforts proceed from and embody a perspective' (Neufeld 1995: 6; Cox 1981). It is post-positivist in moving from associating 'true' and 'reliable' knowledge directly with empirical facts, applying the same research methodology to the natural world and social world, and establishing the value-free nature of scientific knowledge (Neufeld 1995: 33). Instead, this approach aims to be self-consciously reflexive, intentionally interpretative and explicitly critical of the existing global order (ibid.).

While Gramscian perspectives in International Political Economy share broad post-positivist precepts, a consistent Gramscian approach to resistance has not emerged. There has been progress at a meta-theoretical level and there is an expanding literature on Gramscian (Morton 2003), neo-Gramscian (Augelli and Murphy 1988; Cox 2002; Gill 2008; Murphy and Tooze 1991; Rupert 2003; Worth 2011) and alternative Gramscian (Jessop and Sum 2006) approaches. However, progress 'at the level of theoretical analysis of concrete issues', particularly in the case of the politics of resistance, 'remains little more than potentiality' (cf. Neufeld 1995: 125). Hegemony continues to be downplayed in (neo)Gramscian literature in a way that remains entirely coherent with the following critique:

> It is ironic that through their focus on the coherence and expansiveness of these so-called transnational classes, the new Gramscians have down-played one of the central insights provided by Gramsci with regard to hegemony, namely, that dominant and subaltern classes engage in a series of material and ideological struggles which change the very nature of the terrain under contestation.
>
> (Germain and Kenny 1998: 18)

The meta-theoretical and conceptual focus of this book emphasizes reflexive and interpretative modes of knowledge production and the more constructive role of theory to enable criticism of the existing global order and alternative ways of 'seeing' and 'doing' in critical GPE. In reinvigorating this enterprise, the attractions of using Gramsci are acknowledged, such as his insistence on the 'transformative capacity of human beings' and 'radical embrace of human subjectivity' (Germain and Kenny 1998: 5). These attractions help to avoid deterministic and ahistorical structuralism, but they also call for further mediation on Gramsci's meaning. Over-reliance on 'transformative' examples of counter-hegemony, without sufficient attention to the complexity of empirical realities and conceptual adjustment, leads back to the determinism and ahistorical structuralism that most critical theories set out to avoid. This opens up what might be considered a contradictory way forward.

Critical GPE is often defined by what it is not (orthodox, positivist, neo-realist, state-centric) and despite some advances, there is a wider reluctance to facilitate its 'outward' expansion and development. The risks of overproblematizing orthodox theories can be very clearly outlined as:

> the energies of critique get caught up in a backward looking theoretical debate rather than being pushed outward into the exploration of how critical insights may be used to strengthen understanding and explanation in the realm of international politics.
>
> (Hutchings 2001: 87)

There is much from which an 'outward' expansion of critical GPE, as opposed to an inward-looking disciplinary-bounded process, can benefit. Moving from its traditional orientation of critique within IR/IPE opens critical GPE towards new benefits such as: the elaboration of new conceptual frameworks and methodological techniques; the fostering of alternative explanations for phenomena only realism has traditionally approached; and/ or the broadening of research to include phenomena that orthodox theories tended to exclude, such as democracy, social movements and the study of other such areas Global Political Economy has already initiated (ibid.: 87–89). On the one hand, then, the view on critical GPE in this book supports outward expansion. On the other hand, it does not assume that the older debates have been resolved or that having resolved its earlier antagonisms, critical GPE is in a position to definitively move forward. Much further attention, in particular, can be given to periodical reminders of central critical IPE tenets: to address issues such as powerlessness and fundamental change in a 'new IPE' (Murphy and Tooze 1991); and to configure an 'historicist turn' through reintroducing people 'as the agents at the centre of historical change' (Gills 2000: 6).

These reminders are reinforced and hegemony and civil society more concretely understood through the dialectical nexus between concept and reality (Gramsci 1971; Cox 1999). Dialectical practices and forms of thought precede the ancient Socratic method of dialogue which, through the positing of questions and answers, was believed to lead to the advancement of ideas. Meanwhile, a basic definition of dialectics suggests "'the existence or action of opposing forces or tendencies in society" and an understanding of history as "a series of contradictions and their solutions" though not necessarily a unity of opposites as in the Hegelian version of dialectics' (Gills 2003: 93, citing the *Oxford English Dictionary*). It enables a broad appreciation of the theoretical advances of historical materialism in relation to structural Marxism and contributes to the assessment of the core features of critical GPE, and consequently, to review their limitations and avenues for further conceptualization. In the remainder of this chapter I focus on recovering the substantive meaning and advances of Gramscian Marxism through dialectics and drawing on the analysis of 'theory interacting with enquiry' (Thompson 1963, 1978: 275) in a way that facilitates a re-conceptualization of global civil society and hegemony in their relation to contemporary processes of continuity and change. Focusing on the dialectics of concept and reality is alternatively situated, then, to presuppose the unity of opposites as in Hegelian dialectics, as the following shows.

Hegel (1770–1831) brought abstract, empirical thought or ideas on the world towards scepticism or negation, which would, correspondingly, produce a higher plane of complex understanding or 'speculative' thought (van der Pijl 2009). Characterized by negation and resolution, these processes mark Hegel's understanding of dialectics which drives forth historical consciousness in the form of thesis-antithesis-synthesis. The nature of reality (ontology) and methods of understanding reality (epistemology) are based on contradiction so that in its given form reality is 'always constituted by contradiction and the resolution of contradiction' (Patten 2003: 393). Uncovering the sequence of contradictions and resolutions that constructs reality in turn enables greater understanding, according to Hegel.

The Hegelian tradition of dialectics was primarily metaphysical and was critiqued by Marx as a form of philosophical idealism. Nonetheless, Marx inherited from Hegel the meaning of dialectics as an epistemology whereby historical change is interpreted in terms of contradictions at successive levels of abstraction (van der Pijl 2009: 28). However, Marx did not locate such contradictions in the thought process and nor as a principle of nature as Hegel did but within the historical process, in exploitation and domination, in the material world, society and classes (ibid.: 204, 206). Marx, therefore, stood Hegel's dialectic on its head arguing that: 'You must turn it the right way up again if you want to discover the rational kernel that is hidden away within the wrappings of mystification' (Marx 1934, cited in Boucher 1998: 357). To further illustrate, according to Marx, Hegel:

> fell into the illusion of conceiving the real as the product of thought concentrating itself, probing its own depths, and unfolding itself out of itself, by itself, whereas the method of rising from the abstract to the

concrete is only the way in which thought appropriates the concrete, reproduces it as the concrete of the mind. But this is by no means the process by which the concrete itself comes into being.

(Marx 1993: 101)

For Marx 'thought was not self-generating but was "a product, rather, of the working-up of *observation* and *conception* into concepts"' (Thompson 1978: 255, emphasis added).[8] This builds on Marx's well-known line that 'philosophers have only interpreted the world, in various ways; the point is to change it', through pointing to his conception of political practice as integral to his social theory so that drawing on the 'theses on Feurerbach'; the 'dispute over the reality or non-reality of thinking that is isolated from practice is a purely scholastic question' (Marx 1986, cited in Smith 1996: 195). More succinctly, Marx's adaptation of the Hegelian dialectical method integrated theory and practice (Smith 1996).

Hegel's 'philosophical idealism' or the 'doctrine that it is ideas or concepts which constitute reality and not material, physical or existent things', was criticized by Marx for contributing to an uncritical and conservative under-standing of social and political conditions (Burns 2002: 164–65; Marx 1967: 139). However, if philosophical idealism can be extrapolated from Hegel's philosophy, as Engels described, its revolutionary and critical character becomes apparent. Historical dialectics, along this understanding, 'means that subjects (classes, states) "make their own history but not in circumstances of their own choosing" (because of the "objective" circumstances they have cre-ated before)' (van der Pijl 2009: 28). To explain further, as suggested through historical materialism, and here Marx emphasizes his distinction to Hegel, social circumstances determine the ideas of man (ibid.). 'The Idea' is not a subject external to the 'real world' but, rather, 'is nothing else than the material world reflected by the human mind' (Marx 1995: 11). However, while dialectics and contradictions were 'very much alive' for Marx, they do not equate to a principle of nature or formula that can be applied to all circumstances (van der Pijl 2009: 206; Boucher 1998: 360). Marxist dialectics also remain apart from crude forms of dialectical materialism such as put forward by Althusser (2006; Althusser and Balibar 2009), and criticized by Thompson (1978) (see below). In the contemporary context this is worth underlining as the dis-cussion on 'neo-Polanyian optimism' suggests above. Thus, identifying a variety of contradictions inherent in neoliberal globalization does not naturally lead to a delineated rise of human agency apposite to challenging them. Globalization and contestation, in other words, are not mechanical, inexorable forces:

Consequently, we must appreciate that in social life dialectics cannot be reduced to some mechanistic, inexorable force that drives all forward to a rational, progressive synthesis, or hold faith in the power of reason that with the mere recognition of contradiction humankind shall immediately bring forth purposive change.

(Brincat 2010: 9)

Althusser challenged Marx's 'inversion' of the dialectic to emphasize materialism while simultaneously neglecting the material conditions and practices that underlie abstract, philosophical and ideological questions (Townshend 2002: 209). For both Thompson and Althusser the Soviet Communist Party's denunciation of Stalin in 1956 was a formative event. Althusser was subsequently critical of the emerging 'humanist' tendencies in the international communist movement and was strongly critical of 'historicism'. Meanwhile, in *The Poverty of Theory or an Orrery of Errors*, Thompson was immensely scathing of Althusser's 'assault upon "historicism"' (Thompson 1978: 194) as an attempt to construct Marxist science at the level of philosophy through 'the pure refinement of concepts' (McNally 1993). Like Gramsci (1971), Thompson rejects 'Althusserian' forms of scientist or deterministic Marxism in finding an 'orrery of errors' therein.[9] Part of his motivation for doing so may lie in concern for the conceptual 'lethargy' and consequent inadequate responses by historical materialists to Althusserian arguments (Thompson 1978: 191). Consequently, he set forth to demonstrate how: 'In the name of science, Althusser had purged the [Marxian] legacy of its rich dialectical content while imposing a deadening ahistorical finality' (Ashley 1984: 226). Thompson's reading of Althusser demonstrates a clear concern with the *interaction* of concept and reality, elsewhere referred to as the dialectics of concept and reality (Cox 1999). Althusser, in contrast, was concerned to separate the 'order of thought' from the 'order of the real' so that thoughts about the real belong, not to the order of the real, but to the order of thought. On the contrary, Thompson protests, 'the real is not "out there" and thought within the quiet lecture-theatre of our heads, "inside here"' (Thompson 1978: 210). Instead, 'Thought and being inhabit a single space, which space is ourselves ... even as we contemplate the "real" we experience our own palpable reality' (ibid.).

Reminiscent of the working-class experiences extolled in *The Making of the English Working Class* (Thompson 1963), Althusser's failure to attend to the 'thrusting-forth of the "real world"' or to 'the dialogue between social being and social consciousness' is criticized in *The Poverty of Theory or An Orrery of Errors* (Thompson 1978: 200–1, 209). Thompson is critical of the formation of 'static, a-historical categories' such as social class: 'a self-defining historical formation, which men and women make out of their own experience of struggle', but which 'has been reduced to a static category, or an effect of an ulterior structure, of which men are not the makers but the vectors' (ibid.: 238). Rather, historian Marxists are concerned 'every day, in their practice, with the formation of, and with the tensions within, social consciousness' (ibid.: 199), and in a passage that is worthwhile reproducing in full:

> Evidence does not stand compliantly like a table for interrogation: it stirs, in the medium of time, before our eyes. These stirrings, these events, if they are within 'social being' seem often to impinge upon, thrust into, break against, existent social consciousness. They propose new problems,

and, above all, they continually give rise to *experience*—a category which, however imperfect it may be, is indispensable to the historian since it comprises the mental and emotional response, whether of an individual or of a social group, to many inter-related events or to many repetitions of the same kind of event ... what we mean is that changes take place within social being, which give rise to changed *experience*: and this experience is *determining*, in the sense that it exerts pressures upon existent social consciousness, proposes new questions, and affects much of the material which the more elaborated intellectual exercises are about.

(Thompson 1978: 199–200)

The World Social Forum and the World People's Conference on Climate Change (see Chapters 5 and 6, respectively) represent evidence of such 'stirrings' that provoke various tensional responses affecting contemporary social consciousness and give some indication of how 'old conceptual systems may crumble' in the face of general experiences (Thompson 1978: 201). While Thompson was concerned with the experiences of 'fascism, Stalinism, racism, and of the contradictory phenomenon of working-class "affluence" within sectors of capitalist economies', contemporary experiences are once again 'breaking in and demanding that we reconstruct our categories' (Thompson 1978: 217). Thus, there are two 'dialogues' through which our knowledge is formed (and both of which Althusser is accused by Thompson of failing to understand). The first concerns reality or 'the dialogue between social being and social consciousness, which gives rise to experience' and the second concerns conceptualization or 'the theoretical organisation (in all its complexity) of evidence, on the one hand, and the determinate character of its object on the other' (ibid.: 225). In examining these 'dialogues', and in defending historical materialism, Thompson attempts to reinvigorate 'dialectics' from its position as 'the plaything of scholasticism' (ibid.: 235). This attempt to remove historical materialism from its doctrinaire interpretations and from the region of 'Grand Theory' or theoretical truth, appreciates it as 'a developing *knowledge*, albeit a provisional and approximate knowledge with many silences and impurities', which takes place 'both within theory and within practice: it arises from a dialogue' (ibid.: 242, emphasis in original).

Althusser, according to Thompson, is more concerned with establishing the fixity of concepts and is scathing of the 'obvious' 'tautology' expressed by Engels in differentiating between concepts and their 'real object' (Thompson 1978: 247–48). Defending Engels, Thompson uses the concept of feudalism to provide further explanation of the relationship between concept and reality.[10] Even if it was never fully realized in its 'full classical form', feudalism is necessary towards understanding European medieval society (ibid.). In other words, feudalism is 'a heuristic concept which represents (corresponds to) real social formations, but, in the manner of all such concepts, it does so in an overly purified and logical way. The definition cannot give us the real event' (ibid.). According to Thompson, what this comes back to is the far more complex 'cry for "dialectics"', an important part of which is 'that "dialogue" between concept and evidence' (ibid.). It reminds, for example, of 'the particular flexibility of concepts appropriate in historical categories, as expectations rather than as rules', and confirms the view of 'dialectics' that is also carried forward in this book 'not as this or that "law" but as a habit of thinking (in co-existing opposites or "contraries") and as an expectation' (Thompson 1978: 249, 302, 306).

This view on the dialectic contrasts to the negative dialectic. Presented by Adorno and Horkheimer (1944) in *The Dialectic of Enlightenment*, this is reflective of the more pessimistic writings of the Frankfurt School from the 1940s onwards which were sceptical of the Enlightenment and prospects for transformation. This work put critical theory forward as a critique of instrumental rationality. The more optimistic, if not utopian (Hoffman 1987), project of emancipation in critical theory, directed by critical thinkers such as Habermas, Cox, Gill and Booth, provides a complex, but welcome, contrast (Rengger 2001). Much further attention than hitherto given to Gramscian dialectics potentially facilitates greater understanding on the politics of resistance in the global political economy and builds on Gramscian potential to focus epistemologically on the 'intersubjective meanings that constitute human practices and institutions', and on the 'dialectical relationship between consciousness and being' that contributes to the making of global civil society (cf. Neufeld 2002: 3; Cox 1999: 15–16). The inter-related dimensions of Gramscian dialectics may also be understood in terms of ontology, or the nature of historical processes of change leading to new forms of consciousness that replace previously dominant forms (ibid.).

Towards global civil society and transversal hegemony

Movement towards global civil society and transversal hegemony draws on a form of absolute historicism, extending more fully on Cox (1999: 5; Cox 2002) and Gramscian historical and dialectical thought than hitherto and linking Gramscian concepts to his perception of the transitory reality of his time and intellectual consequence of concepts as an instrument for change. The next chapter draws on the concept of civil society not with the intention of freezing a particular moment of history and privileging the prevailing relations of social forces therein, but with the objective of trying '*to understand the historical variations that have altered the meanings of the concept in an ongoing dialectic of concept and reality*' (Cox 1999: 5, emphasis added), as they have consequence for the making of global civil society and relations of force (see Box 2.1) in the politics of resistance.

The dialectics of concept and reality corresponds to the dialectical nexus between categories of research and movement (Gramsci 1971: 178; see Box 2.1). This builds on earlier critiques of determinism in Marxist thought which, through fetishizing capitalist structures and the logic of capital, 'tend to reduce people to interact "rationally" and "instrumentally"', thus equating subjects with objects and making it 'impossible to bring back the subject' (Knafo 2002: 148). While Gramscian approaches avoid the resulting 'deterministic conception of capitalism', a prevailing neo-Polanyian influence makes it more challenging to evade also a 'voluntaristic view of social change' (cf. ibid.: 149). The layers of dialectical interaction between global civil society as a concept and real existing force denote its contradictions at various levels of relations of force and exigency in responding to a binary counterpart or counter-hegemony. The positive impact or outcome of the dialectical interaction between concept and reality can be further outlined to emphasize that:

> Civil society is not just an assemblage of actors, i.e. autonomous social groups. It is also a realm of contesting ideas in which the inter-subjective meanings upon which people's sense of 'reality' are based can become transformed and new concepts of the natural order of society can emerge.
> (Cox 2002: 102)

Thompson recalls the co-option and assimilation of pre-Cold War reforms and their assignment to 'new functions' by the capitalist mode of production during the 'structural stasis' of the Cold War (Thompson 1978: 265), but this is only how it seemed, and reflects only a tendency to 'fall into' the scientific vocabulary of structuralism because this process was 'still the outcome of human choices and struggles' (ibid.).[11] In speaking of 'vocabularies' Thompson refers to 'their sense as ideology', born of the 'pressure of real experience which has seemed to licence the adoption of a particular language of social and political analysis, an ideological predisposition towards one vocabulary or another' (ibid.: 266). Thus, 'the poetry of voluntarism' is preferable to the '"scientific" vocabulary of structuralism' (ibid.: 264). Along similar lines to Thompson's identification of the tendency to 'fall into' the vocabulary of scientific structuralism, Rengger (2001) refers to the 'fateful—and possibly fatal—dilemma' of achieving an emancipatory project of IR theory as the 'Adorno problem' or the tendency towards 'tipping ... back into the clutches of instrumental rationality'. We are reassured, however, that 'there is ... much that critical theory might do to seek to overcome this negative dialectic' and it is suggested that '[t]he various strands of so-called postpositivist theory in international relations do indeed reinforce each other on certain key issues' (Rengger 2001: 106). While Rengger is, nonetheless, sceptical of the possibilities for critical theory to overcome the negative dialectic that is suggested to lie at its centre, the dialectical nexus opens towards further engagement with new ways of seeing.

Notes

1 See Ruggie (1993) on problematizing modernity in international relations. With reference to the discipline of International Relations (IR), he suggests that we are not very good at studying the possibility of fundamental discontinuity in the international system and even lack the adequate language so that '[w]hat we cannot describe, we cannot explain' (Ruggie 1993: 144).

2 ATTAC was founded in 1998 with an explicit objective to generate a tax on financial transactions both to curb market speculation and contribute to a development fund. It is discussed in relation to its role in the World Social Forum in Chapter 5.

3 See also the defence of José Bové, a key personality in the peasant organization Via Campesina, 'against the portrayal of his campaign as reactionary or protectionist' in Birchfield (2005: 589). There is a slight contradiction with Birchfield and Freyberg-Inan (2004) as Birchfield (2005) appears to present a more flattering picture of Polanyian active society when suggesting that only a 'too narrow reading' of Polanyi and Bové may reveal a conservative and reactionary societal counter-movement.

4 See also Amin (2005), who disputes the presentation of a spontaneous and powerful multitude as a real existing force opposing Empire, suggesting that this presentation stems from American liberalism.

5 This phrasing draws on Lacher's critique of contemporary readings of Polanyi for historical permutation and inaccurate application of 'embeddedness' and 'societal protectionism' to GPE (Lacher 1999a: 322).

6 Neufeld (2002: 13) prefers to consider Rosa Luxemburg's conception of revolution as 'the active—but not automatic—resistance of conscienticized masses'. Meanwhile, for an analysis of Rosa Luxemburg's legacy in GPE see Worth (2006, 2012).

7 See Chapter 7 for more on this. Bleiker (2000, 2009), for example, puts forward a more aesthetic approach to world politics and offers a compelling appreciation of a wider set of knowledge practices than social science has traditionally offered.

8 Nonetheless, Thompson finds in parts of the *Grundrisse* aspects of an 'unreconstructed Hegalianism' and a sense that 'Marx's thought is locked inside a static, anti-historical structure' (Thompson 1978: 253–54). Capital, Thompson suggests, becomes Idea which unfolds in history and its development is determined by the innate logic of the category. This is a form of organic structuralism which posits capitalism, or the 'organic system' according to Marx, as a consequent effect of capital. The other side to this is put forward by historical materialism, Thompson suggests, as a real historical process that posits the logic of capitalist process within all the activities of society.

9 Peter Thomas (2009: 25–26) views Althusser and Gramsci as 'two types or poles' of Marxism, whereby 'They should be understood as two significant tendencies or approaches to the question of Marxism and philosophy which have accompanied the tradition throughout its history'. He suggests that the 'apparently decided debate' between Althusser and Gramsci is 'ripe for a re-examination' (ibid.: 35).

10 Thompson's defence of Engels is significant for underlining Thompson's thoughts on the matter and so, for this reason, the particularities of Engels discussion are not examined here. In summary, Engels makes three points: 1 because all concepts are approximations, this does not make them 'fictions'; 2 only concepts can enable us to 'make sense of', understand and know, objective reality; and 3 even in the act of knowing we can (and ought to) know our concepts are more abstract and more logical than the diversity of that reality—and, by empirical observations, *we can know this too.*

11 Ashley (1984: 254) underlines the difficulties of moving beyond positivism in a similar manner through suggesting that 'as positivists, we join them in excluding from the realm of proper scientific discourse precisely those modes of criticism that would allow us to unmask the move for what it is ... we are given to feel that we have stumbled beyond the legitimate grounds of science, into the realm of personal ethics, values, loyalties, or ends'. See also Ashley's discussion on structuralism which draws on Thompson (1978).

3   The making of global civil society

Civil society is a potent expression of post-Cold War concepts and practices and part of coming to terms with global transformations. The rediscovery and legitimation of the term in Eastern Europe and Latin America amid opposition to military regimes in the 1980s is, for example, considered part of a particular conjuncture from which 'global politics' emerged (Kaldor 2003a). Since then, extant and nascent versions of global civil society have been increasingly related to episodes and movements of resistance such as the anti-World Trade Organization (WTO) demonstrations in Seattle in 1999. Receiving less worldwide attention, the World Social Forum, a gathering of opponents to neoliberal globalization, began to convene shortly after. More recently, the reinvigoration of civil society in Egypt and Tunisia in 2011 was considered to signal the 'completion' of the 1989 revolutions in Eastern Europe (Kaldor 2011). Meanwhile, from 15 May 2011, Spanish indignants or *indignados* marched in protest against high unemployment and government policies, 15-M movements camp out in city squares in Madrid, Barcelona and across Spain, and occupy movements mobilize and expand beyond Occupy Wall Street in Zuccotti Park, New York, claiming their position as the 99 per cent within the hierarchies of power and influence.[1]

The longer rise and ebb of the 'historical fortunes' of civil society—from being at the centre of late seventeenth- and eighteenth-century European discourses—to its social and global expansion in the eighteenth and early nineteenth centuries and subsequent crisis during the era of totalitarianism and Cold War is considered in this chapter (cf. Hall and Trentmann 2005: 2). The last decades have seen a revival in the use of the term, increasingly referred to as 'global' and considered to combat state domination and neo-liberal marketization (Wagner 2006), but it cannot yet be understood apart from its historical accumulation of 'different and sometimes incommensurable' meanings (Bartelson 2000: 181). While some scholars have deployed Polanyian active society and Gramscian hegemony to understand this revival, there has been a broader, and not incompatible, tendency for the civil society literature to merge with literature on social movements, alter-globalization and activism to assert the transformative and emancipative capacity of global civil society. Tracing the accumulations of meanings associated with global civil society in this chapter highlights it as a developing—provisional and approximate—form of knowledge (Thompson 1978: 242) which can potentially contribute to a framework towards understanding movements of transversal hegemony and the nexus of global social relations in the global political economy. This does not deny the deep challenges that are implicit in any move towards the 'global' (Walker 2005, 2010), but it does reaffirm the significance of the global political imagination in re-conceptualizing global civil society and detailing its responses to changing patterns of hegemony in the global political economy.

Global inaccessibility

Attempting to integrate global civil society into Global Political Economy (GPE) appears to set up an anomaly. The degree of attention given to a broad conceptualization of civil societal actors in the global political economy has been scantily addressed until recently, with much focus placed on the state, market and large international firms as transnational actors (Williams 2005: 345). Moves towards an increased focus on civil society occur alongside more intensive cross-disciplinary conceptual questioning of orthodox ideas on political community and state sovereignty but much remains to be done. While formal networks of governance, whether national, regional or global, corporate or governmental, are dominant themes, less attention is given to informal modes of governance through which other less visible actors influence policy making in the global political economy. Indeed, when civil society is mentioned, it is often put forward in a contradictory way that fails to break convincingly with orthodoxy established through the field of International Relations (IR). The resulting anomaly between this field and global civil society has led to marginal study of their relationship. This has particularly impacted on understandings of global civil society in studies of global governance and alter-globalization.

To date, much theory on social movements shares a distinctly non-political economy approach, leaving much analysis on the politics of resistance unaddressed. Constructivist-dominated approaches tend to treat social movements as 'theoretically unproblematic units with similar rationales and modes of operation' (Olesen 2005: 120).[2] Consequently, there has been a lack of attention to a 'theoretically informed understanding of social movements and also to the interplay between structure, power and social movements in world politics' (ibid.). The focus of a study on *Constructing Global Civil Society* also expresses concern with the constructivist emphasis on norms rather than power, which produces, it is argued, a weak and selective correlation between increases in non-governmental organization (NGO) and campaign group numbers with an ethical shift in global political norms and principles (Chandler 2004a: 42). This form of analysis leads to susceptibility on the part of social movement studies 'to the illusion that bigger is always better' (Walker 2005: 136). In addition, the constructivist focus on the norms created through neoliberal legitimation of 'global civil society' through allowing activist access to international organizations, is also criticized for drawing attention away from inherent power relations (Chandler 2004a: 53).

Marginalization is also apparent in the distinction between, on the one hand, social movements as an inclusive ontological realm dealing with phenomena that occur within society, and on the other, the field of International Relations as that exclusive realm priortizing state sovereignty or what goes on 'out there' beyond society (Walker 2005: 136; cf. Scholte 1993: 4–8). This binary opposition or 'Great Divide' (Clarke 1998, 1999: 15–33) delineates separate 'international' and 'domestic' fields, often studied through incommensurable frameworks using differing tools of analysis. Accordingly, IR traditionally deals with the study of sovereign states that, in the absence of an overarching authority, exist in a state of anarchy, aspects of which have been carried over to the study of GPE and inherently to delimiting references to civil society from within this remit. As a result, there is 'serious conceptual trouble' with the idea of an emerging global civil society that reinforces, rather than challenges, statist discourse which can itself be seen to exemplify the conceptual complications of any move from IR to world politics (Walker 2005: 139; Walker 2010). However, while global civil society frequently gets caught up in what it is trying to transcend, it still retains an emancipatory purpose. This means, therefore, that:

> Denying the existence of something distinctively global on grounds of its ontological impossibility is not very helpful if we want to understand how present relocations of political authority have been justified with reference to various global imaginaries.
>
> (Bartelson 2011: 290)

Global imaginaries implicate the global political imagination and, in relation to global civil society, this imagination evolves through an accumulation of meanings. However, its contextualized positioning in relation to the global political economy is less considered for reasoning of 'global inaccessibility' (cf. Jameson 1990).

The overview below can capture just some of the complexities of the accumulations of meanings inherent to global civil society but many of them are used to 'condemn us to our current political imagination' (Brasset 2011: 291). In attempting to capture some of the significance of meaning, what emerges is the degree to which global civil society fails to achieve clarity as it oscillates between visions of particularity and universality. Partly, this reflects what is perceived to be the vast complexity and inaccessibility of a changing more 'global' world. The widening structural coordinates of globalization and the accompanying complexity of processes, actors and institutions drive an extensive gap between the concepts that we use and their capacity to capture the intensity of associated experiences (cf. Jameson 1990). Correspondingly, conceptualizations of global civil society, as has been acknowledged by its many critics, fail to achieve a clear articulation of meaning. While global complexity may present one obstacle, the differing and sometimes incommensurable accumulation of meanings of 'civil society' appears to present another. Notwithstanding this, or some might suggest precisely because of its accumulation of meanings, global civil society continues to be used as a 'magical explanatory formula' that is vague and evades definition 'in any illuminating, systematic way or [fails] to explain convincingly why it (or the phenomena it supposedly described) came to assume such overwhelming importance at this particular time' (Buttigieg 1995: 2). However, the conceptual history of civil society, with its frequently incommensurable and ill-defined readings, retains significance and continues to influence modes of relation to the global political economy. At the same time, the exclusivity of state sovereignty is so heavily entrenched and corresponding critique of the vagaries and imaginaries of the global, that global civil society is confined to the innocuous. The task of 'reimagining' civil society in material terms—if 'what matters' is the relationship between matter and global imaginaries—begins with examining accumulations of meanings in relation to varying usages of the concept and its relationship to alter-globalization.

Accumulations of meanings

The concept of civil society has evolved through different historical epochs with individual thinkers 'imparting subtle and distinctive inflexions to the theoretical use of the concept' (Kaviraj and Khilnani 2001: 3). For John Locke (1631–1704), civil society signalled individualist relations of trust and consent based on the rule of law—a social contract—which contrasted with the despotism and violence of the state of nature. Later, during the Scottish and French Enlightenment, civil society and the growing influence of the bourgeoisie were seen to be synonymous, and were influential in melding the pursuit of particular interests with the notion of common welfare (Cox 1999: 6). This reflected the belief in the capacity of a secular commercial civil society to bring individuals together into larger societies and gradually more inclusive groups (Khilnani 2001: 22). The 'social self-cohesiveness' that resulted from commercial society was considered to provide equilibrium and restraint in political power (ibid.). Montesquieu (1689–1755), in a wider extension of this idea, emphasized the 'moral and civilizing effect' of commerce on social and international relations to alleviate prejudices and foster peace and intercultural exchange (Hall and Trentmann 2005: 7). Meanwhile, for Adam Smith (1723–90) the frivolous nature of consumption served to drive further consumption and production while maintaining social harmony. Commercial civil society, it was maintained, achieved a higher form of human association, based not on exclusive and non-voluntary relations such as kinship, which were prevalent in pre-commercial societies, but modelled on 'universal sociability' and the generation of 'an independent social self-cohesiveness and consistency, collectively beneficial and self-regulating' (ibid.). The conceptual denomination of 'commercial' civil society came to mark the opening up of a distinction between the realms of market exchange and personal relations.

In contrast to some of these above-mentioned earlier thinkers, Hegel (1770–1831) maintained in his *Philosophy of Right* that civil society was inherently unstable:

> It threw up acute contrasts of wealth and poverty, created a rootless and discontented 'rabble', and was ridden with tensions and conflicts that it could not itself regulate. It also lacked collective self-consciousness, capacity for collective self-reflection, and a sense of moral direction.
>
> (Parekh 2004: 16–17)

Hegel considered that although civil society was nurtured and regulated by the state, it was still distinguishable from the state and political society—it was both subordinate and distinct to the concept of the state (Bartelson 2006: 377). Some have taken this to mean that Hegel did not view civil society as an entirely autonomous self-organizing realm: 'for him the state remained the higher institution that ultimately held together the social fabric, and maybe even was the guarantor of that civility which society on its own was often enough lacking' (Wagner 2006: 2). These essential tensions are captured in the following extract from Hegel:

> In civil society, the Idea is lost in particularity and has fallen asunder with the separation of inward and outward. In the administration of justice, however, civil society returns to its concept, to the unity of the implicit universal with the subjective particular, although here the latter is only that present in single cases and the universality in question is that of *abstract* right.
>
> (Hegel 1821, reprinted in Hall and Trentmann 2005: 131)

In civil society, the moments of subjective particularity and objective universality are sundered or severed. The corporation, in this instance, 'returns civil society to its concept' because it 'actualizes the unity' of the 'particularity of need and satisfaction' and the 'universality of abstract rights' (Hall and Trentmann 2005: 131). Hegelian civil society embodies particular interests which frequently oppose each other but through the state, for example, it plays a mediating role in accomplishing the universality of its institutions (Bartelson 2006: 377).

Marx (1818–83), frequently referred to civil society in his earlier writings but was more likely to refer to 'material relations', 'relations of production', and the 'economic' 'structure of society' in later writings (Parekh 2004). In contrast to Hegel, Marx argued that 'civil society is both logically and historically prior to structures of authority such as the state ... the state ultimately derives from civil society and thus inevitably reflects the constellation of forces and interests within it' (Bartelson 2006: 377). Civil society is identified with the productive base of capitalist society—bourgeois society—'a realm of contradiction and mystification sustained by relations of power' (Khilnani 2001: 15). Explained further: 'political freedom could only be attained if the working class took over otherwise alienated state functions, while also abolishing the selfish, individualistic, pluralism of civil society' (Baker 1998: 81). This continues the association of civil society with individualism, rights, the pursuit of self-interest, and satisfaction of needs, liberty and equality that earlier writers had also emphasized (Parekh 2004: 17). However, the class structure of the capitalist society had the capacity to render these associations vacuous (ibid.).

For Gramsci (1891–1937), civil society was central and other aspects of his thought—consent/force, war of position/war of movement, ethico-political/economic-corporative—are best understood through the concept (Fontana 2006: 52–53). While often understood as a sphere of freedom, and increasingly in studies focusing on contestation, civil society is best understood as a sphere of hegemony for Gramsci (Buttigieg 1995: 6–7). This is often referred to as a form of 'cultural hegemony' or concern with 'the character and effects of cultural practices within civil society' (Hall and Trentmann 2005: 186–87). Correspondingly, it is considered that civil society predominantly refers to free associational activity including the family, universities, the press, trade unions, cultural institutions, working men's clubs and publishing houses (Parekh 2004: 18).

'Gramscian' readings of hegemony and civil society have been applied to the contemporary context in many ways and the 'many confused and confusing interpretations' (Buttigieg 1995: 6) can partly be attributed to an almost complete shift from considering the material relations of society to considering its voluntary, associational nature. Some imply that Gramscian civil society represents a form of non-state and non-economic social interaction—a strategic 'tool in the revolutionary struggle' (Anheier *et al.* 2001: 13). This interpretation draws on the well-cited paragraph in which Gramsci discusses the differing strengths of state and civil society in Russia and Western Europe (i.e. France, Italy and Germany of the 1920s and 1930s):

> In Russia the State was everything, civil society was primordial and gelatinous; in the West, there was a proper relation between State and civil society, and when the State trembled a sturdy structure of civil society was at once revealed. The State was only an outer ditch, behind which there stood a powerful system of fortresses and earthworks.
>
> (Gramsci 1971: 238)

Largely responsible for the 'prophetic quality' Gramscian civil society was to take on (Buttigieg 1995), this extract has been distanced from the insight that serious attention—through a war of position—should be paid to the culture and ideology of capitalism which supported bourgeois rule in Europe. A contrary form of 'Gramscian bias' has emerged instead to suggest that civil societies are 'havens of communicative solidarity in a heartless world of state organized markets' (Keane 2005a: 26). Gramsci's concern with historical mutations and transformations which consequently alter the meaning of concepts is less attended to. For example, the formula 'State = political society + civil society', constitutes a specific reference to nineteenth-century corporatism in Europe in which the state sought to join with employers and workers, while isolating the powerless and unorganized (Cox 1999: 7) and it is not clear from the *Prison Notebooks* that this formula was intended to be universally applicable.

Further readings drawing on Robert Cox have achieved some clarity and move beyond predominantly 'cultural' readings of civil society. Broadly, they consider Gramscian civil society as the realm in which the existing social order is grounded and in which a new social order can be founded: 'Civil society is both shaper [of the state] and shaped [by the state], an agent of stabilisation and reproduction, and a potential agent of transformation' (Cox 1999: 4). Gramsci was particularly concerned with the emancipatory meaning of civil society and its potential to construct a new state or order according to this formulation. The conflicting elements of civil society as a force both to legitimize and challenge the discourse and practice of global governance is expressed through the following formulation:

> In a 'bottom-up' sense, civil society is the realm in which those who are disadvantaged by globalisation of the world economy can mount their protests and seek alternatives …In a 'top-down' sense, however, states and corporate interests influence the development of this current version of civil society towards making it an agency for stabilising the social and political *status quo*.
>
> (Cox 1999: 10–11)

This follows on from earlier references to social forces 'within and across state borders …[as] a factor in determining the nature of international order and organisation' (Cox 1981, 1987, cited in O'Brien *et al.* 2000: 234). Further readings emphasize Gramsci's consideration of civil society as 'the site of the consensual production of the cultural hegemony of the bourgeoisie—and as the appropriate realm for socialist struggle' (Eschle 2001: 63). This notion of 'cultural hegemony' is based primarily on consent, as opposed to coercion, and is characterized by moral and intellectual leadership. If, however, a residue of 'domination' in Gramscian hegemony is deceptively left over from the processes of material coercion and socialization through ideas and values (Clarke 2011), there is an apparent unease with the conceptualization of a coercive civil society. Depicted primarily as a realm of consensual voluntarism, there is a reluctance to consider how civil society can use coercive power 'to challenge vested interests, remove unacceptable inequalities, fight pockets of coercion in different areas of social life, and increase the freedom and opportunities of its citizens' (Parekh 2004: 23). In practice, while increasingly sophisticated insight into the workings of neoliberal hegemony has emerged through Gramscian studies, accounts of counter-hegemony have given much less attention to the conceptual contributions of (global) civil society. Increasingly, counter-hegemony aligns with neo-Polanyian accounts that gradually dissociate global civil society from the global political economy. The post-Cold War call for a revival and re-elaboration of Gramsci's form of critique in response to the complacency and dearth of oppositional criticism (Buttigieg 1995) remains pertinent in this context as the increasing misalignment of civil society and hegemony moves Marxism toward pluralism (cf. Hall and Trentmann 2005: 187), emphasizes civil society as 'the home of plurality' and upholds a Western image as a universal norm (Parekh 2004: 21). In re-elaborating a form of critique through civil society the notion of hegemony is central to demonstrate that the material relations of society have continued relevance from which the nature of knowledge production is not set apart.

Global civil society and alter-globalization

There is a proliferating body of literature on global civil society, new social movements, transnational protest and global activism seeking to explain and understand movements of global contestation. The conceptual potential of global civil society, its location as a central sphere of hegemony and capacity to encompass the complexity of the globalization-contestation nexus, is made more accessible through relation to its rich accumulation of meanings. The recent history of the alter-globalization movement has been linked to waves of public protest and the steady strengthening of global movements. One such account begins, for example, with half a million farmers marching against the corporatization of agriculture and land reform in Bangalore, India, in 1993 and traces through indigenous demands in Chiapas, Mexico, in 1994; a G8 demonstration in Birmingham, UK, in 1998; the anti-Multilateral Agreement on Investment movement in Paris, France in the same year; the counter-summit at the site of the WTO ministerial summit in Seattle, US, in 1999; and the formation of the World Social Forum in Porto Alegre, Brazil, in 2001 (Pleyers 2010: 1–6). Indicative of just some of the movements for 'another globalization' during this time, each of these examples are locally or nationally based and linked to wider, more global modes of protest such as the world-wide consolidation of *Via Campesina* on issues such as food sovereignty, sustainable agriculture and social justice; the initiation of global street parties to reclaim public space; the formation of other chapters of the Association for the Taxation of Financial Transactions to Aid Citizens (ATTAC, Association pour la Taxation des Transactions financière pour l'Aide aux Citoyens); counter-summits in cities such as Washington DC, Prague, Sydney, Nice and Brussels; and the holding of local, national, continental and thematic social forums (ibid.).

The recent origins of demands for alter-globalization can be located in the crisis of the liberal compromise of the post-Bretton Woods period during the 1970s and in opposition to the consolidation of neoliberalism that followed. Orthodox International Political Economy emerged as a reaction to the practical problems of this time, a response which may be characterized as lying in attempts to explain rather than understand international relations (cf. Strange 1995; Farrands and Worth 2005: 46; Hollis and Smith 1990). The political and economic landscape was transformed during the immediate period as the fixed price convertibility of the dollar into gold broke down, major currencies were floated, and the oil crisis of 1973–74 and 'Third World' debt crises peaked. Gradually, the global political economy moved from a period of crisis of embedded liberalism to the discursive and policy-based consolidation of neoliberalism. The assertion that 'there is no alternative' by British Prime Minister Margaret Thatcher resounded alongside policies to promote deregulation, capital liberalization, privatization, good governance and the internationalization of production, labour mobility and benchmarking. These can be further understood alongside the consolidation of broader neoliberal security, development and governance policies which gave expression to the binding of ideological and material power.

Neoliberal consolidation can be further documented alongside the collapse of liberal and traditional social democratic alternatives, the emergence of the 'new Democrats' under Clinton in the US and the decline of Western European welfare states (Burbach 2001). These changes are part of an 'emergent new consensus or "Third Way"' which 'upholds the basic neo-liberal tenants of an open global economy and the complete mobility of transnational capital', while limiting the state to providing stable market conditions and preparing a new flexible labour market (ibid.: 148). The result has been growing alienation and a general crisis of modern political systems that has, despite 'fragmentation and incoherence', led to 'sustained and continual opposition to the hegemony of the new global order' (Burbach 2001: 11). As a dominant ideology, therefore, neoliberalism is consolidated through tangible policy prescriptions but it also has a wider, less tangible impact on attitudes and values (Payne 2005: 72). In this way, International Monetary Fund (IMF) food riots in the South during the 1980s in response to the curtailing of food subsidies, opposition to World Bank dam projects and Structural Adjustment Programs, and UK poll tax riots constitute just some of the historic precursors to the Global Justice and Peace Movement that took root in the World Social Forum (Waterman 2004a: 57–58).

At this point, global civil society enters the historical fray with increased vigour as the suspension of tension between the two main competing world views of the Cold War was proposed to signal the 'end of history' (Fukuyama 1989). The triumph of liberalism, the free market and democracy, alongside the contrasting ideas of 1989 (Kaldor 2003a, 2003b), signalled parallel characterizations for global civil society as 'an emerging agent and sphere of a nascent world politics' that encompasses a 'medley of boundary-eclipsing actors—social movements, interest groups, indigenous peoples, cultural groups and global citizens' (Pasha and Blaney 1998: 418). In a broadly chronological fashion, global civil society has come to refer to the activities of global advocacy networks or new social movements followed by the anti-globalization movement and more recently by the global justice movement (Falk 2005). Amidst a chorus of voices confirming its capacity to constitute sustained and continual opposition to the consolidation of neoliberalism, global civil society has assembled an accumulation of contemporary meanings.

In addition to contesting state power, during the 1990s, global civil society was also considered to constitute a response to the adverse effects of globalizing tendencies in the form of globalization-from-below (Falk 2005: 125). This was, as yet, considered a restricted form of resistance that rather than challenging globalization can work 'only to alter the guiding ideas that are shaping enactment' (ibid.: 127). In fact, it is considered that globalization 'is too widely accepted and embedded to be reversible in its essential integrative impact' (ibid.). Partly, this is attributed to the absence of a coherent ideological response to neoliberalism in the form of 'a common theoretical framework, political language and programme' (ibid.). Nonetheless, the growth of the global civil society idea has been replicated in practice, or at least tied to the activities of NGOs and popular movements in issue areas such as war and peace, the environment, human rights and gender—activities that have prompted research on global advocacy networks (Keck and Sikkink 1998) and new social movements (Falk 2005: 71–76). The Stockholm United Nations (UN) Conference on the Environment in 1972 was considered especially indicative of the emergence of global, as opposed to national, environmental initiatives, and it has been followed by a proliferation of other conferences. The nature of such activities was, according to Falk (2005: 71), 'generally dialogic and performative with civil society actors mounting transnational pressures demanding *reforms*, not *revolutionary change*'.

The 'globalization of resistance' (Chase-Dunn and Gills 2005) was aided through changes in regulation from the national to regional, international and supranational levels as civil society has been spurred into engaging with, and in some cases contesting, new regulatory measures such as those included within the expanding remit of the WTO (Williams 2005: 355). Financial and trade liberalization have had similar effects as evident through the growing number of advocacy groups which speak for interests unrecognized by state and corporate sectors. Demonstrations and marches condemn IMF and World Bank practices, while movements and organizations such as Jubilee 2000 and ATTAC have formed to initiate a civil society response to globalizing processes. Meanwhile, opposition to the Organisation for Economic Co-operation and Development's (OECD) Multilateral Agreement on Investment (MAI) and the WTO's General Agreement on Trade in Services (GATS) was formalized with the emergence of social movements, NGOs and organizations such as CorporateWatch. These processes are aided through vast improvements in transport and communication. These have spawned a new network-like structure of resistance movements such as the Zapatista Army of National Liberation (EZLN) opposition to the North American Free Trade Association (NAFTA), headed by Subcommandante Marcos in Chiapas, Mexico. The globalization of resistance has enabled the formation of links and networks supported by open communication methods and enhanced by common resistance against neoliberal forms of globalization.

Such developments have led to suggestions that from the strengthening of globalization new forms of 'potential solidarity' have arisen (Rupert 2003: 193). Certainly, the forms and practices of this new politics of solidarity are many and incorporate, among other actors, social movements, the often highly organized NGO, less defined activist networks, indigenous organizations, community groups, political parties and individuals. They express their objectives through dialogue, coordination, networking, information gathering, protest, demonstrations and violence, and along arguments based on identity, gender, equality, environment, democracy, legitimacy and ideology. Though diverse, the new politics of solidarity or politics of connection (Walker 1994) is seen to construct a new common ground or public space from which to instigate a struggle for an alternative world. As examined in more detail in Chapter 5, the World Social Forum is considered to represent a unique social and public meeting place upon which resistance to neoliberal globalization is globalized and new forms of solidarity and contestation are emerging.

In an apparent circumvention of consolidated neoliberalism, 'progressive' perspectives look towards civil society to play an influential role while, to varying degrees, there is some acknowledgement that 'it is important to remember that a strengthened global civil society is itself a goal of neoliberal forces' (Robinson 2003: 169). From the perspective of consolidating neoliberalism, civil society is promoted to comprise the non-profit, voluntary 'third sector' sphere of charities and other voluntary associations that will check state power while also carrying out many previously held state functions (Kaldor 2003a). There has been a consequent proliferation of literature that denotes a benevolent meaning to global civil society such that it is seen to present a counterbalance to global governance institutions, a form of 'societal accompaniment' to globalizing processes (Amoore 2005: 3; Kenny and Germain 2005: 2), or from a more critical perspective; a '"social" wing of neoliberal global capitalism' (Munck 2002: 355).

'Third sector' approaches have emerged alongside the revival of ideas of a Tocqueville-like spirit of association or 'social capital' (Putnam 2000) and the extension of these ideas to the discourse of mainstream development. Civil society forms a component of 'good governance' policies promoted by development policy makers from the World Bank to the IMF and NGOs. The 'virtuous circle' (Archer 1994, cited in Lewis 2002: 570) of state, market and civil society is tied to the construction of democratic institutions and promotion of market reforms in developing countries. This usage has prompted concern that civil society is being used by donor agencies as 'an unproblematic given' in a way that conceals 'intense, ongoing debate about its meaning' (Howell and Pearce 2002: 2). Instead 'mainstream civil society' (also referred to as the 'voluntary sector', 'non-profit sector' or 'third sector') takes on instrumental, functional roles in 'service delivery, social welfare provision and the technical implementation of governance reforms' (Howell and Lind 2009: 7).

The 1989-present conjuncture marks a remarkable change in understandings of civil society from eighteenth- and nineteenth-century conceptualizations to its appropriation by 'those who foresee [for it] an emancipatory role' (Cox 1999: 10). This role is carried out through the distinct realm of 'autonomous group action', as opposed to the realm of corporate and state power (ibid.). Progressive treatments highlight the intensified demands—for autonomy, self-organization and control over life—associated with the global extension of the concept (Kaldor 2003a). This means that a number of dominant features or images can be identified. Notably, these converge to support a virtuous, vibrant and voluntary global civil society, mainly concerned to oppose state domination or neoliberal marketization (Amoore and Langley 2004; Wagner 2006). Related images construct global civil society as a bounded space distinct from governance, the state and market. Global civil society is also frequently aligned with voluntary associations as individuals freely and consensually come together in pursuit of a common aim so that voluntary professional associations, consumer associations and interest groups are considered part of the infrastructure of global civil society to enable the spread of democracy and development (Anheier *et al.* 2001). According to another image, global civil society is an agent of empowerment/resistance or a counter-weight to global capitalism. It is seen to represent the growing connectedness of citizens through internet chatrooms, networks of peace, environmental or human rights activists, student exchanges or global media (ibid.). Within many of these readings, global civil society is an inherently beneficial and transformative force for good. The movements contained therein 'represent the conscience of the world (Willetts 1996), pressurizing nation-states and international institutions to act in more progressive, humanitarian ways on issues such as human rights, the environment, debt, global poverty and arms reduction' (Kiely 2007: 123).

The earlier activities of civil society in opposition to the state are considered representative as civil society loses its direct association with the state and becomes synonymous with struggles for civil liberties, democratic transformations and alternative globalizations. 'The transnationality of influence and the growing leverage exerted by civil society actors' (Falk 2005: 72) have conferred on it further autonomy of action. This popularized understanding places it in opposition to the state, unsettles its historical ties and begets it as a tool with which to overthrow military dictatorships and totalitarian regimes. Civil society has also been proposed to play a role in challenging state power indirectly. Disillusion with party politics and distrust of state institutions has provoked interest in using civil society to extend the boundaries of politics and rejuvenate public life (Khilnani 2001: 11, citing

Keane 1988; Cohen and Arato 1992) in a manner that is entirely consistent with the neoliberal view on global civil society expressed above. In the South, 'civil society incarnates a desire to recover for society powers—economic, social, expressive—believed to have been illegitimately usurped by states' (Khilnani 2001: 12). Here, the constituents of civil society might include private enterprises and organizations, church and denominational associations, self-employed workers' co-operatives, trade unions and NGOs. Through these organizations, civil society is suggested to provide more 'accountable, public, and representative forms of political power' (ibid.). Increasingly, however, the withdrawal of civil society from the state and a move towards global rules and institutions— through human rights legislation, social movements, or global governance—has become more apparent. As a result, civil society is positioned within a unique space associated with the realm of culture, ideology and political debate, the space outside the market, state and family (Kaldor 2003a: 584).

These events and movements are integral towards better understanding the 'globalization of resistance' (Chase-Dunn and Gills 2005), within which 'global civil society' and the *longue durée* of change and transformation offer further insight. This integrates a concern with wider progressive traditions, networks, forums and organizations that, over time, have met with critical junctures such as Third World anti-colonial and independence movements, women's, labour and environmental and indigenous movements (e.g. Chase-Dunn 2011; Chase-Dunn and Gills 2005; Chase-Dunn and Reese 2006; Broad and Heckscher 2003). Partly, a concern with the *longue durée* of resistance challenges distinctions between 'old' and 'new' social movements that tend, even if unintentionally, to set up binary distinctions in explanations of change. Here, critical social movements, for example, are contrasted with more conventional or reactionary nationalist, socialist and political party movements (Walker 1988: 63). Correspondingly, the construction of a new public space is based on a distinction between conventional forms of movements, and 'critical social movements' that emerge in response to structural changes that are underway in the world economy. Conventional movements are seen traditionally to organize around the state and are usually defined in relation to state power. Critical social movements, on the other hand, are movements that 'are able to look beyond the immediacy and specificity of their struggle to understand at least some of the wider connections in which they are caught' (ibid.: 62). They function as responses to 'broad structural problems and transformations' such as economic inequality and also serve to challenge the 'constitutive principles of the existing political order' through rethinking meanings of power, resistance and delegitimation and extending 'the boundaries of the possible' (ibid.: 81–96, 3). While Walker suggests, on a more cautionary note, that critical social movements are open to a 'multiplicity of historical perspectives on the contemporary human condition' and he is careful to dissociate history and unfaltering progress (Walker 1988: 26), comparable distinctions have become implicit, and sometimes explicit, features of studies on globalization and contestation in a reificatory manner that overlooks the historical significance of accumulations of meanings and movements within global civil society.

A global public sphere

Many of the dominant images of global civil society presented above (cf. Amoore and Langley 2004) converge to confront processes of neoliberal consolidation in what is often presented as a unified, but diverse, mode of resistance, located far from the more conflict-ridden terrain of the global political economy, and significantly far from Marxist and Hegelian civil societies which held far stronger ties to the historical emergence of capitalism. Paradoxically then, this image of global civil society aids an analytical spatial and discursive construction of a global public sphere. It conceives global civil society as an autonomous sphere to the state and market, but nonetheless constituent of its own global public sphere, which may even allow it to transcend traditional social science conventions. According to the editors of the *Global Civil Society 2001* yearbook:

> The term takes the perhaps most important social science (re)discovery of the 1990s—civil society—and places it in a framework that ultimately transcends conventional social science categories. The concept posits the existence of a social sphere, a global civil society, above and beyond national, regional, or local societies.
>
> (Anheier *et al.* 2001)

Other accounts also suggest that global civil society exists outside of the state: 'The spatial boundaries of global civil society are different, because its autonomy from the constructed boundaries of the state system allows for the construction of new political spaces' (Lipschutz 1992: 392–93). The growth of global civil society is seen to represent 'an ongoing project of civil society to reconstruct, re-imagine, or re-map world politics', even though 'we are not yet in a position to begin to construct definite guides to global civil society' (ibid.: 391–92). Similarly, the construction of a 'nascent global polity' for global civil society is described as 'already partly extant; yet remains mostly emergent' (Falk 1998: 99). However, despite the absence of a fully formed global polity, the term '*global* civil society' is still entirely justifiable since initiatives proceed from a global orientation and are responses to globalizing tendencies (ibid.). Global civil society may, therefore, be defined as:

> The field of action and thought occupied by individual and collective citizen initiatives of a voluntary, non-profit character both within states and transnationally. These initiatives proceed from a global orientation and are responses, in part at least, to certain globalizing tendencies that are perceived to be partially or totally adverse.
>
> (Falk 1998: 100)

This conceptualization of global civil society is closely tied to democracy which serves to enhance and unify global civil society, a central aspect of the 'normative revolution' in world affairs to integrate ethical concerns into global policy making (Falk 2005):

> To introduce the idea of 'normative democracy' is to offer a proposal for a unifying ideology capable of mobilizing and unifying the disparate social forces that constitute global civil society, and provide the political energy that is associated with globalization-from-below.
>
> (Falk 1998: 106)

While Devetak and Higgott (1999) also identify the emergence of a 'global public sphere' and maintain that it is permissible to extrapolate from civil to global civil society, they are markedly more cautious than Lipschutz or Falk as to the potential of global civil society:

> But increasingly prominent as they may be, it remains to be seen whether non-governmental organisations (NGOs) and global social movements (GSMs) are agents for building a post-Westphalian global civil society and reconstructing a new social bond at the end of the twentieth century.
>
> (Devetak and Higgott 1999: 7)

Merging protest movements and social movements are nonetheless considered in another account to signal the 'rebirth of a democratic public sphere' through igniting demands by the disenfranchised and exploited for a new form of democratic self-determination that moves beyond representation through the right to vote (Richter *et al.* 2006: 10).

Hopeful and critical voices[3]

An enduring vision of a 'community of human beings' (Glasius *et al.* 2005) in global contestation has emerged from the above processes and is reflected cogently in activist interpretations of global civil society that are linked to the publication since 2001 of the *Global Civil Society Yearbooks*, mentioned briefly above. The yearbooks categorize a range of positions that global civil society occupies in relation to globalization which is understood to refer to the spread of global capitalism, global interconnectedness and a 'growing global consciousness' (Anheier *et al.* 2001). These positions are occupied by supporters of globalization such as transnational business and their allies, rejectionists, reformists and alternatives who wish to opt-out altogether. While an operational definition of global civil society is offered in earlier editions of the yearbooks, a more used normative definition emerges to assert that 'civil society is about managing difference and accommodating diversity and conflict through public debate, non-violent struggle, and advocacy' (Kaldor *et al.* 2004). Normative and descriptive representations of global civil society are affirmed together to 'describe a political project i.e. a goal, and at the same time an actually existing reality, which may not measure up to that goal' (Kaldor 2003b: 11).

The yearbooks have been instrumental in influencing wider perceptions and beliefs about global civil society and *inter alia* the 'global spread of fields of contestation' (Kaldor 2003b). They support further work on an 'activist version' of global civil society as an emancipatory realm within a global public sphere where individuals can potentially engage in negotiating a social contract with spheres of authority (Kaldor 2003a, 2005a, 2007). This is a representation of a 'new' civil society that has shed its earlier identification with capitalism and the bourgeoisie to assert an autonomous and emancipative role (Kaldor 2007). The exclusion of markets or constitutional orders from the definition of civil society is deemed to have a certain 'political utility' (Kaldor 2005b: 44) to explain, and enable, the role of civil society in challenging dominant state and capitalist structures. Thus, a recently reinvigorated civil society in Egypt and Tunisia has been suggested to complete the 1989 revolutions so that, for example, 'the Egyptians are reclaiming the values of the *Solidarnosc* and the Civil Forum from the neoliberals who usurped them' (Kaldor 2011).

These hopeful interpretations have, however, met with critical voices on the future of global civil society. A recent forum on 'theorizing global civil society' in *Globalizations*, for example, expands on an earlier study of the dichotomy between 'hopeful and critical voices' (Baker and Chandler 2005) and centres on the argument that the normative nature of theorizing presents an insurmountable obstacle to empirical detail since a normative theory of global civil society 'cannot be empirically measured and disputed, proved or disproved' (Chandler 2007: 291; Chandler 2009a). In a further critique of the 'global ideology', within which 'global' civil society is seen to occupy a central role, claims towards global contestation are described as the reactionary and individualized product of 'hollow hegemony' or the weakening of national politics. In a period of 'hollow hegemony' it is argued that we should not be deceived by attempts to 'use the international sphere for standing and a sense of political purpose' (Chandler 2009a: 49). Such attempts incongruously invert the political to denote conscious political action in global spaces of everyday life *outside* the formal institutions and structures of government: 'The normative project seeks to transform the political not by engaging with politics but by bypassing the political sphere' (Chandler 2007: 295). The resulting space is abstract and 'de-socialized' rather than based on 'actual or concrete social interaction on a global plane' (Chandler 2009a: 115). Equipped with a lack of clear political programmes, this interpretation of 'global' civil society establishes activist interpretations within a vacuous global ideology.

Global accessibility

Reference to global civil society in the previous section as part of a vacuous 'global ideology', however, fails to break convincingly with an orthodoxy that looks for 'identifiable and atomised agents', focuses on institutions as 'fixed structures of political life', and separates levels of analysis 'as though they were actually clearly delineated in everyday life' (cf. Amoore and Langley 2004: 103). This has the effect of further abstracting or removing civil society from structures of power, whether behavioural or structural, and reifying its constituents into bounded studies of NGOs, social movements, other social groupings or citizens. In response to the perception of 'global inaccessibility' there is a tendency to privilege the empirical rather than the normative in a manner that sets up a binary between them. The gap in empirical knowledge is narrowing, to which the evidence of numerous studies on NGOs, alter-globalization and global activism, global networks and processes leading to global agreements attest (Dryzek 2012), but there remains further scope for sustained interrogation of the conceptual assumptions underlying hopeful and critical interpretations of global civil society (cf. Walker 2005; Munck 2006b).

The conceptual potential of global civil society is not realized, however, in its representation as 'mobile, unbounded, fluid political sites' which are 'ambiguous, open to contestation and often contradictory' even if this conceptualization achieves the stated objective of opening the concept up for examination (Amoore and Langley 2004: 103, 102). While in relation to the search for a critical conceptualization of global civil society, an emphasis on its fluidity and ambiguity presents an alternative to both 'hopeful and critical' accounts, it presents a less accessible method of locating resistance movements in and in relation to the global political economy, and makes it more difficult to locate actual or concrete global social interaction. Partly, this is due to the privileging of normative or empirical accounts. Chandler, for example, privileges the empirical in his accounts of global civil society which has the result of abstracting from global civil society both the voice of the academic theorist and social movement activist alike (Patomäki 2007). A similar problem can be found where civil society is conceived to derive from the 'unwilled, non-purposive arena of human interaction' rather than identifying it as a sphere of 'willed action, agency, creativity and resistance' (Pearce 1997: 58).

Challenges to state control by civil society, a feature of the more recent Arab uprisings and demonstrations, are rooted in historical precedents or in the *longue durée* as examined above. These challenges can be located in, for example, progressive Latin American movements against dictatorships in the 1980s or mass movements supporting democratic transitions such as the 'People's Power Revolution' in the Philippines and beyond (cf. Gills and Gray 2012). The precedents of current movements against 'corporate-led globalization' can be traced through historical parallels and contrasts—from the movement to abolish the slave trade and the workers' movement of the 1860s, to the confluence of Third World government and citizen-led resistance in the 1970s, to World Bank- and IMF-sponsored programmes—such that anti-corporate globalization activism can be considered neither spontaneous nor new (Broad and Heckscher 2003). In light of this, therefore, today's movement can learn much from the insights of history (ibid.). From a similar viewpoint, the 'new global left' traces back to the old social movements of the nineteenth century (labour, anarchism, socialism, communism, feminism, environmentalism, peace, human rights), the movements associated with the 1968 and 1989 'world revolutions' (queer rights, anti-corporate, fair trade, indigenous), and more recent movements (slow food/food rights, global justice/alter-globalization, anti-globalization, health-HIV and alternative media) (Chase-Dunn 2011). However, the term 'global civil society' has gained in popular usage in a contrary manner whereupon strategic and tactical insights scarcely intervene.

An agency-centred perception of civil society, in contrast, is 'about the search for new subjects and agents of history' (Pearce 1997: 58) so that the above discourses are not considered to take place within an analytical vacuum. Focusing on the accumulation of meanings inherent in global civil society intends to counter their separation so that they are not treated as distinct, disconnected time- and space-bound projects. Rather, the search for new subjects and agents does not neglect to consider the course of uneasy voluntarism that societal critique of the market and state may take in the absence of understanding both the contemporary continuance of the 'political economy tradition', whereupon spheres of unwilled, non-purposive interaction are continually enacted and acted upon, but also whereby established historical distinctions risk melding one into the other to converge as consensual and voluntary global civil society. This adds to what is perceived to be the central problematic of achieving a coherent theoretical and practical programme for resistance. Neoliberal hegemony, in its behavioural, ideological and material manifestations of power, aligns to the activities of a transnational or global capitalist class that cannot, it appears, but give rise to a 'counter-hegemony' of global civil society. In its quest for theoretical and programmatic coherence, however, counter-hegemony cannot but affirm the coherence of neoliberalism. This coherence gives us 'very little to say about political resistance to transnational neoliberalism' and leaves 'few possibilities for political organization' (Drainville 1994: 111, 121). If, therefore, neoliberalism neglects to show itself as a 'cluster of negotiated settlements, a collection of hesitant, partial and contradictory arrangements' (ibid.: 120), so too does contestation on the part of civil society. The task, taking this into account, is not to achieve a coherent global civil societal project and programme but, rather, to recognize the diversity within differences—a method of translating the matter of global imaginaries— using the historical accomplishments that are the accumulation of meanings of global civil society at hand. This moves from the tendency to highlight 'collectivity' and united fronts in studies of resistance such as seen through the goal of 'globalization from below' and, quite often, counter-hegemony (Chin and Mittelman 1997; Falk 2005). While certainly the search for collectivity implies the presence of organizational structure, fails to account for 'submerged networks' or undeclared everyday forms of resistance (Chin and Mittelman 1997), or masks fragmentation and differences within and between movements, the corresponding task is neither to achieve unity nor introduce further ambiguity or complexity. In this context, consensual and unified visions of global civil society may be disrupted through showing its internal paradoxes and conflicts, highlighting the complex relationships it has with other actors, and demonstrating the effects of competition for power, status and control, and personal rivalries within civil society (Söderbaum 2007). Unsettling contemporary conceptualizations of global civil society, in this context, includes a demonstration of how movements of global civil society may be 'established or co-opted for the satisfaction of more myopic and personal political and economic interests', leading to patterns of 'inclusion' of civil society intimately related to ruling political regimes and 'exclusion' of more critical civil society actors that are marginalized and harassed (ibid.: 335). Through highlighting the denotation of political agency to contemporary movements of resistance, the case studies of the World Social Forum and World People's Conference on Climate Change in Chapters 5 and 6 aim to provide insight into the concrete location of global civil society in and in relation to the global political economy while also attempting to move beyond its 'magical explanatory qualities' (Buttigieg 1995).

Conclusions

There has been a patent flourishing of references to global civil society in academia and activism and a corresponding host of hopeful and critical voices on the concept. Relatively little attention, however, has been given to considering the conceptual potential of global civil society in relation to global contestation or to the reflexive analysis of the role of disciplinary fields in producing and reproducing knowledge on global civil society. Serious academic enquiries into the 'mapping' and measuring of global civil society is carried out, amongst others, by the London School of Economics (LSE) publication of the *Global Civil Society Yearbook*, the Centre for Civil Society Studies at the Johns Hopkins University, and the Centre for Civil Society in Durban, South Africa (Munck 2006b). Empirical concern with mapping and measuring global civil society is significant as its constituents are increasingly purported to play a role in global contestation and, as the next chapter will show, global governance. The recent upsurge in popular protest movements from the Arab uprisings to the Spanish *indignado* movements and American Occupy Wall Street campaign indicates that mapping the spread of these activities is crucial to understanding them. Gramsci (1971: 185), for example, argues that 'schematic definition' can only be achieved through the study of 'fundamental data' related to economic, social and military relations of force. However, studying the fundamental data is only one aspect of an enquiry that finds greater significance in a particular practical activity of 'initiative of will' (ibid.). Inherent to data collection, Gramsci appears to indicate, is the initiative of will that drives forth contemporary movements. This gives two points of insight. First, mapping and measuring global civil society is not a neutral activity. Processes of counting, schematization, categorization and defining are political in themselves: 'any process of counting requires definitions, categorisations and financial resources which puts it firmly into the realm of politics' (de Goede 2003: 92). These are implicitly political acts which necessitate corresponding attempts to find greater clarification on its meaning even as mechanical methods of mapping global civil society are not always used hand in hand with further clarifying political and theoretical meaning (Munck 2006a).

From a conceptual viewpoint, many conceptualizations of global civil society under-specify its nature or derive primarily from the given context (cf. Terrier and Wagner 2006: 227). Many are concerned to underline its transformative, democratic or consensual virtues rather than locate it in and in relation to the global political economy. Consequently, its analytical usefulness has been questioned (Cerny 2006; Germain and Kenny 1998). Rather than signify, clarify or represent the extension of political community, democracy and emancipation to the global level, global civil society is suggested to lack correspondence to the 'particularisms of place' (Chandler 2007: 285; Chandler 2009a: 110). It appears that extrapolations of 'global' resistance and 'global' civil society have failed to engage at empirical and conceptual levels and have reproduced an analogous empirical-normative discursive binary. However, as shown through the brief overview of its accumulations of meanings in relation to alter-globalization and global governance, the focus of the next chapter, it may be as yet premature to draw a conclusion on the proliferation of 'critical and hopeful' voices as instructive for critically conceptualizing global civil society. Rather, their interpretation points towards the benefits of a sustained and critical interrogation of the construction, elaboration and dialectical interaction of global civil society with the empirical realities of the global political economy.

Notes

1 For more on these see, for example, Charnock *et al.* (2012), Brecher (2011) and Albert (2011).
2 For constructivist examples see Keck and Sikkink (1998) and Tarrow (1998).
3 The reference to 'hopeful and critical' voices draws on Baker and Chandler (2005). This section draws on Buckley (2013).

4 Global governance

Constituting global civil society

> A critical orientation calls for not only deconstructing extant knowledge and practice but also constructing new knowledge about what exists and what ought to exist on the basis of transformed relations of power.
>
> (Mittelman 2005: 20)

Global civil society is commonly constituted to represent the extension of moral and political communities, democracy and political emancipation to the international sphere (Chandler 2004a). Met with enthusiasm by post-Cold War theorists, it has also been considered to unsettle the conceptual foundations of orthodox ideas on political community, state sovereignty and disciplinary paradigms. The focus in this chapter centres on reflexive processes of knowledge constitution as they relate to representations of global civil society in global governance. This supports the view that 'the forms and structures that define contemporary society are not immediately available for empirical analysis' (Hardt and Weeks 2000: 4) and further understanding can be achieved through recognizing the influence of activist, scholarly and institutional representations of global civil society (and its constituents) on configurations of 'global contestation' in the global political economy. To this end, therefore, a number of studies on civil society and global governance are examined in this chapter. In addition to presenting varying interpretations and representations of global civil society in relation to global governance, I am centrally concerned to demonstrate how practices of definition and usage constitute global civil society and, in turn, condition possibilities of political thought, imagination and action.

Alongside the normative, philosophical desire to contribute to the making of an activist version of global civil society such as examined in the last chapter, the constitutive effects of functional, instrumental and normative representations are considered. These present challenges for an assessment of the dialectical nexus within and between categories of research and categories of movement, and in particular draw attention to how global civil society engages in 'modes of social relation' in and towards the global political economy (cf. Drainville 2004, 2012). Substantive modes of social relation, from dialectical presence to civic ordering, are considered alongside scholarly and institutional practices in constituting global civil society. This method seeks to address the envisaged lacuna between the philosophical promises and empirical realities of contestation and considers that it is through negotiating the dialectical relationship between the promise and reality of global civil society that most potential for a politics of contestation can be found. The privileging of normative and instrumental conceptualizations and the failure to demonstrate their interactions with material realities, it is argued in this chapter, delimits and decontextualizes the concrete range of possibilities for contestation and change and fails to articulate the potential of global social relations and hegemony in understanding global contestation.

Modes of social relation

The Gramscian/Coxian predisposition on civil society presents an account of its dual role in global governance. Civil society in global governance, for example, provides more accountable structures and adds legitimacy to the practices of hegemony while, as an emancipative or counter-hegemonic movement, potentially effects real and positive change by turning back and transforming the neoliberal direction of the global economy (Cox 1999). Introducing a specific focus on modes of social relation to the global political economy, however, potentially moves beyond the double binary of civil society and hegemony that is most evident in applications of Coxian approaches.[1] The immediate and fashionable meaning of 'modes' may be outlined, but 'modes' are also used in the social sciences to refer to 'relatively invisible but enduring, and structuring, products of specific historical circumstances' (Drainville 2004: 11):

> Dialectically, they are both artefacts of historical struggles and part of the conditions under which histories are made. Born of the meeting of social forces, they structure, inform, shape or over-determine historical conjunctures ... Thinking about modes, then, will encourage us to reflect on what is being born of present circumstances that may later set limits to political possibilities ... What are being constructed in the present juncture are ways to enter the world economy and to organise the occupation to the new terrain; modes of social relations, then, not *in*, but *to*, the world economy.
>
> (Drainville 2004: 11–12)

Two modes of social relation, civic-consensual and unitary, can be specified, although specification of these modes does not preclude the creation of others through the context of the world economy and, indeed, further modes of social relation, creative dislocation and dialectics of presence can also be specified (Drainville 2012; Drainville 2004: 32, 163). Modes of relation are 'part and parcel of the practice of all social forces that are taking themselves to the world economy, or that are being taken to it' (Drainville 2004: 160).

The civic-consensual mode is dominated by global neoliberalism in which the form and functions of social forces may, for example, be detailed by institutions of global governance. Insight from the Internationale Situationniste critique of urbanism can be applied to conceive the mapping, gridding and levelling of social spaces in the global political economy by neoliberal governance.[2] Similar to 'creative dislocation', this is a mode of relation to the world economy that aligns with most ease to hegemonic projects for world order (Drainville 2012: 35). The unitary mode, in addition, represents the flight of social forces to the world economy and is 'rooted in both concrete and situated struggles and … constitutive of a broader, more political sense of place' (ibid.: 95). Examples include the global street parties organized by groups such as Peoples' Global Action in protest against World Trade Organization (WTO) policies, or attempts to create a virtual and actual meeting place for the convening of a World Social Forum. This is closer to world-situated counter-hegemony or 'dialectics of presence' (ibid.: 35). The making or constituting of global subjects is addressed through examining the relations between concretely situated social forces in an indicated geographical space or site of struggle on the one hand, and the whole world on the other (ibid.: 30).

Much academic and policy-based discussion on global civil society is polarized between tendencies towards establishing binary positions, making it increasingly difficult to maintain a dialogue between contending positions. Through circumventing the dual presentation of global civil society, modes of social relation offer a more effective viewpoint for understanding contestation in the global political economy. Engaging with modes of social relation reinforces the presence and agency of global civil society in the global political economy so that 'all social forces present on the terrain of the world economy, whether constituted as NGOs, local unions or social movements, are necessarily involved in both modes of relation to the world economy' (Drainville 2004: 155). Beyond this, modes of relation are not prescribed, intangible, nor static in the last analysis:

> That is not to say, of course, that modes have already gelled into some-
> thing that can over-determine the movement of social forces, that they
> have been reflexively integrated into strategies of power and counter-power,
> or that they can be directly transposed into practices.
>
> (Drainville 2004: 160–61)

I am not concerned to 'name' global civil society so that it can be circumscribed according to lists of who enters into 'civil' as opposed to 'uncivil' society. Nor am I primarily concerned to critique 'the faultlessly global Us-object, the perfectly innocent thing of global governance' (Drainville 2012: 38). Rather, I intend to articulate the provisional nature of modes of social relation entered into by global civil society so that it can be considered a state of becoming through the constitution of knowledge, while retaining tangible qualities, rather than a statement of being. Global civil society engages in modes of social relation, which are not pre-determined, in and towards the global political economy. It is the case that in the midst of a large body of literature on understanding the contemporary world we have very little knowledge of 'how political subjects actually make themselves in the world or in relation to it' (ibid.: 25). Through modes of social relation and other conceptual instruments, including global civil society, the tasks of identification and situation may be enabled. Partly, then, my objective is to re-conceptualize global civil society as a sphere of transversal hegemony so that, in drawing attention to how it is constituted, it may also recover the capacity to re-make itself.

Contesting global governance

The co-authored *Contesting Global Governance* by O'Brien, Goetz, Scholte and Williams (2000) forms the basis for illustrating critical processes of constituting global civil society and provides critical insight into scholarly and institutional representations of global civil society and the concrete elaboration of modes of social relation in and towards the global political economy. This study provides an important empirical snapshot of civil society interactions with key global governing institutions but, particularly in its conclusions, contains some key normative statements on the role of civil society in global governance. This presents evidence of a significant lacuna in research between the philosophical promise and empirical reality of global civil society.

Contesting Global Governance focuses on relations between global social movements (GSMs)—women's, labour and environmental groups—and 'multilateral economic institutions' (MEIs)—the World Bank, International Monetary Fund (IMF) and WTO. Predominant attention is given to a narrow range of non-governmental organizations (NGOs) and traditional international environmental, women's and labour movements rather than on peasant, indigenous, micro- or other forms of resistance. The narrow focus is qualified by reference to those global social movements that do not operate on a global terrain and since they do not interact with MEIs, are considered to fall outside the remit of discussion (O'Brien *et al.* 2000). For example, the assessment of interactions between environmental social movements and the World Bank is reduced to focus mainly on environmental NGOs since they are more prominent at the international level compared to the more local, regional and national activities of the vast majority of environmental groups. In addition, this study provides a partial view of 'global governance'; in isolating the 'trinity' of dominant international institutions (World Bank, IMF, WTO), emerging private, public, informal and alternative modes of global governance are not alluded to.

The limitations of interactions between 'global social movements' and 'multilateral economic institutions' are examined in *Contesting Global Governance* through, for example, putting forward the constraints faced by certain social movements in attempting to influence policy making at the World Bank, IMF and WTO. This evidence confirms the need to consider civil society replication and reproduction of the 'neoliberal governance agenda' (Munck 2007: 89) and provides insight into empirical evidence of civic-consensual modes of relation to the global political economy. Overall, this study demonstrates that while MEIs were obliged to address the grievances of global social movements during the 1990s, GSMs occupied a subordinate position as MEIs refused to compromise their own policy objectives. Meanwhile, the study also reveals deep political divisions among global social movements (see also, Colás 2002: 156).

The influence of politico-economic environments

In *Contesting Global Governance*, a comparison of the contrasting environments offered to civil society by the WTO and International Labour Organization (ILO) leads to the suggestion that:

> It may be the political environment rather than the issue area which is most influential in determining the degree to which civil society actors are integrated into international institutions. More specifically, the degree to which civil society actors are capable of aiding or frustrating the ideal of these organisations is key.
>
> (O'Brien *et al.* 2000: 103)

This view equates the militancy of workers at the time of the formation of the ILO in 1919 and the perception that this unrest posed a threat to world order, with the decision to integrate civil society into the International Labour Organization's decision-making processes. It draws attention to the importance of the social, economic and political contexts in which international organizations are formed and in which social movements seek change. In general, global social movements find it difficult to alter the operation of multilateral economic institutions partly because of the shortage of modes or structures through which they can participate in governance (O'Brien *et al.* 2000). Yet, even where these structures are provided, such as in the ILO, particular ideological and environmental conditions can also affect the degree to which civil society can 'frustrate' the ideal of the ILO and instead contribute to civil society 'aiding' of this ideal (ibid.: 103). Despite the unique input allocated to workers in the ILO, the organization lacks the teeth to protect workers (ibid.: 77). Instead, as suggested in the concluding chapter of *Contesting Global Governance*, the prevailing influence of the 'trinity' of the World Bank–IMF–WTO dominates the global governing arena.

Thus, the politico-economic environment constitutes an important factor affecting modes of relation between global civil society and global governing structures. More precisely, the dominant ideology, in this case the predominance of neoliberalism in the 'trinity', represents a key limitation to those seeking to change entire ideological outlooks (O'Brien *et al.* 2000: 190). In general, economic liberalism is the dominant organizational ideology of multilateral economic institutions, which correspondingly affects institutional structure.[3] In the case study on the IMF in *Contesting Global Governance*, it is suggested that the 'monolithic' character of the IMF tends to exclude global social movements while the much larger World Bank shows some degree of openness: 'In contrast to the Bank, the Fund has had little division on the inside and porosity toward the outside' (ibid.: 191, 215). In the IMF and WTO, '[t]here is a much clearer governing ideology and expression of dissent or controversy within the institution is less likely and certainly less visible' (ibid.: 215). This consensual governing nature reflects the core concerns of the institutions, finance and trade respectively, which can include sensitive negotiations with or between states and a high degree of secrecy. In some cases MEIs have an evident preference towards interacting with structured trade unions and are reluctant to engage GSMs that are deemed to be insufficiently legitimate or democratic. Nonetheless, while GSMs may only have limited success in influencing MEIs such as the IMF, for example, according to the authors of *Contesting Global Governance*, some benefits can be drawn from even limited interaction: 'Resistance by social movements to IMF sponsorship of neoliberalism has therefore played a vital role in sustaining some elements of diversity and critical debate in global economic governance' (ibid.: 205).

Prevailing civic-consensual modes of social relation

While the dominance of neoliberal ideology in MEIs presents a key limitation to GSM integration into global governance, on the other hand, as shown by O'Brien and co-authors (2000: 116), neoliberal aspects of globalization encourage NGO formation. The emergence of NGOs, as explained in a case study on the World Bank, came about in the 1980s largely as a result of the gap opened up by neoliberal policies that reduced state involvement in the delivery of welfare services. NGOs play a particularly important role in the field of development due to their ability to lobby donor governments and mobilize resources. This explains relative openness towards non-governmental organizations by the World Bank and is reflected in Bank rhetoric on NGOs that stresses 'collaboration, mutual benefit and enhanced effectiveness' (O'Brien *et al.* 2000: 121). However, from the point of view of environmental groups, the World Bank's record produces a more perceptibly mixed result, neither one of 'tokenism' nor a 'complete victory' (ibid.: 122). By and large, however, both environmental and development groups remain 'unconvinced' by the rhetoric of the Bank (ibid.: 131). The above evidence prompts the authors to question the sincerity of World Bank rhetoric, especially when it is compared to conflicting reports from GSMs: 'From the perspective of social movement activists the reality is one of confrontation, conflict and co-option', which prompts the suggestion: 'To some extent it can be argued that what the Bank seeks is not so much partnership as a form of co-option' (ibid.:121).

Multilateral economic institutions are well aware of the benefits of presenting a public veneer of co-operation. From the point of view of the WTO, to take a further example, co-operation may be employed in an effort to halt growing public opposition to its policies (O'Brien *et al.* 2000: 155). This perspective is reinforced by the only moderate success of GSM strategies or generally ambiguous results of MEI–GSM interaction (ibid.: 220–25). The authors conclude that, in general, 'the goal of MEI interaction with GSMs is to neutralize their opposition so that the policy process can function smoothly' (ibid.: 217). This position contrasts sharply with the goals of even less radical global social movements, to seek out some sort of social protection and reorientation of policy so that the costs are not borne by the weakest in society (ibid.: 220).

In addition to the above delimiting factors that govern relations between global social movements and multilateral economic institutions, the level of institutional openness towards global social movements affects the remit of discussion in *Contesting Global Governance*. In all examined cases, GSM involvement is restricted by the MEIs themselves. For instance, in practice, much World Bank policy is geared towards NGOs despite institutional rhetoric of civil society or 'stakeholders' (O'Brien *et al.* 2000: 118). Effectively, groups who do not wish to register officially as NGOs are excluded from World Bank projects—the example given of Chilean *poblador* groups explained the subsequent depoliticization and exclusion from World Bank-funded projects experienced by the groups as a result of their reluctance to register officially as NGOs with the Chilean state (ibid.: 58).[4] NGO accreditation guidelines by the WTO also serve to exclude those groups with activities that cannot be directly related to trade. NGOs were allowed to attend the WTO ministerial meeting in Singapore in 1996 on the basis that their concerns could be directly related to the trade activities of the WTO (ibid.: 93). Sixty-five per cent of NGOs registered for the meeting were business organizations (ibid.). Thus, a complete analysis of GSMs (and also global civil society) is not possible as, on the one hand, not all GSMs choose to operate on the global level with institutions and, on the other hand, GSM involvement is limited to those elements—mostly NGOs—that the institutions of global governance choose to admit or allow.

Increasing signs of fragmentation and polarization of global social movements are observed in *Contesting Global Governance*, with a split between GSMs that operate comfortably within the loop of multilateral economic institutions and more radical movements that seek to effect change from outside the 'trinity'. Within MEIs the degree to which certain NGOs replicate the terms of global governance appear significant:

> It is mistaken to think that the ESM [environmental social movement] represents voices from the periphery ... At the level of interactions with MEIs the ESM is characterised not only by diversity but also by a highly sophisticated policy elite which shares more than access to modern

technology with those who run the institutions. In order to be heard representatives of social movements must of necessity enter into a dialogue with (speak the language of) the holders of power.

(O'Brien *et al.* 2000: 156)

As this suggests, a single unified global environmental movement cannot be mooted, while the differing strategies and standpoints of radical and reformist environmental groups are significant and can become intensified as a result of MEI–GSM interaction. The absence of some social movements at the global level of MEI interaction and divisions and conflicting goals of movements limit the capacity of GSMs to influence MEI agendas. The differing objectives of labour movements are illustrated by reference to the International Confederation of Free Trade Unions' (ICFTU) desire to include core labour standards in the WTO remit and the conflicting views of developing countries such as those put forward by the Third World Network (ibid.: 88).

In part, global social movement fragmentation and ability to influence MEIs are further frustrated by social hierarchies not only within MEIs but also GSMs. Exasperations of social hierarchies are visible in MEI subordination of Southern and Eastern interests and among the constituency of global social movements. Even when crossovers between Northern and Southern social movements are initiated, a lack of North-South collaboration between the grassroots and under-classes is noted (O'Brien *et al.* 2000: 194). In terms of resources, GSMs are severely restricted in comparison to MEIs. Inadequate or sporadic resources affect staffing levels (especially continuity of service which limits the potential to build relationships with MEI officials), funding, and information and coordination capacity. The ability to lobby MEIs, for example by Northern and Southern environmental groups, differs considerably according to their size, material and ideational resources.

Lacunas in contesting global governance

The evidence presented above appears to confirm the view of governance sites as 'anchoring points of order' rather than places full of possibilities (Drainville 2004: 139) and the assessment of *Contesting Global Governance* as a 'sober empirical study' (Helleiner 2001: 129). The studies carried out in the study present a rich analysis of formal interactions between global social movements and multilateral economic institutions. They notably highlight not only contextual constraints of time, place and ideology, but also the dialectics of internal social movement processes. Conceptually, the making of global subjects can be applied to the 'making' of global civil society through the modality of social relations. The evidence presented in the O'Brien *et al.* (2000) study appears to confirm the aim of 'neoliberal governance ... to create a global civil society that is a strategic site of decontextualization, occupied by a politically neutered humanity, held to purpose and efficiency, never whole except when fulfilling appointed duties' (Drainville 2004: 22).

The purpose of governing civil society appears to be to 'contain politics' and put 'in place the social and political infrastructure of a sustainable global order free of irritants and resistance' or, to phrase it another way, to effect a 'revolution by solutions' (ibid.: 136). While civic-consensualism or creative dislocation do not preclude the possibilities for a dialectics of presence or alternative modes of social relation, they effect a significant gridding and levelling of the terrain of contestation which challenges the capacity of global civil society to 'manipulate' social structures.

A post-Seattle strategy

A further study on the World Trade Organization's 'post-Seattle strategy' (Wilkinson 2005) extends the time-frame of MEI-GSM interactions and assesses the impact of the 1996 WTO *Guidelines for Arrangements on Relations with Non-Governmental Organizations*. Focusing on further applications of modes of relation in which global civil society engages during the post-Seattle period of governance also enables a wider conceptual and contextual analysis of global civil society. For example, a comparable, and more extensive, vision of the conduct of governance on the part of the WTO is put forward in Wilkinson (2005) which, in summary, outlines the following:

- The WTO equates global civil society with NGOs and further qualifies them as organizations that share similar trade concerns to the WTO.
- The role NGOs can play in increasing public awareness and, thus, transparency of the WTO is emphasized. The WTO objective is on what NGOs can do for the WTO and not vice versa.
- The WTO commits to making more documents available on its website in lieu of making its actual working procedures more transparent.
- Relations with the WTO are to be developed though vague symposia or other informal ways, largely keeping NGOs at arm's length.
- Discussions and meetings with NGOs are conducted by WTO officials in a personal capacity, unless otherwise decided.
- The primacy of national-level relations with NGOs is established and the intergovernmental character of the WTO is underlined.

In a discussion of civil society participation in WTO ministerial meetings since the establishment of these guidelines, it is suggested that NGOs have not gained meaningful access to the WTO. Furthermore, the impact of the above guidelines is suggested to 'have locked the WTO into a particular kind of relationship with civil society that is, for both sides, deeply constraining' (Wilkinson 2005: 171). The groups that are accepted by the WTO would have been most likely to gain access to global decision-making procedures anyway. Poorly resourced groups or those that would probably refuse collaboration, such as the direct-action group Peoples' Global Action, are not involved which, it is suggested, only serves to reinforce the Western bias of the WTO and global governance. In summary, the relationship between the WTO and civil society is seen to be largely developed and 'managed' by the WTO (ibid.), a view that confirms creative dislocation:

> This ... dimension of the WTO's post-Seattle strategy drew upon and took forward a relationship that the Organization had begun to develop with NGOs—those institutions the WTO treats as synonyms for civil society ... This relationship has, in turn, shaped and constrained the WTO's dealings with 'civil society' in a manner that best suits the Organization's interests. But the operationalization of this relationship and its projection to the international policy-making community has influenced wider perceptions of what constitutes global civil society.
>
> (Wilkinson 2005: 157)

The above draws attention to the effects of institutional conceptualizations of global civil society whereby civil society-WTO relations are influenced by particular configurations of state-society relations but also produce wider assumptions concerning global civil society. The WTO view and instrumentalization of civil society feeds into and influences wider visions of global civil society.

The effect of such transnational 'upstreaming' and mainstreaming of global civil society through, for example, NGOs, coordinating bodies of non-governmental organizations (CONGOs) and donor-organized non-governmental organizations (DONGOs) in order to 'solve global problems, restore authority and ensure efficiency' results in an NGO *'nébuleuse'* (Drainville 2004: 118–20).

> In contrast to conjunctural places of transnational struggles, governance sites are not made by social forces answering tactical solicitations. Rather, they answer to the ordering spirit of civil reformism. They are apolitical locations, set aside for purposes of political and economic efficiency, where citizens, community leaders, stakeholders, shareholders and other partners assist in the delivery of services and facilitate social adjustment. Rather than places pregnant with possibilities, they are anchoring points of order in the world economy.
>
> (Drainville 2004: 139)

As part of this *nébuleuse*, civil society has been integrated into European Union (EU) institutional and scholarly discourse in a variety of ways that further presses the task of finding the relation within and between categories of research and movement. The inclusion of civil society in the European discourse is attributed to the European Economic and Social Committee (EESC) in the late 1990s (Smismans 2006). However, it was only in 2001 with the Commission 'White Paper of Administrative Reform' that the 'idea of civil society participation as a way to improve both the efficiency and legitimacy of European governance [became] a recurrent part of policy discourses'

(Smismans 2006: 5). Thereafter, the concept of civil society became integrated into the European integration literature (cf. Armstrong 2002; de Schutter 2002; Smismans 2003), although the concept raised questions among those who were troubled by the contradictory claims of the democratic potential of civil society (Armstrong 2002; de Schutter 2002), or questioned the extent to which civil society is really involved in European governance and can thus make the EU more democratic (Warleigh 2001).

Troubled by the introduction of civil society to the European discourse by two non-elected EU institutions, it has been argued that some EU institutions 'use the civil society discourse above all to further their institutional interests' (Smismans 2006: 5). The EESC initially introduced the concept 'to redefine its proper role and combat the risk of marginalisation within the European institutional set-up', while the European Commission took it up 'to build support for policy initiatives in the social sphere and subsequently to respond to the legitimacy crisis of the Brussels bureaucracy' (Smismans 2003: 482). The background to this was the perceived legitimizing role of social NGOs to further European social policy in the 1990s (ibid.). It is suggested that the main view of civil society is of functional representation, whereby civil society provides expertise in European policy making while fulfilling a form of democratic representation of all the different groups within society. This view is privileged in the two aforementioned institutions over that of civil society as politicization, a view to which both the European Parliament and Committee of the Regions are closer. This representation of civil society stresses the impact of 'social capital', reciprocity, civil engagement and the building of social trust, and is closely linked to theories of deliberative democracy, stressing the formation of a public sphere of informal deliberations. The last view of civil society as decentralization, it is suggested, is not addressed at the European level: 'While proposals are made to strengthen the consultation of civil society organizations in the formulation of new policy measures, no concrete proposals are made to delegate policy tasks to them' (ibid.: 498). In summary, current representations of civil society by European institutions create assumptions that: civil society will support integration; it is all-inclusive; it enhances 'participatory democracy'; there is no gap between the European and local level; and that the EU provides for the transnationalization of politics rather than the Europeanization of domestic politics.

This analysis is particularly important as it establishes similar impediments for civil society interaction with regional organizations as identified in relation to international organizations such as the WTO. It is illustrative of the range of institutional interests that prompt a reaching out to civil society to satisfy a number of conditions and demonstrates that dissenting interpretations of the role civil society plays are also expressed at the regional level of global governance as there is much to indicate a weak dialectics of presence and more to suggest creative dislocation in relation to the global political economy. Most significantly, however, these studies point to the functional uses of 'global civil society', not to explain changes in governance or processes of socio-economic change in the global political economy (cf. Amoore and Langley 2004), but to further institutional and/or scholarly interests.

Democratizing global governance

Returning to *Contesting Global Governance* (O'Brien *et al.* 2000), despite presenting a wide-ranging analysis of constraints faced by global social movements in their relations with multilateral economic institutions, a somewhat contradictory conclusion is presented. 'Complex multilateralism' is argued to 'capture real world changes' or a transformation in the nature of governance away from an exclusively state-based system, and is more fully explained through mediation between the short and long term:

> At present the transformation primarily takes the form of institutional modification, although some policy innovation is occurring. Such changes explicitly acknowledge that actors other than states speak on behalf of the public interest. While signalling an alteration to the method of governance, it is less clear that there is a change either in the content of governing policies or in the broad interests they represent. In the short run the MEI-GSM nexus is unlikely to greatly transform institutional functions. In the longer run, there is the possibility of incremental change in the functioning and ambit of these key institutions depending upon the outcome of continued political conflict.
>
> (O'Brien *et al.* 2000: 206)

In the short term, the authors point to a process of increased engagement, exchange of information and mutual learning in the MEI–GSM relationship (ibid.: 229). In the long term, a range of possibilities are mooted for the MEI–GSM relationship from 'atrophy to effective partnership' (ibid.: 230). While acknowledging that global social movements have a modest rather than substantive impact on multilateral economic institutions, it is suggested that continuing incremental change could, in the long term, result in the incremental pluralization of governing structures (ibid.: 3, 232; Wilkinson 2005: 8). The authors indicate the wider applicability of their study and implications for understanding international organization and IR. One such outcome is to show from a Coxian perspective that social forces are a factor in determining the nature of international order and organization. Another is to support studies (e.g. Murphy 1994) that link changes in economic organization, the move to neoliberalism for example, with forms of governance (ibid.). As demonstrated in the text of *Contesting Global Governance*, global social movements experience significant constraints in their interaction with the World Bank, WTO and IMF which may indicate creative dislocation in relation to the global political economy. The optimism with which O'Brien and co-authors end their study dissents, to a certain extent, with the evidence of conflicting objectives, institutional co-option and neoliberal ideological dominance in the MEI–GSM relationship presented in the course of the study.

Similar studies present the 'potentials and limitations of civil society as a force for democracy in global governance' (Scholte 2002: 281). They aim to demonstrate how civil society activism offers significant possibilities to reduce major democratic deficits while offering the proviso that civil society does not automatically deliver democratic benefits but must be actively nurtured in order to do so (ibid.). Based on empirical research regarding civil society and global, especially economic, governance, the democratic promise of civil society is outlined: 'Engagement between civil society and regulatory mechanisms can—if it gives stakeholders voice, bolsters public education, promotes debate, raises transparency, and increases accountability—enhance the respect that citizens accord to global governance' (Scholte 2002: 294). The main points may be summarized as the potential of civil society to:

- Give voice to stakeholders;
- Enhance democracy through public education activities;
- Fuel debate in and about global governance through raising issues;
- Pressure global governance to increase public transparency;
- Monitor regulatory agencies; and
- Foster legitimacy through the above points.

While some noteworthy achievements of civil society to enhance democracy to date, such as opposition to the Organisation for Economic Co-operation and Development (OECD)-sponsored Multilateral Agreement on Investment, are noted, the returns are described as 'relatively modest' (Scholte 2002: 295). Thus, the democratic challenges for civil society that can serve to undermine its democratic legitimacy are outlined as follows:

- Privileged civil society claims to speak for the subordinated, often with only limited, if any, direct consultation with the would-be constituents;
- Western-styled, Western-funded NGOs led by Westernized elites tend to dominate;
- Standards in public education are neglected or not provided;
- There is a tendency for co-option, top-down or authoritarian management;
- Opaque organizational structures lack public transparency; and
- There is little democratic accountability as regards issues such as funding and leadership (Scholte 2002: 299).

In relation to *Contesting Global Governance*, an optimistic assessment might be presented in terms of future possibilities for the development of unitary modes of social relation or a dialectics of presence that outweigh the evidence of historical antagonism and co-option—essentially prioritizing promises over limitations. More concretely, however, as the limitations above suggest, the strategic site of 'global governance' is further levelled and decontextualized. These contrasting views appear to co-exist uneasily with the intention of scholarly interest to nurture the role of civil society in influencing and democratizing global governance (Amoore and Langley 2004; Lipschutz 2005a; Linklater 1996).

From the viewpoint of conceptual history, the potential of GSMs to effect incremental change, alongside evidence of co-option and fragmentation, results in a complex definition of social change that further conditions theory and practice. The extent to which *Contesting Global Governance* shows social forces could constitute a determining factor in international order and organization is limited by the partial and mediated picture on global social movements that is presented and the delimiting of global social movements to a collection of NGOs, for example. While not wishing to detract from the important empirical analysis of women's, environmental and labour social movements and their interactions with institutions of global governance that is put forward in this study, the corresponding widening of the perceived gap between the philosophical promise of resistance and its empirical realities can, nonetheless, be highlighted.

While presenting an important empirical analysis, the conclusions are significant for demonstrating the role of scholarly interpretations of global civil society. When a post-positivist perspective is applied to GSMs, it can be suggested that they are constitutive of both the world around them (contextual, ideational, material, political and institutional conditions) and scholarly interpretations (normative support to enhance the democratizing potential of global social movements). The tension between the normative promise and empirical realities of resistance through GSMs notwithstanding, this study also points towards the functional, instrumental manner in which global civil society is constituted through and by 'global governance'.

However, the dialectical nexus between voluntarism and instrumentalism is not readily distinguishable. Despite describing civil society as a 'political arena' and asserting that civil society operations are 'steeped in struggles to affect the ways that power in society is acquired, distributed and exercised' (Scholte 2007a: 11), there is a tendency to find functional efficiency and promote the capacity of civil society to legitimize global governance rather than address the failures of 'unjust, incompetent, and corrupt' national and global governance (Lipschutz 2008: 72) or, as referred to above, the mutually constraining influence of the civil society-WTO relationship (Wilkinson 2005). Also evident in some interpretations of civil society is the failure to consider the relevance of the state and the structure of the global economic system in generating global issues of concern or influencing civil society (Lipschutz 2008). Closer to the empirical realities of contestation is consideration of sceptical views on the role of global civil society in democratizing European governing structures and the institutional 'management' of global civil society to further institutional interests (Smismans 2006). The notable insistence on greater and more intense civil society involvement in global governance can tend to occur without consideration of more concrete or substantial measures both to increase and improve this involvement (Martens 2008). Similarly, the abundance of scholarly literature on the topic somehow neglects to address the 'specific governmental functions fulfilled by the different institutions and practices of global civil society' (Bartelson 2006: 384). While the absence of more concrete measures may reflect the general rather than specific nature of some studies, as has been explained in response to a similar criticism (Scholte 2008), if civil societal engagement of global governance can lead to worth-while improvements in people's lives, it is not clear from more general accounts how this can be achieved. Equally evident is the clear mismatch between objectives, results and drawn conclusions in *Contesting Global Governance* (O'Brien *et al.* 2000).

This method of analysis tells us more about the problems of global governance—in terms of democratic deficit, legitimacy gaps and narrow remit that only just extends to consider levels of analysis from the local to the global—than about the co-constitutive or contradictory relations of neoliberal globalization and contestation. Partly, this can be explained through reference to how ideas of civil society are engaged 'less as they have appeared in the history of political thought and more as they might contribute to a theory of contemporary globalization and governance' (Scholte 2002: 283). Although qualified by a concern not to deny the historical importance of Western liberal and Marxist notions of civil society, this is over-shadowed by adaptation of the notion to fit contemporary politics: 'The issue is not to determine a definitive definition, but rather to craft a concept of civil society that is intellectually and politically relevant to the context at hand' (Scholte 2004: 213). As a result, a theory and history of civil society is not put forward in this assessment of the 'global accountability problem' (ibid.: 233). A politically relevant concept of civil society is also absent as the 'political' attributes of civil society in global governance are not examined. The selectivity of this conceptualization of civil society is also evident in the 'Building Global Democracy' programme, which, launched in 2008, receives its core funding from the Ford Foundation; 'ideas of "civil society" must be employed carefully and critically so that the activities in question are not captured for hegemonic and imperialist ends—and thereby detract from democratic accountability' (Scholte 2011: 36). It is not clear, however, how ideas of civil society can be abstracted from the workings of hegemony—which necessarily includes 'counter-hegemony'—and how, in this context, the democratic challenges for civil society that are listed above in greater detail such as its privileged and Western-centred nature, will be addressed, other than through functional and procedural changes. Also impacting on activist interpretations of global civil society, conveners of the 'Building Global Democracy' programme have held workshops on the theme of 'rebuilding global democracy' at the 2009 World Social Forum in Belém, Brazilian Amazonia, and at the 2011 World Social Forum in Dakar, Senegal.[5] However, the contested nature of civil society in, for example, combating neoliberalism or through 'alter-globalization', is not clear in the four-fold schema of 'contemporary uses' of civil society that are outlined (Scholte 2011: 33–34).[6] In common with activist representations of global civil society discussed in Chapter 3, Habermasian theories of a political space or 'public sphere' where 'citizens congregate to deliberate on the actual and prospective circumstances of their collective life' are drawn upon (Scholte 2011: 33). As a result, the clear concern with adding to a new framework of global governance and demonstrating how 'global scale regulation' can 'secure decent human lives for all in a more global world' (Scholte 2007b: 305), in the absence of a theoretical, historical, contextual and political conceptualization of civil society risks leading to a somewhat transparent exercise in how to mould a more democratic civil society and legitimate global governance. This critique gives substance to the shortcomings of conceptualizations of global civil society which, while acknowledging its historical accumulation of meanings, over-rely on current contextual conditions, and under-develop its theoretical and practical potential.

The plethora of conceptualizations of global civil society prompts further research to clear up related conceptual confusion. One such focus attempts to reinstate the market within conceptualizations of global civil society through its location within 'cosmocracy' (Keane 2001, 2005b, 2003). Global civil society is described as plural processes that are evident in charities, lobby groups, small and large corporate firms, independent media, trade unions and sporting organizations, which, through interaction with states, international organizations and non-state bodies, 'help to conserve or to alter the power relations embedded in the chains of interaction linking the local, regional, and planetary orders' (Keane 2001: 24). An influential definition of global civil society is given as: 'the contemporary thickening and stretching of networks of socio-economic institutions across borders to all four corners of the earth' which are propelled by the transnational energies of turbo-capitalism (ibid.).

Global civil society occupies a middle ground between competing national sovereign states and world government. It has a 'constitutional agenda' to 'find new governing arrangements that enable something like effective and democratically accountable government, the rule of law and more equitable and freer social relations to develop on a global scale' (Keane 2005b: 35). This agenda, however, is shared (and mostly directed it appears) by cosmocracy—an overlapping and interlocking conglomeration of power—which both integrates global civil society under governmental power and, due to its 'clumsy' nature, provides multiple openings for civil society to manipulate or exploit certain policy areas.

While reinstating the market within conceptualizations of global civil society, Keane's approach is blunted by a failure to move beyond the frameworks of 'liberal' global civil society. On the one hand, global civil society is not presented as a naturally occurring or spontaneous phenomenon and so this account avoids voluntarism, but, on the other hand, the structure of 'cosmocracy' appears to detract from any possibility, unless determined through chance, of global civil society influence. The agency of global civil society is lost amid multiple and competing power structures that resemble an anarchic picture of world order rather than shedding any light on the proposed function of civil society to reorder relations between the state, market and society—such that it is proposed to wield a constitutional agenda. Cosmocracy, from this point of view, fails to shed significant light on relations of governance and contestation in the global political economy. It is not clear how global civil society can carry out its agenda and alter power relations particularly in the face of numerous threats. These include: dominant neoliberal forces that champion free market turbo-capitalism; forces that promote stronger nationalist territorial states or forms of 'deglobalization' with a view to re-empowering the local and national (Bello 2000); and, finally, the 'far-fetched thinking' that heralds the arrival of world government, and 'stimulating, but unconvincing' portrayals of 'cosmopolitan democracy' (Keane 2005b: 49). It appears that in avoiding what are considered one-sided accounts of civil society which emphasize the resurgence of market economies and subsequent searches for a new ethical order in Marxist writings (Keane 2003: 3, note 3), and on the other hand, in avoiding dubious cosmopolitan accounts of global civil society, the conceptual clarification of global civil society becomes subsumed and mediated by a '"neo-medieval" mélange of overlapping legal structures and political bodies' (Keane 2001: 37). The problem with this account, and here agreement may be found with Lipschutz, is that scholarly interest in 'fostering the efficiency and transparency of non-governmental participation and process' can be associated with a liberal worldview that accepts power as a given and is 'less interested in the normative implications and consequences of how power is exercised and the results of that exercise' (Lipschutz 2005a: 183). While it is argued that the market may be integrated into conceptualizations of global civil society, the position of global civil society in relation to prevailing structures of power is less clear. Even the promise of its 'constitutional agenda', we soon learn, might only be achieved through manipulating the more 'clumsy' structures of cosmocracy.

Cosmocracy takes on much of the statist discourse of IR which has considerable difficulty in formulating a meaningful conceptualization of global civil society in relation to states and markets. The relationship between civil society and the market is highlighted but there is a tendency to delimit from the start the agency or 'willed action' (Baker 2002b) of civil society by situating it outside governmental structures and as a subject of 'cosmocracy'. Equally, even if it successfully points to problems of global governance, this account ultimately succumbs to the shortcomings that are therein critiqued through failing to explain relations of governance and contestation at work in the global political economy.

While according to this account global civil society is located 'outside the boundaries of governmental structures' (Keane 2001), a contrasting account contests the axiomatic autonomy of civil society from state institutions (Colás 2002). Rather, states are considered to mediate and constitute *international*, as opposed to *global*, civil society. The 'politics of accreditation' denoted by globalization theorists to transnational civil society is critiqued for representing the latter 'as a fairly homogeneous, non-hierarchical and disinterested counterpoint to the power-driven system of states' or 'disenfranchised "global citizenry" which stands outside the realm of inter-state relations', which, it is argued, leads to inflated hopes of change (Colás 2002: 139, 152). The United Nations (UN) Economic and Social Council (ECOSOC) framework that gave NGOs consultative status and has, since 1972, led to UN world conferences on issues such as the environment, human rights and gender, is provided as an example of the politics of accreditation. On the one hand, it is acknowledged that these conferences have provided a significant point of convergence for civil society with the attendant benefits of expanding the number, scope, networking opportunities and representative functions of NGOs and raising global awareness of their issues through the media (ibid.). The pervasive influence of states in such gatherings is highlighted but:

> on closer inspection, the form, content and eventual outcomes of such gatherings are so heavily circumscribed by the interests of states that it is difficult to see how the agents of global civil society can be said to be genuinely representative of an autonomous and undifferentiated 'global citizenry'.
>
> (Colás 2002: 153)

Since the state devolves its legitimate monopoly over political rule to international organizations, the state ultimately determines whether an NGO will receive consultative status. This often means that Third World NGOs, or NGOs with few material resources and/or explicitly political goals, may not receive consultative status or, if they do, may not hold an adequately influential position in relation to other, more established and influential NGOs such as Amnesty International (ibid.).

Although drawing on alternative theoretical influences, it has been elsewhere argued that the focus should change to how 'particular forms of society and governmentality are constituted and reconstituted, sometimes through the very agency that, at first glance, appears to be a means of opposition and resistance, if not liberation' (Lipschutz 2005a: 183). A contrasting body of literature on global governmentality maps out a compliant global civil society in relation to discursive governance. In contrast to the above, global civil society is proposed as a site of government—'a place where the global political economy is shaped, regulated or deregulated, disciplined or sustained'—and dominant representations of global civil society are considered to enable neoliberal conceptions of global governance to flourish (Amoore and Langley 2005: 147). It is, nonetheless, contradictory and ambiguous as it 'simultaneously holds out the potential for resistance, while it closes down, excludes, controls and disciplines' (Amoore and Langley 2004: 100). It is, therefore, a form of 'government from a distance' prescribed by global governance while also having the capacity to 'open itself to challenge and contradiction' (ibid.).

In seeking to interrogate conceptualizations of global contestation and to reopen debate on global civil society, these studies, even while failing to affirm the emancipative potential of global civil society in global contestation, open toward further critique of articulations of resistance and the tendency to treat resistance and power and global order as analytically separate (Coleman and Tucker 2011: 400).

Conclusions

In conclusion, the above studies give particular insight into the hegemonic production of global civil society as an object of global governance while implicitly contributing to 'counter-hegemonic' knowledge on global civil society in ways that can, even unintentionally, limit its possibilities. Many of them demonstrate that global civil society is: 'a site that is used instrumentally by different actors, whether within the civil society realm or without, for different ideological, political and organisational purposes' (Howell and Lind 2009: 5). Applying categories of research—from instrumental to voluntarist— to conceptualizations of global civil society draws attention to modes through which it is constituted in studies of global governance. Its prescience is clear as, for example, the 'building global democracy' gathers momentum and pushes the boundaries of activist and governance representations of global civil society. Instrumentalism points towards its functional constitution in consideration of democratizing, legitimating, educating or representative roles. Voluntarism tends more towards an activist constitution, as discussed in Chapter 3, which highlights emancipative purpose. Instrumentalism and voluntarism are each productive of contrasting conceptualizations of global civil society but each is also capable of overestimation and exaggeration. If global civil society is, or can be, 'a battlefield upon which different values, ideas and political visions are debated, contended and struggled over' (Howell and Lind 2009: 5), it may first be useful to acknowledge the dialectical nexus between scholarly, institutional and activist categories of research and movement that serve to thus constitute it. A critical orientation, as evoked at the beginning of this chapter, highlights the relationship between knowledge and material and political conditions. One way of responding to the latter lies in seeking out modes of social relation engaged in by global civil society in and towards the global political economy, from a dialectics of presence to creative dislocation or unspecified other. Focusing on *Contesting Global Governance* (O'Brien *et al.* 2000) in this chapter enabled a conceptual and contextual analysis of global civil society in global governance, alongside a textual examination of the processes of authorial and institutional knowledge construction. These were extended through drawing attention to further studies which gave greater understanding into how narratives of meaning are generated through the practices and institutions of current and envisioned structures of global governance (cf. Drainville 2004; Wilkinson 2005; Smismans 2006, 2003; Scholte 2002, 2011; Keane 2001). An analysis of the constituting of global civil society has an effect on conditioning the 'possibility of thought and action' since 'conceptual history attends to what the practices of definition and usage *do* to a concept, and what the concept in turn *does* to the world into which it is inscribed' (Bartelson 2000: 181–82).

These studies demonstrate that substantive involvement of global civil society in the policy-making processes of various international institutions is limited and may, as a result, place constraints on all parties. Thus, the nature of WTO-civil society relations is 'deeply constraining' for both—an observation that may be used to challenge creative dislocation and civil society 'management' but which, nonetheless, influences wider perceptions of what constitutes global civil society (cf. Wilkinson 2005). Many of these studies effectively reveal how certain dominant conceptualizations of global civil society can feed into a more general understanding of the term, a process that may result in depoliticizing and limiting civil society to those functions and boundaries prescribed by institutions of global and regional governance and also by scholarly accounts. The constitutive outcome of institutional conceptions of global civil society has led to general assertions concerning the all-inclusive, democratic and bridge-building characteristics of global civil society (ibid.). This confirms the expectation that definitions of global civil society condition possibilities of thought and action (Bartelson 2000). The democratic and non-state credentials frequently attributed to civil society by dominant world views are often composed in a self-interested light which may, for example, highlight the functional uses of global civil society to further institutional interests (Smismans 2003, 2006). Feminist perspectives evoke similar possibilities in terms of the position of the academic through showing that by engaging in academic analysis of the social movement the scholar is also engaged in its construction (Eschle 2005: 22). The academic, as outlined in this chapter, is also responsible for the construction of varying conceptualizations of global civil society in relation to the institutions of global governance from optimism for long-term pluralization of governing structures (O'Brien *et al.* 2000) to the more modest and limited conceptualization of *international* civil society (Colás 2002). Further critiques of autonomous representations of global civil society examined above draw attention to the tendency for many conceptualizations to represent resistance, power and global order as analytically separate (Coleman and Tucker 2011: 400). There is a significant lacuna between the philosophical promise and empirical realities of global civil society alongside evidence of institutional co-option, movement fragmentation and ideological, and structural, dominance. While these processes contribute to the gridding and levelling of the global terrain, they do not automatically preclude, or guarantee, a dialectics of presence, which is extended further in the next chapter to consider the World Social Forum as a terrain not only of resistance but of power and global order. In sum, the practices of defining global civil society and the ways in which academic and policy practitioners use the concept, are important indicators of how global civil society is understood in relation to the practices of globalization and contestation within the global political economy, and in turn, the impact this has on the parameters, and possibilities, of thought and action.

Notes

1 Drainville's critique of transnational historical materialism and scepticism concerning the making of 'grand absentee subjects' should be noted here. For more see Drainville (2004: 11–15, 71–103).
2 The Internationale Situationniste (IS) used concepts such as *dérives* and *situations* in order to criticize radically the alienation and *ennui* of modernity. From 1957 to 1962 the IS was specifically concerned with a critique of urbanism as a process that disempowers citizens and with breaking down the distinction between public and private. For more on the IS see Drainville (2004: 33–36).
3 In relation to the World Bank see O'Brien *et al.* (2000: 117), on the IMF (ibid.: 159, 202), and WTO (ibid.: 141).
4 The origin of Chilean poblador groups is located in women's protests against the Pinochet regime in the mid-1980s. As funding from the World Bank Social Investment and Solidarity Fund (FOSIS) is only through officially registered organizations, these informal *poblador* groups are pressurized to become more formal and institutionalized. Many women's groups, however, are reluctant to register as statutory bodies under the state. They fear possible depoliticization and pressure to move their focus from protest against the state to colluding with the state through using FOSIS funds for projects related to reconstruction and poverty reduction (O'Brien *et al.* 2000: 58–59).
5 For further details on WSF workshops such as on 'How to Build Global Democracy?' held in Dakar see: www.buildingglobaldemocracy.org.
6 This four-fold schema of civil society includes: 'civil' society based on trust, openness, tolerance and non-violence; associational life following Tocqueville (1945) and also the idea of social capital (Putnam 2000), including non-official, non-profit organizations outside the family that are not overtly political; civil society as the aggregate of NGOs or as a third sector; lastly, the definition Scholte claims to mainly adopt, civil society is identified as a political space or 'public sphere' drawing on Habermas where 'citizens congregate to deliberate on the actual and prospective circumstances of their collective life' (Scholte 2011).

5 'Dialectics of presence' at the World Social Forum

There was an ambiguous dialectics of presence at the 2011 World Social Forum (WSF) in Dakar, Senegal. An array of colour and festivity accompanied the opening march of about 60,000 to produce an upbeat expression of diversity and celebration that was later disrupted through organizational chaos and confusion at Cheikh Anta Diop University, where thousands of people from an estimated 130 countries gathered from 6–9 February.[1] Revolts and protests in Tunisia, Egypt, Algeria, Jordan, Yemen, Saudi Arabia and Sudan formed a backdrop against the unfolding of the forum. There was a sense, expressed by some participants, that Senegalese authorities reacted through deploying riot police at the opening march and stepping back from earlier support for the forum. Nonetheless, President Wade of Senegal was in attendance, President Evo Morales of Bolivia played a part in the opening ceremonies, and the forum culminated with the news that Hosni Mubarak had resigned in Egypt. In a view confirmed by many participant accounts, the forum was marked by 'confusion, *confounded*' with 'classrooms filled with students, inadequate signage, tents that lacked facilities (chairs, interpretation and audio-visual equipment), programmes—late and insufficient' (Kumar, in Alloo *et al.* 2011: 220). Non-governmental organizations (NGOs) 'and men speaking on behalf of the down trodden populace across the globe', rather than social movements, dominated the space according to another account (Longwe, in Alloo *et al.* 2011: 225). It was also innovative according to the main decision-making, non-deliberative body of the forum, the International Council (WSF 2011). The Assembly of Social Movements was vibrant and well attended; large caravans of people arrived from West Africa and the Maghreb; remote participation with people in South Africa, Zambia, Zimbabwe and other countries was facilitated through the Dakar Extended project; and the forum was freely open to the public, in contrast to, for example, the 2007 Nairobi, Kenya, WSF in the south of the continent.

Seeing the World Social Forum through 'global civil society' in this chapter offers a wider conceptual lens through which to consider modes of social relation towards the global political economy than focusing on social forces, anti-globalization movements, new social movements, global social movements, multitude, or the post-modern prince might enable alone. Present also at the forum are often neglected individuals, indigenous peoples and members of non-governmental organizations, trade unions, political parties, cultural and religious groups.[2] While seldom conceptually interrogated, global civil society is frequently conjectured in relation to the World Social Forum. According to one assessment, the inception of the WSF captured progressive civil societal developments which were already underway 'across continents, nations and cities and around a variety of themes' (Wainwright 2005: 109). The WSF, we are also told, has fulfilled critical functions for global civil society through providing a physical and temporal meeting space; allowing it to retreat, energize and chart future directions; and providing a site and space to discuss, debate and elaborate an alternative world order (Bello 2007). If we want to speak of global civil society, although challenging in the absence of a mechanism to ensure global civic rights, the forum would be the site of an 'emancipatory', as opposed to 'liberal', global civil society (Santos 2006a: 42–43). It is considered, nonetheless, that 'the WSF is one of the most promising civil society processes that may both contribute significantly to global democracy initiatives, and possibly constitute such an initiative itself' (Patomäki and Teivainen 2004a: 124) and that 'the WSF is the most substantial initiative of the counter-hegemonic and emancipatory global civil society' (Caruso 2007: 105). Confirming this significance, it has also been suggested that '[g]iven its scope and breadth as well as its focus on some of the most urgent conflicts of our day, the WSF is arguably the most important social and political development of our time' and calls for far more attention from social scientists (Velitchkova et al. 2009: 194).

However, global civil society at the forum merits much further consideration, particularly if the WSF is considered to stand out as 'a new major space created by and for global civil society' (Patomäki and Teivainen 2004a: 212), or indeed if the 'pre-figurative politics' of the WSF is thought to enact the world which it envisages through presenting a new form of global governance and civil society (Smith et al. 2008: 25, 132). I consider such representations in this chapter through the WSF 'strategy of convergence' for 'another possible world' to bring together groups and movements of global civil society and facilitate the contested creation of an 'open space' or 'movement of movements'. In looking for a 'dialectics of presence' at the World Social Forum, the sense of 'place' of global civil society and the social relations in which they are engaged are construed in this chapter as part of the dialectics of order and change in the global political economy (cf. Drainville 2004: 163, 32). The more recent consolidation of the strategy of convergence, whereby reconciliation appears to have been reached between contending perspectives, presents some real challenges for any assessment of the 'creative tensions' and 'new politics' of the forum process (Smith et al. 2008; Velitchkova et al. 2009), particularly in the context of preparations for the 2013 WSF in Tunisia as the forum attempts to address its perceived disconnection from the Middle East and North Africa (MENA) uprisings.[3]

Global convergence at the World Social Forum

The WSF Charter of Principles, adopted in April 2001, describes the forum as 'an open meeting place for reflective thinking, democratic debate of ideas, formulation of proposals, free exchange of experiences and interlinking for effective action, by groups and movements of civil society that are opposed to neo-liberalism and to domination of the world by capital and any form of imperialism' (WSF 2002a). It further affirms that the forum does not intend to be a 'locus of power to be disputed by the participants', but does represent 'a permanent process of seeking and building alternatives' within a 'plural, diversified, non-confessional, non-governmental and non-party context' (ibid.). 'Open space' was promoted in the context of a new optimism on the capacity of movements of civil society to converge on the principle of anti-neoliberalism and in the more threatening context of the closure of spaces and suspension of civil liberties as the 'war on terror' got underway. Consequently, there has been much reluctance to delimit the concept of open space through transforming the forum into a 'more unified and delineated movement' (CACIM and CCS 2007). Instead, the idea of open space conceives the WSF as 'a space for relatively free association and for the free and creative exchange of ideas and experiences' and, furthermore, as 'a significant and radical polemical challenge to empire and to hegemonic politics' (ibid.).

Proponents of open space, among them some WSF founders and members of the Organizing Committee (OC) and International Council (IC), affirm the creation of '*non-deliberative* political spaces where a wide range of movements converge and where the only requirement is their shared opposition to neoliberalism' (Conway 2005: 427).[4] Here, open space is likened to an ideal Habermasian public sphere implying 'a singular discursive arena ... where diverse networks and groups converge to share ideas and develop proposals' (Juris 2008a: 255). Cándido Grzybowski, director of the Brazilian Institute of Social and Economic Analyses (IBASE), an early OC organization, underlines the capacity of open space to facilitate global convergence:

> It is impossible to understand the Social Forum without linking it to the growing wave of public protests against globalisation, as occurred in Seattle, Washington, Prague and Nice. The people behind the Forum are the same actors in the same struggles, movements, associations and organisations, however small or large, local or national, regional or global. It is this global convergence of diverse networks and movements that creates and sustains the World Social Forum.
>
> (Grzybowski 2001)

The forum can be understood as 'only partly a culmination of the "Seattle effect" and its internationalization' (Munck 2007: 70). The proposal for a counter-forum to the World Economic Forum is attributed to a suggestion by François Houtart at a Tri-Continental Centre (CETRI) meeting in

Louvain-la-Neuve, Belgium in 1996 (Fisher and Ponniah 2003: 4; Sahabandhu 2006). This was followed by an anti-Davos meeting in 1999 under the auspices of the World Forum for Alternatives. In 2001 the first World Social Forum was held for five days at the Catholic University of Rio Grande do Sul in Porto Alegre, Brazil, a town renowned for its participatory budgetary process and a seat of the Brazilian Workers Party (Whitaker 2004). Further key figures were involved in its formation in Europe and Brazil including: Bernard Cassen, editor of the French newspaper *Le Monde Diplomatique* and president ATTAC, France; Oded Grajew, coordinator of the Brazilian Association of Entrepreneurs for Citizenship (CIVES); and Francisco Whitaker of the Brazilian Justice and Peace Commission (Teivainen 2002). Table 5.1 and Table 5.2 detail the composition of the initial and expanded Organizing Committees.

Global convergence was a significant originating rationale for the WSF and its location in the South—in Porto Alegre, Mumbai, Bamako/Caracas/ Karachi, Nairobi, Belém, Dakar—and continued resistance to holding a World Social Forum in the North, can be understood as integral to the strategy of convergence through processes of 'intercultural translation'; diverse 'traditions of critical knowledge, transformative practices, and conceptions of a better society' beyond, although not excluding, the already existing, and more hegemonic, movements of the Western left and imperial South (Santos 2008: 258–59). The forum was conceived to draw on emerging Latin American 'new social movements' comprising women, indigenous peoples, Latin Americans of African heritage and others organizing on issues such as religion and human rights, while serving to link them to the globalized struggle for economic and social justice (Prevost *et al.* 2012). Thus it is considered conducive to a new political era that enables new social movements to assert 'autonomy from traditional political parties, to practice horizontal and participatory processes in decision-making, and to seek social justice based on race/ethnicity, gender, and/or traditional marginalization from the political process or economic benefits' (ibid.: 4–6). In this way, the open space of the forum is compared to a footpath that traverses the modern

Table 5.1 Initial composition of the World Social Forum Organizing Committee

ABONG	Brazilian Association of Non-governmental Organizations
ATTAC-Brazil	Association for the Taxation of Financial Transactions for the Aid of Citizens
CBJP	Brazilian Justice and Peace Commission
CIVES	Brazilian Association of Entrepreneurs for Citizenship
CUT	Unified Workers Confederation
IBASE	Brazilian Institute for Social and Economic Studies
	Social Network for Justice and Human Rights
MST	Landless Movement

Source: (Adapted from Santos 2004; Whitaker 2004; Fisher and Ponniah 2003)

Table 5.2 Composition of the Brazilian Organizing Committee, 2005

ABONG	Brazilian Association of Non-governmental Organizations
AMB	Association of Brazilian Women
ATTAC	Association for the Taxation of Financial Transactions for the Aid of Citizens
Conam	National Confederation of Residents Associations of Brazil
	Cáritas Brasil
CAT	Central Autônoma de Trabalhadores
CBJP	Brazilian Commission of Justice and Peace, part of the CNBB
CIVES	Brazilian Association of Entrepreneurs for Citizenship
CLACSO	Latin American Council of Social Sciences
CMP	Central de Movimentos Populares, Popular Movements
	Organizing Committee of the Intercontinental Youthcamp
	African Committee of the WSF
CUT	Central Trade Union Federation
FBOM	Brazilian Forum of NGOs and Social Movements for Environment & Development
GTA	Amazon Working Group
IBASE	Brazilian Institute of Social and Economic Analyses
IPF	Paulo Freire Institute
	Jubilee South Brazil
WMW	World March of Women
MST	Landless Movement
	Social Network for Justice and Human Rights
UJS	Union of Socialist Youth, youth wing of Brazilian Communist Party
UNE	National Student Union

Source: (www.forumsocialmundial.org.br)

city allowing locally bound people consciously and unconsciously to communicate, exchange information, and accumulate global knowledge and understanding as they go about their everyday lives. This process of 'sustained' exchange, it is suggested, allows for the emergence of a new culture 'of more open, horizontal social relations and politics' (Sen 2007: 510).

At an International Council meeting in 2002 the forum was affirmed as a space for 'convergence and synthesis' that, in alignment with the Charter of Principles 'does not take positions or define types of political action' (WSF 2002b). The strategy of convergence is a distinguishing feature of the forum which, as I will examine in this chapter, appears to strengthen alliances between similar groups while also marginalizing or excluding others. Many of the examples I use draw on participant observation at the 2007 Nairobi WSF and I refer to some forum panels and workshops that I attended to show how many of the conceptual discussions on global civil society, strategy and future of the forum play out at its site. Convening approximately 57,000 people, the Nairobi forum was organized by the Eastern Africa Organizing Committee (EAOC), composed of representatives from the Kenyan, Ugandan, Tanzanian and Somali Social Forums.[5] The secretariat of the EAOC was based in Nairobi, Kenya, and hosted by the Social Development Network (SODNET).

The EAOC was to work in close collaboration with the International Council of the WSF, its working groups, the WSF secretariat in Sao Paulo, Brazil, the WSF India Organizing Committee, the African Social Forum Council and organizations active in the European Social Forum. Prominent themes of this forum focused on the fight against AIDS, the debt burden, food sovereignty and the need for fair trade agreements, and activities were organized around:

- Building a world of peace, justice, ethics and respect for diverse spiritualities;
- Liberating the world from the domination of multinational and financial capital;
- Ensuring universal and sustainable access to the common goods of humanity and nature;
- Democratization of knowledge and information;
- Ensuring dignity, defending diversity, guaranteeing gender equality and eliminating all forms of discrimination;
- Guaranteeing economic, social, human and cultural rights especially the right to food, health care, education, housing, employment and decent work;
- Building a world order based on sovereignty, self-determination and rights of peoples;
- Constructing a people-centred and sustainable economy; and
- Building real democratic political structures and institutions with full people's participation on decisions and control of public affairs and resources (WSF 2006b).

The World March of Women (WMW), a WSF IC member, engages actively with the strategy of convergence through coalition building with social movements and other feminist organizations at the site of the forum. The origins of this particular movement can be traced back to a mass march organized by Québec feminists to protest deepening poverty in Québec (Conway 2012b). Later developed through the fourth United Nations (UN) World Conference for Women in Beijing in 1995 and subsequent local, national and global activities, the WMW demands the elimination of poverty and violence against women (WMW 2004; Dufour and Giraud 2007). It is now a movement of over 6,000 diverse groups from grassroots women's organizations, to labour unions and leftist political parties in 150 countries (ibid.).

The WMW has been involved in each of the World Social Forums, and in many regional and national forums, through organizing roundtables, seminars and actions. It describes the World Social Forum as 'a privileged space for building alliances with other anti-globalization social movements' and, according to a recent assessment, 'they approach the WSF ... pragmatically and instrumentally as a "convergence space", rather than as a place for encounter' (Conway 2012b: 387). The WMW has worked with Via Campesina and Friends of the Earth in the struggle for food sovereignty and engaged in political training activities with the Committee for the Abolition of Third World Debt (CADTM). It has acted jointly with regional organizations that work on related issues such as the Latin American Network of Women Changing the Economy (REMTE) and Lesbian Gay Bisexual and Transgender (LGBT) South-South Dialogue, although because of the institutionalized and lobbying nature of many international feminist organizations, from which the WMW distances itself, it claims to have difficulty building alliances with feminist movements on the international scale (WMW 2008a). The WMW also plays an active role in the Assembly of Social Movements (ASM), which seeks to 'amplify alliances between social movements through analysis and common actions' at the site of each forum and possibly beyond (WMW 2007).[6] Through the ASM, the WMW has worked with Via Campesina, the Central Única dos Trabalhadores (United Workers Confederation, CUT), ATTAC, Focus on the Global South and CADTM. It joined with Via Campesina and the Brazilian Movimento dos Sem Terra to organize a dialogue with presidents Evo Morales of Bolivia, Hugo Chávez of Venezuela, Rafael Correa of Ecuador and Fernando Lugo of Paraguay at the 2009 Belém WSF.

However, while the World March of Women actively facilitates convergence across these groups, the presence of anti-choice organizations at the 2007 Nairobi WSF, with which they are ideologically opposed, was viewed as an impediment towards achieving their objectives. On the one hand, therefore, the WMW states that 'convergence needs to be at the heart of the WSF ... We need more interaction among movements to live out our alternatives, to discuss them, to integrate them into our praxis' (WMW 2008). On the other hand, following the Nairobi WSF they state that there is 'a blatant lack of coherence between the organization of the WSF and our social transformation objectives. The commercialization of the event, the presence of anti-choice groups, etc., are impediments to building alternatives and must be tackled' (ibid.). This confirms an earlier critique of the WSF Charter of Principles for being 'so broad that it allows the adhesion of groups that have opposing ideological view points, such as around the issue of abortion' and, furthermore, that '[w]e cannot hope to build a better world and at the same time allow space for hatred and misogyny in the WSF' (WMW 2007).

To illustrate further, a statue supporting reproductive rights for women was a source of considerable controversy at the Nairobi WSF. This statue, called 'In the Name of God', depicted a pregnant teenager nailed to a crucifix.[7] According to Art in Defence of Humanism, the crucifix is a symbol of opposition to the 'Christian fundamentalists' crusade against contraception and sexual education', a policy of sexual abstinence promoted by the George W. Bush government 'with disastrous consequences for the AIDS situation in Africa' (AIDOH 2007). One of its locations during the forum was near the prominently located large tents of the Caritas-All Africa Council of Churches (AACC) ecumenical platform. There was a strong ecumenical presence at the 2007 Nairobi WSF, especially compared to other forums. It is estimated that 50 per cent of the participants were from churches or church-related organizations (World Council of Churches 2008), while 400 Caritas delegates from approximately 40 member organizations attended (Caritas 2007). A speech by Anglican Archbishop Desmond Tutu and an ecumenical rally preceded the official start of the forum. Giving some insight into the role of the Church, Francisco Whitaker explains to the national conference of the Brazilian bishops:

> how the Forum has emerged by initiative of some civil society organizations in Brazil with the intense participation of our Church, by way of our Commission of Justice and Peace, to become a repeated event growing into what we now call the ongoing World Social Forum Process ... I would like to ... [call] attention to the direct relationship there is between the values that the Forum has been consolidating around the world and the Christian social, political and economic thought. My reason for doing this is that we may discover we have, as Church, a special responsibility to resume this quest, as it still is quite far from completion.
>
> (Whitaker 2003)

At Nairobi, the organization behind the statue 'In the Name of God' later removed the crucifix from the statue in response to conservative religious criticism that religious symbols were being used for political purposes and, the group behind the statue claims, to refocus attention onto the issue of contraception (AIDOH 2007). The apparent reification of the many complex issues that the statue embodied, in response to significant contention, gives disturbing insight into how a strategy of convergence deals with diversity. It appears that forum strategy tends to facilitate convergence between like-minded groups while also folding in or creatively dislocating contention.

The Porto Alegre consensus

As it becomes increasingly difficult to suggest that the forum fosters an 'ideological Disneyland' (Engler 2005, citing José Fogaca, Mayor of Porto Alegre), another form of convergence among like-minded groups, perhaps unsurprisingly in the context of the above, has led to the drafting of unified programmes for action. Still captured within the strategy of convergence, this consolidates the World Forum for Alternatives focus on 'convergence in diversity' through programmatic formulations (Amin 2007). While the ASM regularly issues calls at the end of forums, the Manifesto of Porto Alegre of January 2005 and the Bamako Appeal of January 2006 each received far more attention on their release.

According to a signatory of the Manifesto, its purpose was to find expressions of convergence among the diversity of organizations at the WSF: 'the WSF should present itself to the world as being the major manifestation of a counter-hegemonic globalization and the bearer of an alternative global consensus, the Consensus of Porto Alegre' (Santos 2006a: 123).[8] To this end 'twelve proposals for another possible world' were drawn up. The majority are concerned with the implementation of new economic and social measures such as: cancellation of the external debt of Southern countries; the restitution of money stolen by corrupt leaders; the implementation of a wide range of international taxes and their direction (along with 0.7 per cent of the gross national product (GNP) of rich countries) towards social services such as clean water, energy and health; the progressive dismantling of a wide range of fiscal, juridical and banking havens; the right to employment and social protection; equal rights between men and women; equitable trade; the exclusion of education, health, social services and culture from the General Agreement on Trade in Services (GATS); alimentary sovereignty; elimination of subsidies and dumping practices; enabling sovereign power to forbid the production and import of genetically modified organisms meant for consumption; and the prohibition of the patenting and privatization of common goods such as water.

The Manifesto also focuses on the sustenance of community life, peace and justice. This includes a bid to use public policies to fight all forms of discrimination and racism and to recognize indigenous populations. An alternative development model based on efficient use of energy and democratic control of natural resources is proposed to tackle environmental destruction. The dismantling of all foreign military bases and the removal of troops without a UN mandate from all countries is also proposed. The final two proposals in the Manifesto advocate the creation of another possible world through the promotion of democracy from the 'neighbouring' or local level to the global level. Legal rights to freedom of information are proposed alongside support for a non-profit alternative media monitored by national and international media institutions. Lastly, according to the 12th proposal, international institutions must be reformed and democratized through respecting the broad rights stipulated in the UN Declaration of Human Rights. Democratization includes the incorporation of the World Bank, International Monetary Fund (IMF) and World Trade Organization (WTO) into the 'decision-making mechanism and systems' of the UN and the possible transfer of the UN headquarters from New York to a Southern country.

Upon its release the media were quick to interpret the Manifesto as an expression of the political will of the WSF despite the assertion within its text that 'We, the signers of the Porto Alegre Manifesto, by no means pretend to speak in the name of the entire World Social Forum, but speak on a strictly personal basis' (Group of Nineteen 2005). This is a reference to the Charter of Principles emphasis on the non-deliberative nature of the WSF under which individuals cannot express positions on behalf of all participants and decisions cannot be taken by the WSF as a body. Nonetheless, the Manifesto was viewed by some as a violation of the principle of open space and just one of many other proposals presented at the WSF by participant groups and the Assembly of Social Movements (Whitaker *et al.* 2006). The Manifesto is substantively criticized for reformism and for failing to integrate gender perspectives into its proposals (Bond 2005). According to critics, the profile of its signatories—consisting of 18 white men and one African woman—betrays intellectualism and elitism. Among its signatories are social theorists, a philosopher, a journalist, Nobel Prize winners, novelists, theologians, economists and political sociologists. Santos (2006a), a signatory of the Manifesto, accepts the legitimacy of some of these criticisms such as the absence of a developed gender perspective in the proposals. However, he goes on to stress that eventually the current strength of the WSF—its diversity—may become its weakness, which will lessen its impact. He accepts that some proposals are reformist although this is justified through the suggestion that social revolution is not on the cards in the short to medium term. The importance of the Manifesto and its location within the debate on the space/movement debate is also highlighted:

> The 'incident' of the manifesto highlighted the cleavage between those who conceive of the WSF as a social space and those who conceive of it as the embryo of a global civil society, constituted by a wide range of global or globally linked social actors.
>
> (Santos 2006a: 125)

Meanwhile, the Bamako Appeal, an initiative of the World Forum for Alternatives, the Third World Forum, the Malian Social Forum, and Environmental Development Action in the Third World (ENDA), was prepared at a meeting just before the 2006 polycentric WSF in Bamako and, not unlike the Manifesto, it raises the controversial question of developing a political programme for the WSF. It too has been criticized for contrasting sharply with the representation of the forum as an open and horizontal process in the WSF Charter of Principles. Key figures involved in this initiative, and also signatories of the Manifesto, include Samir Amin, director of the African office of the Third World Forum, an international NGO for research and debate, and François Houtart, director of the Belgian NGO Centre Tricontinental and lecturer at Louvain University. The Appeal has invited broader support than the Manifesto and has been signed by 21 collective entities and 66 individuals (Open Space Forum 2006).

The authors of the Bamako Appeal want to move the WSF from a place of dialogue to 'a base for coordinated anti-imperialist and pro-socialist action' (Sen *et al.* 2007: 19). According to the text of the appeal it 'aims at contributing to the emergence of a new popular and historical subject … one that is diverse, multipolar and from the people', thus turning people into 'protagonists of their history' (ibid.). The appeal includes commitments to internationalism and solidarity and aims towards the construction of a political, economic and cultural consensus for an alternative to militarized neoliberal globalization. The following principles are outlined in the Appeal:

- Construct a world founded on the solidarity of human beings and peoples;
- Construct a world founded on the full affirmation of citizenship and equality of the sexes;

- Construct a universal civilization offering in all areas the full potential of creative development to all its diverse members;
- Construct socialization through democracy;
- Construct a world founded on the recognition of the non-market-driven law of nature, the resources of the planet and its agricultural soil;
- Construct a world founded on the recognition of the non-market-driven status of cultural products and scientific acquisitions, education and health care;
- Promote policies that closely associate democracy without pre-assigned limits, with social progress and the affirmation of autonomy of nations and peoples; and
- Affirm the solidarity of the people of the North and South in the construction of an internationalism on an anti-imperialist basis.

The Bamako appeal for a new 'collective consciousness' includes medium- and long-term goals and methods of action:

- For a multipolar world system founded on peace, law and negotiation;
- For an economic reorganization of the global system;
- For regionalization in the service of the people which reinforces the south in global negotiations;
- For the democratic management of the planet's natural resources;
- For a better future for peasant farmers;
- To build a workers' united front;
- For a democratization of societies as a necessary step to full human development;
- For the eradication of all forms of oppression, exploitation and alienation of women;
- For the democratic management of the media and cultural diversity; and
- For the democratization of international organizations and the institutionalization of a multipolar international order.

Actions under each of these proposals include a mixture of long-term and short-term goals to create working groups, observer groups, networks of researchers, establish contacts, launch campaigns, reinforce solidarity, disseminate information, develop databases and internet sites. According to Amin, the idea of a Fifth International expressed partly through the Bamako Appeal 'should contribute to the internationalism of the peoples' of the North and South, to include not only the proletariat 'but all social classes and popular strata that are victims of the system whose survival is threatened' (Amin 2007: 141).[9]

These more comprehensive reassertions of the left in alter-globalization brought to the forefront a precept of the strategy of convergence that is central for WSF organizers—that the forum would reinvent the hierarchies, violence and authoritarianism of the traditional Left and facilitate global convergence against neoliberalism. However, like the Manifesto, the Appeal has been seen by critics as a top-down attempt to define a political programme for the WSF rather than allowing programmes to emerge from political struggle or simply not imposing programmatic ideas on fluid movements and campaigns (e.g. Bond 2010: 333). There is a 'contradictory impulse' at work whereby the promotion of egalitarian relations and diversity within the architecture of the forum, by promoters of open space, for example, may present an obstacle to the development of political programmes and actions (Juris 2008a: 265). Indeed, the main opposition to the Manifesto and Bamako Appeal has come from supporters of open space, but as argued below, a strategy of convergence tends to preclude diversity at the forum. While the clear political motivation behind the Bamako Appeal makes it stand out from the less detailed and more tentative Manifesto, and the merits of its location in socialism, anti-racism/colonialism and national development have been commended, it has not had a significant impact on the working principles of the WSF. In addition, the broad scope and depth of the Bamako Appeal, if it were to be enacted upon, would require considerable resources and motivation that are beyond the remit and capacity of the forum.

These proposals do come at a curious point in the development of the WSF as the prospects of Left politics play out favourably in Latin American politics and begin to demand answers to how successfully the forum has influenced global convergence of progressive movements. Added to this is the sense that perhaps it is time for the WSF to 'give way to new modes of global organization of resistance and transformation'—a view that found greater support following the 2007 Nairobi WSF which, for some, appeared to confirm that the forum is not anchored in 'actual global political struggles' and has turned into 'an annual festival with limited social impact' (Bello 2007). Lastly, the Manifesto and Appeal both brought to the forefront a much-neglected aspect of positing an 'open space' without privileged actors which concerns the position, role and influence of academics, theorists, journalists, philosophers and theologians, all signatories, therein.[10]

The World Social Forum in 2012

Panels, roundtables and workshops to discuss the challenges facing the forum are, however, increasingly included in WSF programmes. Formed partly with the intention of opening up discussion on the strategy and future of the forum process, I will outline in this section the background and process of one session on 'The future movements of the forum', which I attended at the 2007 Nairobi WSF. Critical discussions on 'open space' can be traced back to the 2004 Mumbai WSF and at least part of their motivation has been that 'there had been too little critical self-reflection and too few public debates on the future of the process' (Patomäki and Teivainen 2004b: 149). Nonetheless, the WSF was very quickly to 'become both the subject and the site of intense reflection concerning its own significance, nature and future' (Waterman 2004a: 59). In Porto Alegre, in January 2010, more recently, an international seminar entitled 'Ten years later: Challenges and proposals for another possible world' was held by the Group for Reflection and Support for the WSF Process (GRAP) which included IBASE, Ethos and Instituto Paulo Freire.[11] The Indian Institute for Critical Action: Centre in Movement (CACIM) from New Delhi, India, and the University of KwaZulu-Natal Centre for Civil Society (CCS) in Durban, South Africa, have also been active in raising debate through organizing panels at WSF, publishing books (e.g. Sen and Kumar 2007), running the CACIM listserve, WSFDiscuss, and webspace OpenSpaceForum. The World Forum for Alternatives and Third World Forum have been similarly involved.

The 'WSF 7 Years Group' organized sessions at the Nairobi WSF to discuss the extent to which the forum has fulfilled its promise to make another world possible. Partners to this initiative include: Kepa or the Service Centre for Development Cooperation, comprising Finnish NGOs; the Network Institute for Global Democratization (NIGD), an IC member initially based in Finland but since expanded to an international network of almost 100 researchers and practitioners working to promote democratization; the Inter-Press Service (IPS), a communications institution and global news agency that seeks to give a fresh perspective on development and globalization; and Transform! Italia, a network of the critical and alternative Left in Italy.[12] The results of small-group discussions at a session organized by the 'WSF 7 Years Group' on 'The future movements of the forum', and gathered through experience of participant observation at the forum, are presented here. The first discussion during this session was based on the following question: 'What are the main achievements or successes of the World Social Forum?' The following answers were given:[13]

- Providing a space for groups who would otherwise not be heard;
- Providing a platform;
- Giving a source of hope and inspiration;
- Providing a space for concrete wins and struggles;
- Thinking of alternatives at a global level;
- Strengthening social movements;
- Helping localized struggles to connect to other levels;
- Giving Americans a fresh perspective originating outside of the United States;
- Mobilizing social movements in the US; and
- Setting up of a youth forum as part of the WSF.

The second discussion at this WSF session was based on the following questions: 'Where would you like to see the WSF in 2012 and how can we make the WSF more democratic?' Answers included:

- A more democratized forum where women are represented equally;
- More prominent regional forums;
- A process, not just an event with nothing in between annual meetings;
- A process that continues without ending on the last day of the WSF;

- A main focus is needed—overarching broad inclusive goals and programme;
- A programmatic vision featuring a broader programme;
- A longer event giving more time to issues;
- A more all-inclusive forum;
- A more publicized event by the mainstream media so messages can be more successfully transmitted;
- A forum that translates words into action in terms of sponsors and vendors of food and beverages at the event;
- Divisions transcended to focus on only one enemy;
- A permanent space facilitating discussions between (not just within) many different groups and issues;
- Better coordination of NGOs, community-based organizations (CBOs), etc. and discussion on them;
- Not just a talk shop;
- Improved translation facilities to facilitate and enable cultural diversity;
- A democratic organization that is structured and self-sustaining, financially speaking;
- Bring the Forum to the grassroots;
- Bring theory and practice together;
- Emphasize marches and protests;
- A political programme that emphasizes human rights; and
- A new political approach—a new Left or political vision is needed.

Past achievements of the WSF are largely predicated on the extension of a global space for debate, discussion and networking among social groups. The suggested outcome has been to energize and motivate participants to think about alternatives to neoliberal globalization. However, while the achievements of open space were highlighted at this session, the challenges are also apparent in calls for a more inclusive, programmatic, proactive, focused, co-ordinated and democratic forum. Some of the reasoning for this may stem from structural, relational and substantive frictions that quickly became apparent from the holding of the first WSF in 2001. Visions of the WSF in 2012 broadly bifurcate into those that emphasize a more permanent and inclusive WSF space and those that focus on the emergence of a new political programme or vision for the WSF. Many of the proposals for a more democratic WSF in 2012 focus on enhancing the 'open space' of the forum through more equal representation of women and other minorities, emphasising the space as a process rather than an individual event, and achieving better co-ordination of and discussion on the constituents of global civil society. Others, in what has become a familiar dialogue, emphasized the need for a more programmatic vision, overarching goals and expansion of the forum beyond a 'talk shop'.

The holding of panels and sessions directed towards discussion on the future of the WSF may, on the one hand, be seen to reflect the ongoing processes of adaptation or methodological evolution in which forum has engaged.

However, there has been some scepticism concerning the capacity of seminars, panels and roundtables to have large consequences or to leave the rooms or sites where they take place 'to become topics of conversation among the activists that have been joining the WSF process' (Santos 2008: 268). There is a contrast between such panels and others at the 2007 Nairobi WSF where, for example, women from contending cultures worked to prepare a second draft of the manifesto on reproductive and sexual rights (ibid.). Some may point towards the benefits that such diversity between panels indicates but this does not automatically translate into a concrete dialectics of presence. At the 2009 Belém WSF, CACIM organized a seminar entitled 'Critically engaging with the principles underlying the WSF', which without a small measure of irony in light of continued debate on the attendance of heads of state at forums, was scheduled at the same time that Presidents Lula da Silva (Brazil), Chávez (Venezuela), Correa (Ecuador), Morales (Bolivia) and Lugo (Paraguay), addressed participants at Belém (CACIM 2009a, 2009b).[14]

Creative dislocation: where global civil society meets world ordering

The World Social Forums are significant for what they can tell us about 'real' lived sites of global contestation as they take place at, for example, the Moi Sports Centre in Kasarani, Nairobi or the Cheikh Anta Diop University in Dakar, where those present engage in modes of social relation in and towards the global political economy. This potentially gives insight into spaces of the forums as 'real lived places' with their own cores and peripheries (Osterweil 2004b: 187–88) for which the strategy of convergence does not appear to account. Understood in this way, contrasting and complementary modes of social relation traverse the site of the WSF. While some may be indicative of a dialectics of presence, 'creative dislocation' works to destroy and integrate existing subjectivities where 'subjects incapable of autonomous action are made by being bound to a false sense of global purpose and unity' (Drainville 2011: 416). The organizational chaos that according to numerous accounts traversed the site of the 2011 Dakar WSF, circumscribed and disrupted the activities of the forum. While some accounts refer to the capacity of some movements to self-organize and overcome the disruption of organizational chaos, this does not appear to have been a generalized outcome. Rather than facilitate the innovations of new social movements and networks, the site of the forum appears to appeal more to traditional organizational structures, and large NGOs which rather than engage in a dialectics of presence tend to neglect their positioning in and in relation to the global political economy. This terrain is far more complex when understood as where '*social forces meet world ordering*' (Drainville 2011: 414) than the dynamics of self-organization within specific movements can account for.

The Nairobi WSF, in particular, gives expression to the suggestion that simple co-presence in open space 'does not automatically produce mutual intelligibility, however, much less genuine dialogue across cultural, class and colonial divides' (Conway 2011: 226). Among other points of contention examined below, this highlights and echoes a critique of the forum from DAWN prior to the 2003 Porto Alegre WSF that the forum neglects the 'critical geo-political issue' of abortion (cited in Eschle and Maiguashca 2010: 31). The WMW, while actively engaging in strategies for convergence with some groups, refers to the 'struggle to get feminism recognized as an answer to neoliberal globalization' within the WSF organizing process (Diane Matte, cited in Conway 2011: 226). The experience of the World March of Women is indicative of the 'fluctuating feminist fortunes' within the forum (Eschle and Maiguashca 2010: 32), which persist despite participation in the International Council by the WMW, Articulación Feminista Marcosur (AFM), Development Alternatives with Women for a New Era (DAWN) and other feminist groups for a least a decade.

The mere presence of contention, often presented as significant in its conspicuousness, may not be sufficient to suggest a dialectics of presence. The tensions within the strategy of convergence have also been played out through the setting up of 'autonomous spaces' and 'intentional spaces' in relation to various forums (Juris 2008a, 2008b). Opposing 'autonomous' spaces are frequently set up in an attempt to retain the political autonomy and specificity of smaller, networked spaces, e.g. the Peoples' Parliament at the Jeevanjee Gardens in Nairobi was held 15 kilometres away from the main event of the 2007 WSF; Mumbai Resistance comprised Maoist and Gandhian peasant movements and the Peoples Movements Encounter II led by the Federation of Agricultural Workers and Marginal Farmers Union at the 2004 Mumbai WSF; and Intergaláctika and Life after Capitalism organized by *Z Magazine* at the 2003 Porto Alegre WSF. The presence of such autonomous spaces has been suggested to enrich and expand the WSF experience (Sen 2009), but when considered alongside the sense of marginalization expressed by feminist, dalit and indigenous movements participating in the forum (Conway 2011: 234; Conway 2012b: 390),[15] the strategy of convergence appears inadequate towards sustaining a strong dialectics of presence. Similarly, the experience of 'intentional spaces' at the US Social Forum (USSF) in 2007, whereby organizers targeted grassroots communitarian groups, led to an unprecedented high level of diversity in terms of race and class but to the exclusion of larger NGOs, liberals, white radicals and anarchists, organized labour and mainstream environmentalists and feminists from the organizing process (Juris 2008b).

The significance of the WSF is not as forum organizers tend to present it— that locating the forum in the global South integrates the South into 'global contestation' and moreover that the explosion in forum attendance demonstrates the success of the strategy of convergence (cf. Pianta *et al.* 2004). The strategy has been added to through a continual focus on technical or 'methodological' fixes such as self-organization of forum activities or the introduction of Global Days of Action (GDA) every two years. These are a primary focal point for post-forum assessment by IC members and at IC meetings. These have been the main format of responses to 'logistical crises', such as occurred at the 2011 WSF in Dakar. Such logistical crises carry clear political costs and hinder communication and contact between established networks of European and Latin American activists and newer, less well-established and/ or local activists (George 2011). There is a sense that 'In every Forum the mistakes are repeated' (WSF 2011), even if some group activities, such as those associated with the World Forum for Alternatives and Third World Forum, were well facilitated in Dakar and reported strong attendance by African and Asian participants (Amin 2011).

Methodological fixes, however, have not been entirely successful in restricting the emergence of hierarchies or resolving the early contradictions of the forums as outlined here:

> The organizational structure of the forum was so opaque that it was nearly impossible to figure out how decisions were made or to find ways to question those decisions. There were no open plenaries and no chance to vote on the structure of future events. In the absence of a transparent process, fierce NGO brand wars were waged behind the scenes—about whose stars would get the most airtime, who would get access to the press and who would be seen as the true leaders of this movement.
> (Research Unit for Political Economy 2003, citing Naomi Klein)

Following sustained criticism for allowing media personalities and celebrities among whom women were poorly represented to dominate the forum, self-organization was introduced to allow participants to organize and participate in self-governed activities without the particular involvement of forum organizers. The new methodology, however, also opens up a power vacuum which benefits well-resourced and funded groups while leaving gender and territorial representation unchecked (WSF 2005a: 17). This has inadvertently given the WSF IC organizations and individuals a greater voice and emphasized its authority over discussions on the future of the forum.

At the 2007 Nairobi WSF the exclusion of local and weakly financed and resourced groups contrasted greatly with the high visibility and conspicuous nature of commercial sponsorship of the event. Mobile phone company CelTel, the primary commercial sponsor of the forum, conducted a highly visible marketing campaign. Large NGOs and organizations such as the Caritas-AACC Ecumenical Platform were strongly represented. Meanwhile smaller and less well-financed and resourced groups and individuals were disadvantaged by relatively high admission prices and pricing within the WSF grounds.[16] In response, the forum became a site of resistance itself. Protests, for example, were held to allow local Kenyans to enter the forum free of charge. Demonstrations to reduce the price of food and drink at the site of the forum took place, led by a banner proclaiming 'Expensive Food Violates People's Rights', and the Windsor Golf and Country Club food stall was taken over and its food distributed to children.[17]

Certainly a potent theme in Nairobi, inadequate funding is a constraint of forum organization and frequently a theme of WSF IC meetings. The resource commission of the WSF IC has stressed that over time the WSF should reduce its dependency on funding from governments, the private sector and foundations (WSF 2005b). This is reiterated in the 'Guiding Principles for Holding WSF Events' adopted by the IC in 2008 (WSF 2008b). This document, hereafter referred to as the 'Guiding Principles', emerged partly as a result of the controversy surrounding the commercial sponsorship of the WSF in Nairobi. It deals with the three sources of funding for a WSF event:

- Raised by the organisers from foundations and other agencies;
- Raised through registration and other fees, for space etc.;
- Raised by the participating groups for their events, travel etc. (WSF 2008a).

The 'Guiding Principles' recognize that 'raising funds from foundations etc. is a major resource', and also that 'it is deeply political' and differs according to country and region. It is worth quoting at length:

> Following the Charter of Principles however, one may conclude that sources that are champions of neo-liberalism must remain excluded, namely: International Financial Institutions, multinational commercial agencies and corporations, and sources with known links to drugs, mafia and crime.
>
> (WSF 2008b)

The 'Guiding Principles' also refer to the 'grey areas' of funding from governments and public-sector enterprises and suggest caution when accepting funds from these sources. The tentative language of this document resembles that of numerous IC discussions on the issue of funding such as the suggestion that a 'common pool of solidarity funds' to which all participating organizations contribute should be set up. The Charter of Principles remains as the definitive reading on the position of the forum in relation to multinational corporations and governments and international institutions that serve corporate interests:

> The alternatives proposed at the World Social Forum stand in opposition to a process of globalization commanded by the large multinational corporations and by the governments and international institutions at the service of those corporations interests, with the complicity of national governments.
>
> (WSF 2002a)

The failure to consider questions of funding in a comprehensive manner that deals with issues of power and inequality is a reflection of the wider reluctance to address the political economy of the WSF. Recalling the high price of food and drink on sale from 'official' sources at the Nairobi WSF, it certainly appears an anomaly that the political economy of the forum has been little critiqued, despite the attendance at forums of many political economists (Waterman 2009: 13).

The necessity of this critique is especially relevant when the following figures are compared to the sparse and limited references to funding in the Guiding Principles (WSF 2008b). Between 2001 and 2005 the following approximate total contributions/income to the World Social Forums came from local government sources in Brazil (US$3.6 million, although probably much more according to the WSF report on financial strategy), federal government ($1.1 million), international NGOs and foundations ($7.1 million), registration fees ($2.2 million) and from corporations ($1.8 million) (WSF 2006a). International agencies such as the Netherlands Organization for International Assistance (Oxfam NOVIB, $1.9 million) and Inter-Church Organisation for Development Cooperation (ICCO, $573,000) consistently supported the WSF between 2001 and 2005 (ibid.). Among others, significant contributors include the German (Protestant) Church Development Service (EED), the French Catholic Committee against Hunger and for Development (CCFD), and ActionAid, while the Rockefeller Brothers contributed also in 2005 (ibid.).

The Ford Foundation in particular has been a prominent WSF financial contributor, directly to the WSF and indirectly through participant organizations (Parmar 2006).[18] It contributed approximately $1 million to the WSF between 2001 and 2005. It did not contribute directly in 2004 because the Mumbai WSF OC declined to accept financial support from the Ford Foundation. Even indirect support, however, allows foundations such as Ford, Rockefeller and Carnegie, widely viewed as carriers of American globalization and foreign policy, to become involved in the discourse of creating an alternative globalizing project (ibid.). This prompts criticism from the far Left that continued dependency on external funding allows the WSF to resemble 'an international network of liberal-reformist globalisers' (ibid.; cf. Armstrong 2006). This example illustrates clearly that not only is it important that a critique of the political economy of the WSF is initiated but also that the WSF cannot be viewed as an exclusive forum for 'emancipatory global civil society without also considering the presence of "liberal" global civil society' (cf. Santos 2006a).

Forum organizers do not give adequate attention to the presence of capitalist power relations within the WSF (Teivainen 2007). Rather, they approach the issue of funding as a technical issue. For these reasons it is 'important to ask to what extent the WSF itself reproduces economism and creates apparently non-political structures in its mode of organisation' (ibid.: 77). The drawing up of 'Guiding Principles' appears to be a primarily technical rather than political exercise. The following issues also fall within the political economy of the Nairobi WSF, although they were primarily addressed by organizers as technical issues: the location of the forum 15 kilometres outside of Nairobi; the positioning of food stalls run by the Windsor Golf and Country Club and the Norfolk in a prominent position compared to the peripheral location of less well-resourced food courts; and the high prices of food, water and admission for local Kenyans. A failure to consider global civil society in relation to not only the political economy of the concrete location of each WSF, but also in relation to the wider global political economy gives disquieting expression to global civil society, at least on the part of the IC and OC, as 'a type of court jester, one that may have a colourful appearance, but only serves to entertain, rather than realise, the potential of transformation' (Worth and Buckley 2009: 650).

Conceptualizing global civil society at the site of the forum

Building on the context of a courtly global civil society, the site of the Nairobi WSF gave rise to some more specific conceptualizations of global civil society. During my attendance at the forum, I attended the following panel on 'Global Civil Society: More or Less Democracy?' which was organized by the Committee on Civil Society Research, Sweden.[19] It aimed to discuss historical and social perspectives on civil society within the context of contemporary globalization (Committee on Civil Society 2007). A core question that was posed to the panel of speakers was: what implications do NGOs, social movements and private foundations have for democracy, whether we choose to conceptualize them as 'civil society' or not?[20]

An assessment of this session gives insight into how global civil society was constituted at the site of the forum. The discussion that followed affirmed the ambiguities of global civil society with speakers using the concept in differing and sometimes vague ways. In the introduction, the dual uses of the concept were put forward as either a project for elites to compete for political representation or a social space for grassroots organizations and carrier of the democratic learning process. Other speakers suggested that the meaning of the civil aspect of global *civil* society should be interrogated before its implications for democracy can be understood. A number of other factors were highlighted by the various speakers, e.g. the danger that corporatization could lead to unequal relations; the position of the state in relation to civil society and the impact this has on the location of the WSF in Porto Alegre or in Africa; and the paternalistic nature of society in Russia and the challenges of a Western-influenced civic society in this context. Global civil society is also conceived as a post-national concept that unaffected by political boundaries, does not subscribe to any one template, much like global democracy.

In the brief question and answer session that followed it was suggested that nobody seems to know what civil society is and that none of the speakers had addressed the question of democracy. This further confirms, responded a speaker, the need for a critical interrogation of the concept of global civil society. The ambiguous nature of global civil society and the remaining gaps in its meanings were apparent throughout this discussion. The nature of the relationship between civil society, the state and the market, it may be inferred from the discussion, delimits the inherent capacity of civil society to engage with hegemonic relations of incivility, paternalism and corporatism.

In further discussion at this session it was suggested by Jan Aart Scholte, one of the speakers, that it is acceptable to use the concept of civil society in different ways, as other speakers had done, as long as the political implications of alternative conceptualizations of civil society are thought through. Furthermore, Scholte mentioned that meaning also depends on context, which presently refers to counter-hegemonic potentialities. He went on to say that the democratization of 'anti-globalization', or whatever we choose to call it, can be related partially to the person through, for example, provoking their sense of political debate or enabling them to do so. Another aspect of democratization is institutional which, at a deeper level, concerns how far institutions challenge structural hierarchies that cover our lives such as cultural dominance, sexuality and gender, and how far institutions open spaces for political identities to emerge.

The proposal to apply definitions of civil society carefully, rather than recourse to its accumulation of meanings, revisits the above discussion on the problematic aspects of the functional and restricted usage of the concept according to a particular context. While in this panel discussion the inclusion of counter-hegemonic potentialities relating to the present context was referred to, the position of global civil society was not discussed specifically. The issue of democratization was also referred to in relation to 'anti-globalization', rather than civil society, but the speaker, nonetheless, provided a broad understanding of democratization. This was followed on a cautionary note by Teivo Teivainen of NIGD that general use of the term 'global civil society', or when used as a watchdog for corporate capitalism, can do more harm than good and does not give us good answers.

In conclusion, this was a full session with little opportunity for audience participation as most of the time was allocated to panellists and invited speakers. The academic content of much of the discussion, coupled with limited opportunity for audience participation, leads to questions concerning the capacity of the forum for popular education, or at the very least suggests that much more time should be given to allow wider and more inclusive discussions to take place.[21] This is not a new suggestion and demonstrates many of the challenges of scholar activism and inclusivity in similar events. Towards the end of this WSF session an interpreter was found to translate the views of a participant, dressed in tribal clothing, who spoke out against homosexuality on religious grounds. Following this, the session was quickly ended. In general, during this session, there was apparent reticence to engage with the conceptual difficulties that global civil society entails and practical challenges in its application to the forum that, for example, might be linked to academic reticence to engage further with the concept. It seems, in sum, that the task of effectively conceptualizing global civil society in relation to the forum and contestation more broadly remains to be accomplished.

Convergence and strategy

If the WSF is where global civil society meets world ordering, the capacity of the forum to foster diversity and global convergence in this context appears to be limited. Suggestions that the forum is an expression of globalization from the middle rather than globalization from below (Waterman 2004b: 87), or that the 'NGOization' of the forum is reducing its radical potential, also confirm this observation. Whether conceived as a space or movement, and despite the diversity of movements in attendance, the structure and organization of the forum fails to foster diversity, and is more conducive to convergence across goals, in a way that facilitates further forms of elitism and exclusion. During the early years of the forum much was made of the general divergence of opinion among participants. A number of axes were identified such as revolution versus reform; environment versus economy; human rights versus protectionism; universal or Western values; and varying degrees of focus on the local, national or global level (Fisher and Ponniah 2004). Some activists advocated greater economic development and job creation while others wanted to reduce current production and consumption levels to protect the environment. Activists in the global North held differing ideas on trade, redistribution, environment and labour policies to activists in the global South (Chase-Dunn and Reese 2006). While not wishing to suggest that diversity is no longer a feature of the forum, I would challenge the capacity of a strategy of convergence to maintain 'diversity in difference' while moving the forum forward. Increasingly, it appears that the Charter-based 'opposition to neoliberalism', broad as it might appear, and much as one might question the attachment of all attending movements of civil society to this principle, has functioned to exclude, or at least entrench ambiguity, towards the political economy and power relations at the site and through the processes of the forum. While 'neither party representations nor military organizations shall participate in the WSF' (WSF 2002a) according to the Charter of Principles, the emphasis on non-violent resistance and closure to military organizations has resulted in disagreement among WSF participants which, like the issue of funding, has become a recurrent source of tension. At the 2009 Belém WSF, the exclusion of the aforementioned Zapatistas due to their past links with violence, despite being considered a key ideological influence on the formation of the WSF, was a strong topic for debate (CACIM 2009a, 2009b). Meanwhile, convergence was strongly emphasized in the format of an 'Assembly of Assemblies' that took place on the final day of the Belém forum. The assembly was organized to encourage convergence among participating organizations. It was preceded by self-managed thematic assemblies in the morning of the final day and in the afternoon, at the Assembly of Assemblies, the conclusions of each thematic assembly were presented in addition to the final declaration of the Assembly of Social Movements (Imbach 2009). It remains to be seen whether the contradictory impulse (Juris 2008a) may yet work to consolidate what might be called the 'self-proclaimed "plural left"' within the forum. Its objective is to legitimize the principles of liberalism, capitalism and imperialist globalization 'through a minimum of "social demands" (such as the "struggle against poverty")' and '[a]ssociations (as apolitical as possible) of the so-called "civil society" are considered instrumental in the formulation of such demands' (Amin 2007: 142). The evidence of convergence towards the centre gives growing credence to the Gramscian process of *trasformismo* whereby divergent ideologies from the conservative right (represented through the open space position) and traditional left (represented through the 'movement' position), conform towards a new civic-consensual middle ground.

The 'creative tensions' of the forum, according to many close to the forum process, work to challenge organizers and help to propel the process forward (Smith *et al.* 2008: 25, 132). At the plenary of the Utrecht IC meeting in 2005 there was some recognition of the need for the forum to adapt to geo-political and economic world situations, beyond methodological 'fixes', and beyond merely reporting on increases in WSF attendance (WSF 2005a; WSF 2005b). Further insight can be gained through reference to written proposals discussed in the Strategies Commission of the IC. Roberto Savio of the Inter-Press Service proposed that the IC should be more broadly representative of anti-globalization actors and constitute a more transparent and reactionary organization that can respond to globalization, for example, through the use of referendums at each forum to decide on which campaign to follow (WSF 2005b: 14). The Conferencia de Naciones sin Estado de Europa (CONSEU) referred to a sense of crisis in a WSF model that lacks the vitality and enthusiasm required for discussion and debate (ibid.: 15). There exists, according to CONSEU, a failure to define and reach consensus on the meaning of terms as central to the forum as 'another world is possible'. Thus, discussion is needed within the IC on whether the forum should continue as before or adopt an entirely new model. Such conflicting views were also apparent in the ambiguous conclusions on the outcome of the 2007 Nairobi WSF. At the Berlin meeting of the International Council in May 2007 some argued that 'the "failure" of Nairobi was not a failure of the Africans but of the whole process, the lack of connectedness with local initiatives, the lack of political clarity' (Mestrum and Bacal 2007).

These criticisms of the WSF indicate several areas of tension which parti-cularly after the Nairobi WSF could no longer be overlooked. A formal 'strategy debate' was initiated in 2008. In advance of the debate, documents on WSF strategy were circulated.[22] Many of these contributions were by prominent WSF organizers and IC members and the space/movement debate was a key concern in many of them. Nonetheless, some of the issues that had been highlighted at the Utrecht IC meeting, such as the changing socio-political context, were addressed in the strategy debate during discussions of working groups. The evolution of social movements at the centre of the WSF, the debate on open space, and the future of the WSF were other key issues. However, it is argued here that rather than result in meaningful strategic outcomes, the outcome of the strategy debate further confirms what has been referred to as the 'dilemmas of decision making' within the WSF IC (Teivainen 2006). At the IC meeting in Abuja where the debate took place, little consensus was reached on changing the strategic direction of the WSF.[23] Instead it was decided that the Charter of Principles would not be changed. More piecemeal future actions and topics for discussion were planned through changes in methodology, the adoption of guiding principles for hosting WSF events and further Global Days of Action. A form of consensus appeared to emerge on the space/movement debate that confirmed the earlier WSF IC position that political positions and calls for action—such as the Bamako Appeal—would continue to be expressed, but not on the authorization of the WSF.

It was decided that 'Guiding Principles for holding a WSF event' (WSF 2008b), discussed above, would be prepared and adopted by the IC. It was envisaged that this document would address a host of controversial decisions that the WSF has been unable to resolve since its inauguration such as: criteria for participation, rules on military organizations, parties, international institutions and violent movements, the question of funding and other internal rules. Early drafts of the document and the final 2008 version suggest that it merely reaffirms some Charter Principles and puts forward some general advice on holding WSF events. The rationale for adopting Guiding Principles, as it is outlined in the document in disquieting language, centres on the emerging popularity of the WSF 'brand' alongside a lack of awareness of the Charter of Principles and consequent concerns that the basic principles of the WSF are not being upheld in events adopting the WSF 'label' (ibid.). Where confusion persists and further clarification is required, it is suggested that: 'The organising committee of an event may seek the help and support of the International Council, through its Liaison Group or the concerned Commissions' (ibid.). The impact of the Guiding Principles, and indeed Strategy Debate, has so far been marginal and has not, for example, prevented further controversy on the unresolved issues of the WSF relationship with the state and violent movements.[24] The outcome of the 'strategy debate' is not reflected in concrete decisions and appears to be more indicative of a failure to address, in a substantive or creative manner, the key tensions that have been outlined in this chapter.

Conclusions

Success at the forum level is suggested to have been achieved through advance preparation and networking among activists to strengthen regional and global alliances on shared issues. This is reflected in the reaffirmation of the strategy of convergence as an 'important trend in global activism' and part of the success of the 2011 Dakar WSF (Caruso 2011). To facilitate practical convergences, a mobilization process was carried out prior to the forum at national, African and international levels. Caravans and other forums (e.g. World Charter of Migrants, Forum of Peasants, Forum of Science and Democracy, World

Trade Union Forum) were part of this process to raise awareness particularly in Western Africa (WSF 2011). Convergences, it is suggested, are located 'at the heart of [the] WSF's mission' and are considered potentially to indicate a 'trend towards consolidation of struggles at the global level' (ibid.):

> If it is premature to state it confidently, it is nonetheless something to be closely observed in the months and years to come to capture the spirit of both converging and networked alliances, encounters, interactions and practices that could influence both the awareness of and the underlying values of a truly emancipatory global cosmopolitan society.
>
> (Caruso 2011)

However, the resolution of the strategy debate may confirm what has been referred to as a 'contradictory impulse' whereby the promotion of egalitarian relations and diversity within the architecture of the forum, through the strategy of convergence, for example, may present an obstacle to the development of political programs and actions (cf. Juris 2008a: 265). In this context, it is not clear whether the WSF could become Gramsci's 'modern Prince' or revolutionary party that allows new organic intellectuals to steer a new hegemony and leadership within civil society (Sehm-Patomäki and Ulvila 2006), or whether it could contribute to a new form of global governance and civil society (cf. Smith *et al.* 2008). Therefore, while 'many people regard Social Forums as important political spaces, with the potential to radically transform politics—and therefore society itself' (Böhm *et al.* 2005: 98), important limitations towards achieving radical transformation as discussed in this chapter still exist.

While the clear political motivation behind the Bamako Appeal makes it stand out from similar initiatives, and it draws on a multifaceted location in socialism, anti-racism/colonialism and national development, it has failed to change the working principles of the WSF or find inclusion in the Guiding Principles. This suggests that while the strategy of convergence rhetorically supports diversity and encourages broad movements of global civil society to come together, it may also act to preclude diversity and strengthen the position of the Left to articulate alternative strategies. This confirms apprehension that the diversity of the WSF, considered by many to be its strength, may become its weakness and lessen its overall impact (Santos 2006a). Indeed, some of the examples in this chapter suggest that rather than encourage a horizontal and inclusive space for debate and dialogue across diverse groups, activities and themes, the strategy promotes similar-minded groups to work together. Broad processes of *trasformismo* delimit the possibilities for global civil society to form a new transformative social force that is rooted in an ethico-political mode of consciousness (Worth and Buckley 2011).

The representation of the WSF as a 'space that vigorously encourages disagreements' (Anand 2004: 140) is arguable in the context of strong efforts towards convergence between movements in the organization of the forum.

While public discussions on the future of the forum are to be welcomed, they are largely conducted and dominated by forum founders and regular commentators and academics. The narrow range of contributors to the Strategy Debate and muted responses by forum participants in making their own written contributions to the debate illustrates this point.[25] In addition, current WSF preoccupations, as reflected in the Manifesto, Bamako Appeal and Strategy Debate point to the continued salience of the space versus movement dichotomy that has resulted in insufficient attention being given to addressing the real challenges that face the forum. The protraction of this debate lends much appeal to suggestions that a compromise or coexistence of both visions of the forum has been reached (Chase-Dunn and Reese 2006; Wallerstein 2007; Whitaker 2007). However, the evidence that is presented above suggests that any reconciliation of conservative and traditional Left social forces is more likely to occur through passive modes of *trasformismo* than through a self-conscious and transformative mode of contestation.

It does appear, however, that more optimistic assessments persist amidst hope that the 'creative tensions' and 'new politics' of the forum process will have a positive impact (e.g. Smith *et al.* 2008; Caruso 2011). It has also been suggested that having achieved the goals of aggregation and articulation, a new, more high-intensity phase of aggregation, articulation and consistent promotion of alternatives can come into being (Santos 2008: 262). These may even, it is claimed, challenge the prior-asserted identities and autonomy of participating social movements and NGOs (ibid.). To have any impact, however, representations of the forum as a site for the global convergence of global civil society would integrate a more effective strategy of praxis based on dialectical modes of social relation towards the global political economy in a manner that does not consider global contestation at the forum to be representative of 'global contestation'. The continued, even if ambiguous, dialectics of presence at the site of the forum nonetheless contests the possibility that resistance at the more global level of the forum leads to a 'loss of social connection' or expressions of political aspirations in 'increasingly abstract and unmediated forms' (cf. Chandler 2009b: 531). Furthermore, while the resolution of the strategy debate appears to lessen any impact of the Manifesto and Appeal, activities on their basis continue to be organized at forums each year and new programmes and strategies have emerged which will be considered further in the next chapter. The dialectics of presence at the WSF, although impacted by civic-consensual modes of social relation, does not directly preclude the possibility of transformative modes of contestation.

Notes

1 See, for example, a special issue of *Development* in which members of the WSF International Council (IC), Fatma Alloo, Corinne Kumar, Samir Amin, Yash Tandon, Sara Longwe, Giuseppe Caruso and Chico Whitaker document their impressions of the forums which, broadly speaking, acknowledge the organizational

problems while affirming the forum as a positive, in some cases 'exhilarating', 'fulfilling' experience (Alloo *et al.* 2011). Documents from International Council meetings in Dakar and Paris also give a sense of how the forum unfolded, e.g. following the IC Meeting in Dakar a Working Group was formed to evaluate the 2011 WSF and initial results were presented at the IC Meeting in Paris (WSF 2011). Further assessments are provided by George (2011), FNTG (2011).

2 Data from a survey carried out by IBASE (2009) of the 2009 Belém WSF captured participant membership of organizations (multiple answers were given): social movements (27 per cent), NGOs (17 per cent), religious groups (12 per cent), associations (11 per cent), culture groups (10 per cent), trade unions (8 per cent) and, among others, political parties (8 per cent). Some 30 per cent reported no membership, with this figure being particularly high among Brazilians (33 per cent of interviewees).

3 For more on the 2013 Tunisia WSF, including the Preparatory Assembly to the WSF in Monastir in July 2012, see: www.fsmaghreb.org. Agathangelou (2012) discusses the MENA uprisings, while Amin (2011) notes this sense of disconnection.

4 Francisco Whitaker of the Brazilian Justice and Peace Commission (CBJP), Oded Grajew chair of Ethos Institute, and Cândido Grzybowski, director of IBASE, all founding organizers of the WSF, strongly advocate the WSF as a space rather than a movement.

5 For an overview of southern African social movements and national forums preceding Nairobi see Larmer *et al.* (2009).

6 For the text of the ASM declaration in 2009 see: www.marchemondialedesfemmes. org/alliances_mondialisation/asamblea-movimientos-sociales/declaration2009/en?set_ language=en& cl = en.

7 The statue was created by Danish sculptor Jens Galschiot, and is an initiative of Art in Defence of Humanism (AIDOH), an informal network of artists who want to use their work to promote social change. See www.aidoh.dk.

8 For the texts of each see Sen *et al.* (2007). The Manifesto was signed by Aminata Traoré, Adolfo Pérez Esquivel, Eduardo Galeano, José Saramago, François Houtart, Boaventura de Sousa Santos, Armand Mattelart, Roberto Savio, Ricardo Petrella, Ignacio Ramonet, Bernard Cassen, Samir Amin, Atilio Boron, Samuel Ruiz Garcia, Tariq Ali, Frei Betto, Emir Sader, Walden Bello and Immanuel Wallerstein.

9 Hugo Chávez, President of Venezuela, proposed a new Left International composed of social movements and left-wing parties. It has been endorsed at an international conference of Left parties in Caracas in 2009 and at another conference in Caracas in 2010.

10 In 2005, 29 per cent of participants from 'other countries' (outside of Latin America and the Caribbean) had Masters or PhD qualifications compared to 27 per cent in 2009 (IBASE 2005, 2009). From approximately 150,000 participants at the 2009 Belém WSF, 120,000 (80 per cent) were Brazilians; another 20,000 (13 per cent) came from Latin America and the Caribbean and 10,000 (7 per cent) came from other countries (IBASE 2009: 3). A further study by Chase-Dunn and Reese (2006) found that NGOs, Latin American and European activists, affluent people with high levels of formal education and whites were over-represented at the 2005 Porto Alegre WSF.

11 See www.grap.org.br.

12 For further information on Kepa see www.kepa.fi/English/; on NIGD see www. nigd.org; on IPS see www.ips.org; and on Transform! Italia see www.transform-network.net. Other partners include the Alternative Information Center Jerusalem-Bethlehem, Enda, Ethos, Centre for Civil Society (Durban), Centre of Indian Trade Unions (CETRI), Liberdade Brasil, Paolo Freire Institute, Program on

Democracy and Global Transformation, SODNET, Travola della Pace and the World Forum of Civil Society Networks (UBUNTU).

13 Groups were organized according to language. My group was one of two English-speaking groups, while other groups were composed of Swahili, French, and Spanish and Portuguese speakers, and each was facilitated by an organizer. There were some difficulties in hearing the final proposals of groups at this session and some possible loss of meaning through translation difficulties.

14 See, for example, the 'Heads of State' debate held in advance of the 2009 Belém pan-Amazonic WSF: openfsm.net/projects/wsfic_fsmci/heads-of-state-jefes-de-estado. At this forum there were two 'events' at which presidents spoke. One, organized by the WMW, Via Campesina and the MST, included four presidents but not President Lula of Brazil. The other, organized in conjunction with but not as an official part of the WSF, was attended by approximately 10,000 people (Velitchkova *et al.* 2009).

15 See Conway (2012b) for her assessment of the 'relative success' of coalition-building tactics of the WMW in contrast to 'dialogues across difference' engaged in by alternative groups of feminist movements. See also Conway (2012a).

16 In order to meet the US$5 million cost of the event entrance fees were deemed necessary. These were set at different rates varying from $110 (€80) for Northern nationals, $28 (€20) for those from the South, and $7 (€5) for Kenyans. According to the WSF organizing committee (WSF OC 2007), participation from Africans was lower than envisaged as the solidarity fund (which would have funded participants in need) had to be foregone due to resource constraints.

17 A contentious issue also was the directorship of the Windsor Golf and Country Club by John Michuki, former minister for environment and mineral resources in Kenya, former minister for transport and communications, and minister for provincial administration and internal security. Human rights groups, including Kenya's Human Rights Commission, criticized the issuing of an order by Michuki in 2005 for police to shoot anyone found with illegal firearms (BBC 2005). The police raid of the Kenyan newspaper *The Standard* and the Kenya Television Network (KTN) in 2006 also prompted local and international condemnation (BBC 2006), while Michuki is also notorious for his loyalist activities during the colonial period for torturing Land and Freedom Army (Mau Mau) detainees (Larmer *et al.* 2009: 54).

18 See an Open Democracy interview with L. Jordan (2004) 'The Ford Foundation and the World Social Forum', Open Democracy, www.opendemocracy.net/globalization-world/article_1678.jsp. For information on grants see the Ford Foundation website: www.fordfound.org.

19 I attended this WSF session at the Nairobi WSF. The Committee on Civil Society Research is a group composed of academics of 10 universities and research institutes as well as members of civil society organizations in Sweden and is funded by the Bank of Sweden Tercentenary Research Foundation (Committee on Civil Society 2007).

20 Many academics and researchers addressed this question including: Håkan Thörn, Jai Sen, Moema Miranda, Alla Glinchikova, Patrick Bond, Jan Aart Scholte and Teivo Teivainen. Papers by each, based on this WSF session, have since been published by the Dag Hammarskjöld Foundation in a special issue of *Development Dialogue* (*Development Dialogue* 2007). Analysis on this seminar is, nonetheless, primarily based on field notes written during my attendance at the seminar.

21 In general, within the WSF, many panels and sessions are led by academics and researchers, which in part ties to the pedagogical content of the WSF Charter of Principles which takes on some influence from Brazilian educationalist Paulo Freire (Sen 2010: 998). I also attended a 'Colloquium on global civil society movements: Dynamics in international campaigns and national implementation',

organized by Thandika Mkandawire of the UN Research Institute for Social Development (UNRISD) at the 2007 Nairobi WSF, where much of the discussion was academic in content discussing issues such as debt relief (Katarina Sehm Patomäki), fair trade (Murat Yilmaz), international trade rules and barriers (Manuel Mejido), and the currency transaction tax (Heikki Patomäki).

22 Prior to the meeting, political-strategic assessments of the WSF process, the anti-globalization movement, and the international context from movements, organizations and IC members were circulated: 51 general texts and interviews, 19 contributions from IC members, five from GDA participants, and one from the commissions and workgroups. During the meeting five working groups discussed the strategic future of the WSF.

23 It was decided that the WSF event should be held every two or three years while the GDA (Global Day of Action) should be continued. The form and periodicity of GDAs were not agreed upon and so it was decided that a working group would carry out further discussions on the issue. For the IC report on the Abuja meeting see WSF (2008) and for the text of the Guiding Principles see WSF (2008b).

24 See WSFDiscuss (online), mail.openspaceforum.net/mailman/listinfo/worldsocialforum-discuss_openspaceforum.net (accessed 14 August 2008).

25 Initial texts to be considered included contributions by Walden Bello, Chico Whitaker, Thomas Ponniah, Francois Houtart, Boaventura de Sousa Santos, Samir Amin, Roberto Savio, Jose Correa, Jai Sen, Janet Conway, Peter Waterman, Francois Polet, Francine Mestrum.

6   Situating contestation at the World People's Conference on Climate Change and the Rights of Mother Earth

Lived or situated experiences of contestation through articulations of climate justice at the World People's Conference on Climate Change and the Rights of Mother Earth (WPCCC) at the Universidad de Valle campus in Tiquipaya, Cochabamba, Bolivia in 2010 are a focal point of this chapter. While the World Social Forum (WSF) was envisaged to bring together northern- and southern-based movements of civil society to contest neoliberal globalization primarily through the dynamics of open space, the WPCCC was an initiative of the government of the Plurinational State of Bolivia in response to the perceived failure of the 'Copenhagen Accord'. It called for activists, social movements, scientists, academics, lawyers and governments to come together to address the pressing issue of 'climate justice' and absence of attention to 'buen vivir' and 'rights of Mother Earth' at the 15th Conference of the Parties (COP15) to the United Nations Framework Convention on Climate Change (UNFCCC) in 2009. Reflecting its reception by global environmental governance, scholarly responses to Cochabamba have been muted thus far. Nevertheless, Cochabamba remains a key referent point for climate justice activism as it secures a position in 'global' activism for social and environmental justice that, in the declaration of the People's Summit at Rio+20 in July 2012, is inserted alongside contestation at Rio 1992, Seattle, the WSF, COP17 in Durban, and mobilizations against the G8-G20. In what follows, articulations of working groups at the Cochabamba conference and the final production of the People's Agreement are assessed in terms of deepening debate on the politics of contestation that moves from but remains related to the World Social Forum. The conceptual potential of 'global civil society' and 'Mother Earth', however, is constrained by symbolic, metaphorical usage which, it is argued, delimits their capacity to represent an alternative politico-ethical worldview.

The People's Agreement: articulation of alternatives through Mother Earth

The People's Agreement was adopted at the World People's Conference on Climate Change and the Rights of Mother Earth (WPCCC) in April 2010, which was attended by more than 30,000 activists from more than 100 countries and financially supported by the governments of Bolivia and Venezuela (Chase-Dunn 2011). The People's Agreement can be seen as a direct response by a group of states led by Bolivian President Evo Morales and social movements to the 'Copenhagen Accord' that had emerged from COP15 in 2009.[1] The substantive content of the People's Agreement is assessed in this section through highlighting the interaction between alternative articulations of climate change and commitments to current structures of governance that are represented in the agreement. The agreement refers to the Copenhagen Accord as 'illegitimate' because it imposes the views of developed countries on developing countries. The potentially divisive practice of classifying developing countries according to their vulnerability to climate change, as the accord seeks to do, is highlighted as a factor that could generate disputes, inequalities and segregation between developing countries.[2]

The People's Agreement attempts to present an 'alternative' articulation of climate change, a term which, in this spirit, is also referred to as climate justice.[3] In the agreement, the capitalist system is put forward as a key cause of climate change through its imposition of 'a logic of competition, progress and limitless growth', and an extension of this logic is seen to result in a preoccupation on the part of corporations, governments and the scientific community with the rise in global temperatures. These foci are contrasted in the agreement through references to humanity's 'path of harmony with nature and respect for life' and proposals for a new model for:

> the recovery, revalorization, and strengthening of the knowledge, wisdom, and ancestral practices of Indigenous Peoples, which are affirmed in the thought and practices of 'Living Well,' recognizing Mother Earth as a living being with which we have an indivisible, interdependent, complementary and spiritual relationship.
>
> (People's Agreement 2010)

This is a restatement of principles which, drawing on the human rights paradigm, accords rights, such as the right to be respected and the right to be free of contamination and pollution, to Mother Earth (or *Pachamama*). In turn, developed countries are obliged to address their 'climate debt' and 'adaptation debt' and act towards effecting 'restorative justice'—restoring greater integrity to Mother Earth—to supplement financial compensation.

These articulations co-exist in the text of the People's Agreement with a commitment to the already well-recognized principle of historical common but differentiated responsibilities. The agreement not only extends the Western language of human rights to Mother Earth but also commits to stabilize more effectively greenhouse gases in the atmosphere as outlined in Article 2 of the UNFCCC. In this sense, the contributions of the agreement rest on supplementing current negotiations on climate change with a new language of Mother Earth, rather than re-articulating the entire terms of negotiations. In a paragraph that deals with technology transfers this approach is clear: the benefits of technology transfers are not disputed but the terms of the discussion are changed to acknowledge knowledge as 'universal' and not the object of private property or private use.

> The world must recover and re-learn ancestral principles and approaches from native peoples to stop the destruction of the planet, as well as promote ancestral practices, knowledge and spirituality to recuperate the capacity for 'living well' in harmony with Mother Earth.
>
> (People's Agreement 2010)

To examine the call for a global referendum, plebiscite or popular consultation on climate change which is included in the agreement, it is useful to examine the more detailed documents of the working group that examined this issue at the site of the WPCCC at the Universidad de Valle campus in Tiquipaya, Cochabamba. These documents refer to the setting up of a committee system, consisting of both international and national committees, to facilitate a global referendum. This suggests a commitment to more universal forms of decision making while also utilizing the structures of the current national/international system. In the absence of national governmental support for a global referendum it is proposed that civil society organisms, student groups, social organizations and social networks could support a plebiscite or referendum. The global referendum would address many of the key demands in the People's Agreement such as changing the current capitalist system, debate on the level of emission reduction by developed countries and transnational corporations, and the level of financing to be offered by developed countries. This proposal is accompanied by a call to reallocate all funds spent on war to defending Mother Earth.

The People's Agreement proposes the creation of a Global People's Movement for Mother Earth 'constituting a broad and democratic space for coordination and joint worldwide actions'. It includes specific climate justice targeted proposals to, for example, set up an International Climate and Environmental Justice Tribunal which, to be more effective and ensure compliance, is linked to deep reform of the United Nations. Drawing on the People's Agreement, a number of practical measures emerged from the WPCCC that were submitted by the Bolivian government to the COP16 in Cancun:

- That all industrialized countries should ratify the Kyoto Protocol;
- CO_2 emissions should be halved from their 1990 levels by 2050;
- Temperature increases should be limited to 1 degree centigrade, and not 2 degrees as proposed at Copenhagen;
- A charter of rights for climate migrants;
- Support for education on climate and environmental issues;
- A universal declaration on the rights of Mother Earth and Humanity (drafted by Fr. Miguel d'Escoto, former president of the UN General Assembly);

- A universal referendum on climate change; and
- An International Climate and Environmental Justice Tribunal (Houtart 2010).

This brief overview of the People's Agreement serves to highlight some core substantive tensions that suggest the co-existence of demands for new global structures and agreements (such as reflected in the last three points above) and willingness to work within the current system of governance to achieve these objectives (commitment to the Kyoto Protocol and to the UNFCCC process). The negotiation of these tensions presents clear problems for detailing accessible accounts of the immediate lived experiences of resistance as they were carried out at the WPCCC and straightforward conceptualization of these resistances. For example, re-articulations of climate change in the People's Agreement and a reliance on forms of 'universal knowledge' aim to challenge the language and practices of global environmental governance. The alternative language of the agreement is reflected in references to 'Mother Earth', nevertheless a term that a year previously the UN General Assembly had denoted to 22 April, the Day of Mother Earth. While generally welcomed by participants at the conference, some called for more conceptual depth on 'Mother Earth' to emphasize the particularity of its usage at the WPCCC. This recognizes an explicit tension in the People's Agreement, between the concept of Mother Nature—as a metaphor for closer engagement between humanity and nature—and its application in reality—to take on human characteristics such as the ability to listen and react (Houtart 2010). The issue here, examined further below, is not that 'Mother Earth' is a problematic concept—in the sense that the harmony between nature and humanity should be questioned—but rather, that it is problematic to privilege its symbolic importance over its practical application.

The World People's Conference on Climate Change (WPCCC): situating alternatives

The People's Agreement is more fully contextualized—and greater accessibility to the immediate lived experiences of contestation is enabled—through examining the processes through which the agreement was constructed at the site of the World People's Conference on Climate Change in Cochabamba. Gaining international recognition from the anti-globalization movement for its 'water war' in response to the privatization of the city's water system in 1999, Cochabamba was the site of mass protest against Aguas del Tunari, a transnational consortium and subsidiary of the US Bechtel Corporation (Morales 2012: 55–56). Present at the WPCCC were two heads of state, Evo Morales and Hugo Chávez, two vice-presidents of Cuba and Burundi, 47 official delegations, and international organizations such as the secretariat of the United Nations (Houtart 2010). Some 35,500 participants of 147 nationalities were present, while it is estimated that more than 800 Europeans and a number of Africans and Asians were prevented from attending due to air traffic restrictions in response to a volcanic ash cloud (ibid.). The Bolivian Foreign Minister David Choquehuanca announced that of 35,000 participants, 9,254 foreigners had come from 142 countries and official delegations from 47 states (Chávez 2010).

Prior to the conference an estimated 5,000 intellectuals and activists collaborated via online sessions (Chávez 2010). Seventeen working groups (see Table 6.1) were formed and each had an open email list. The aim was to include those who would not be able to attend and to produce a draft document to begin working on at the conference. The 'migration' working group comprised approximately 400 registered for the online pre-conference consultation, while about 50 participated in the first day of the working group in Cochabamba (Ayya 2010). An assessment of the online process on the part of a group of eight participants notes that:

> whilst this online process deserves merit for its attempt to include those who could not attend, from our experience the process was ineffective. While people sent reports and position papers, there was very little analysis or debate and the lack of translation was also an obstacle
> (Building Bridges Collective 2010)[4]

A similar online process was carried out in advance of the World Social Forum Strategy Debate in 2008 and the outcome restated forum principles and processes.[5] Prior to the WPCCC a government-appointed moderator synthesized the outcomes of the online consultation into an initial working group text. The pre-conference texts from each of the 17 working groups,

Table 6.1 World People's Conference on Climate Change working groups

Working groups
Structural causes
Harmony with nature
Mother Earth rights
Referendum
Climate justice tribunal
Climate migrants
Indigenous peoples
Climate debt
Shared vision
Kyoto protocol
Adaptation
Financing
Technology transfer
Forest
Dangers of carbon market
Action strategies
Agriculture and food sovereignty

according to Climate Justice Action participants, were disappointing and did not go far enough (Brien *et al.* 2010). A pre-conference was also held, organized by CONAMAQ, a national indigenous council in Bolivia, bringing together representatives from Bolivian grassroots movements, several ministerial representatives and Evo Morales.

At the WPCCC 17 working groups worked to produce a final group document. An 18th unofficial working group, Working Group 18 or Mesa 18, discussed a theme that was not addressed at the conference: the contradiction between the defence of nature and extractive policies of progressive Latin American countries (e.g. oil, gas, mining). The formation of an official working group on this theme was blocked by the Bolivian government (Redman 2010). During the WPCCC, Mesa 18 was also involved in direct action protests at the site of Bolivia's largest mine, San Cristóbal. Meanwhile, alongside the 17 official working groups, self-organized workshops were held by social movements and organizations at the conference. Panels were also held during the conference hosting figures such as Vandana Shiva, Naomi Klein, Bill McKibben, Martin Khor, Jose Bové, Bernard Cassen and François Houtart. On the last day a common assembly was held to bring together the reports of the working groups in a final declaration—the People's Agreement discussed above—which, according to Climate Justice Action (CJA), was much more ambitious, in rejecting Reducing Emissions from Deforestation and forest Degradation (REDD), genetic modification and market-based solutions, than the pre-conference working group documents.

The working group texts that had been drafted during the pre-conference preparatory and mediation processes were the focus of two and a half days' discussion and debate in the 17 working groups. Each working group elected two secretaries to document the proceedings and two chairs to facilitate the discussions with representation by a male and a female and a national and an international (Building Bridges Collective 2010). Working groups took differing formats and just some are discussed here. Janet Redman, a founding member of Climate Justice Now, describes the process of working in her working group of more than 150 members on 'climate finance' (Redman 2010). This working group was directed to focus on the sourcing and amount of financial resources necessary to combat climate change in developing countries in addition to ensuring efficient and sustainable management of these resources over time directed towards mitigation, adaptation, development, transfer of technology and capacity building in developing countries (WPCCC 2010). The first day of work within the working group was spent collecting proposals from students, indigenous elders, municipal officials, community organizers, labour leaders and representatives of non-governmental organizations (NGOs). These were heated exchanges during the 'town hall-style discussions' with the issue of using carbon markets as a source of climate-related funding as particularly controversial amid concerns of the potentially devastating impacts of the commodification of nature (Redman 2010). On the third day a consensus was reached and a three-page draft was produced. It was put to a gathering of several thousand people in the local university's coliseum, 'where an open microphone offered the opportunity for voicing approval, disagreements, and questions about the text'. The production of the final text was reached after facilitators had incorporated 'commonly raised issues', after which each working group's work was 'summarized in a few paragraphs highlighting the most essential demands and principles' (ibid.).

The controversy over forests and the issue of REDD was a contentious issue within the 'forests' working group. According to one report, indigenous organizers and leaders from the Indigenous Environmental Network wanted to include a condemnation of REDD in the working group text but met with opposition from Bolivian government representatives and southern indigenous leaders (Negrón-Gonzales 2010). The initial text that the moderator presented to the working group supported the REDD mechanism, despite evidence of opposing views in the course of online preparatory work (Building Bridges Collective 2010). Nonetheless, REDD was condemned in the final text of the People's Agreement:

> We condemn market mechanisms such as REDD (Reducing Emissions from Deforestation and Forest Degradation) and its versions + and ++, which are violating the sovereignty of peoples and their rights to prior free and informed consent as well as the sovereignty of national States, the customs of Peoples, and the rights of Nature.
>
> (People's Agreement 2010)

In contrast to the 'Action Strategies' working group which largely left their initial text intact, the forests working group 'went through a process, at many times conflictual, of information sharing, heated discussions and consensus building' (Building Bridges Collective 2010). This may be reflective of the presence at Cochabamba of people who had been negatively affected by climate change mitigation actions, so-called 'false solutions', such as the construction of mega dams and carbon offset projects (Powless 2010a). Working group final texts were submitted to a closed meeting comprising the secretaries, chairs, the moderator of each group and government officials who edited the document to four pages and presented it to a large assembly the following day. Each was read out and assembly participants queued to make comments, additions or rejections. The amended texts were then taken to another closed meeting in which the 'People's Agreement' was produced (Building Bridges Collective 2010).

Initial assessments of the WPCCC were positive on the part of the United Nations Non-governmental Liaison Service, for example, which emphasized that 'the particularity of this meeting was its democratic and citizen-oriented structure, and its aim to give voice to those directly affected by climate change' (UN-NGLS 2009). While recognizing the contradictions between the Bolivian government's rhetoric and actions regarding the environment and indigenous rights, it is also suggested that 'Bolivia's experiment with democracy opens up new ways of thinking about multilateralism' (Redman 2010). It was considered by another participant to present the opportunity to 'start a discussion', inform and mobilize around future actions which 'with a bit more time, resources, and representative participation … could have been more powerful' (Powless 2010a, 2010b: 27).[6] More broadly, the WPCCC advances the deepening of debate on the politics of resistance that moves outside of the World Social Forum and opens towards ideas of the formation of a new global Left which includes not only civil society entities such as social movements, individuals, social movement organizations and NGOs, but also political parties and progressive national regimes (Chase-Dunn 2011).

Following the WPCCC the content of the People's Agreement and draft proposal for the Universal Declaration of Mother Earth's Rights were presented to the Ad hoc Working Group on Long-term Cooperative Action (AWG-LCA) to contribute to the draft negotiating text for its session in Bonn, Germany, in June 2010 in advance of COP16 in November 2010.[7] A delegation including President Evo Morales and representatives of social movements presented the agreement to the UN Secretary-General Ban Ki-moon, the G77 and China.[8] However, the impact of the WPCCC has been muted. Its call for a Global People's Movement for Mother Earth constituting 'a broad and democratic space for coordination and joint worldwide actions' met with difficulties at the site of the Cancun Conference of the Parties where three physically fragmented gatherings took place under the format of: a) a Klimaforum of mostly European constituents; b) *Espacio Mexicano* comprising larger Mexican networks, larger NGOs, Climate Justice Now, International Hemispheric Social Alliance; and c) Via Campesina and the Assembly of Climate Affected Communities in Mexico (Kim 2011). Following COP16 the Bolivian negotiating team noted the proposals that were submitted to the UN, including the proposal for a Climate Justice Tribunal, had been systematically excluded from the negotiations (Bond 2011).

Nonetheless, the People's Agreement is supported by the Bolivarian Alliance for the Peoples of the Americas (ALBA) countries and Union of South American Nations (UNASUR) (Bullard 2010).[9] This highlights the particularity of the call for inclusivity at the WPCC which aims to create alliances between states and social movements. Some social movements have expressed concern that the ALBA governments will attempt to control the formation of a Global People's Movement and restrict the autonomy of social movements in the process (Lander 2010). In Bolivia, a closer alliance between the state and social movements formed within the Movement Toward Socialism (Movimiento al Socialismo, MAS) alliance, led by Evo Morales. Described as a 'hybrid socialist-indigenous-populist movement turned political party' (Morales 2012: 51), it calls for radical national social change and has benefited electorally from decentralization and participation reforms. This is not without controversy particularly once MAS moved from being an oppositional force and entered government (Teivainen 2012; Kennemore and Weeks 2011; Morales 2012; Petras and Veltmeyer 2009) although social movements and indigenous peoples have met with some success in articulating their demands through the Morales government (Prevost *et al.* 2012: 14). Concern with the mismatch between government rhetoric and action was expressed in response to controversial plans to construct a highway through the Isiboro-Sécure Indigenous Territory and National Park (TIPNIS) ecological reserve. This deepened following violent police action against lowland indigenous families who had left their homes in TIPNIS in a 360-mile march to the capital La Paz to protest Bolivian government plans to build the road (The Democracy Center 2011). As the presence of Mesa 18 at the WPCCC indicates, the role of Bolivia as a carrier of climate justice values has been questioned as it continues to focus on resource extraction as a basis of its economic model to fund social programmes (Kennemore and Weeks 2011).

Spaces and movements of global contestation: World Social Forums and the World People's Conference on Climate Change

An Assembly of Social Movements (ASM) was also held at the start of the WPCCC in Cochabamba.[10] As discussed in Chapter 5, the assembly has its roots in the World Social Forum where it aims to bring together a variety of movements to construct an agenda for future actions. The presence of the ASM at the WPCCC highlights the differing nature of the forum and People's Conference, aside from being convened by a state and social movements— the forum, unlike the WPCCC, does not constitute a 'locus of power to be disputed' (WSF 2002a) by its participants and does not issue statements in its name or provide a space for the elaboration of a document such as the 'People's Agreement'. According to a member of Via Campesina the assembly in Cochabamba was important 'in order to have common policies to construct an agenda of struggle, resistance and proposals' (Via Campesina 2010a). This reflects the social-movement position which promotes the WSF as an 'action platform' for social movements to coordinate and strengthen global actions rather than simply as an 'open space' for dialogue (Raina 2008; Teivainen 2006).[11] At the WPCCC ASM prominent issues also considered in the final People's Agreement were raised, particularly the need for systemic change, climate justice and the inadequate solutions to tackle climate change proposed by northern governments and industries.

The ASM was founded at the WSF to 'strengthen the voice and the political agenda of social movements from all over the world' (Kenfield 2010). It issues a single statement following each WSF and has been attributed with coining the term 'Global Justice and Solidarity Movement' (GJSM) and in constructing a common agenda against the World Trade Organization (WTO), the war in Iraq and, following the WPCCC, climate change (Waterman 2010; Via Campesina 2010a). A WSF International Council participant points to the less coherent aspects of ASM statements in a description of the ASM as a 'haphazard and motley collection of people who happen to be present at the WSF who read out a fairly hastily prepared statement—it is more like using the opportunity of being present together than any sustained organizational or well-thought out conceptual positioning' (Raina 2008). Jubilee South, however, point to the ASM as 'the most important element of the WSF' as a usage of space that 'is used for mobilization by movements and networks with goals and dynamics more rooted in ongoing processes' (Jubilee South 2008). Nonetheless, it is considered that since the full strategic significance of the ASM is not captured through the predominantly promoted 'open space' of the forum, its strength would lie in making it independent of the forum (ibid.). The ASM was, however, but one event among many others at the WPCCC and the 17 working groups were primarily involved, during the conference, in producing draft texts for consideration in the final agreement. It does, however, underline some key differences between the WSF and WPCCC.

The more explicit and broader, arguably inclusive, drawing up of the People's Agreement can also be compared to the processes through which the Manifesto of Porto Alegre, at the time of the 2005 Porto Alegre WSF, and the Bamako Appeal, the day before the 2006 Bamako Polycentric WSF, were produced (see Chapter 5 also).[12] The Manifesto, containing 12 proposals for another possible world, was prepared by a group of 19 individuals including just one woman. The Bamako Appeal was prepared by a larger group of movements of civil society including Forum for Another Mali, World Forum for Alternatives, Third World Forum and ENDA.[13] Samir Amin and François Houtart were key associated figures with this initiative while also being signatories of the Manifesto. Both documents met with criticism for the manner in which they were drawn up. In the case of the Bamako appeal those who attended the meeting were presented with a draft which was 'complemented' by working groups and edited by Amin, Houtart and Rémy Herrera, a French political economist (Waterman 2006). In particular, attention has been drawn to the process through which the final version was produced and, while more explicitly inclusive, this raises some questions that are applicable to the final production of the 'People's Agreement' at the WPCCC. While recognizing that the subsequent 'endorsements' of the Bamako Appeal give some indication of its international appeal to Left intellectuals, social movements and NGOs, Waterman expresses his own 'discomfort about a document *produced* by a tiny group of individuals, *complemented* by an invited audience, *edited* by the original group, and "accepted" (whatever that might mean) at the event, and apparently, at (not by) the WSFs in Bamako and Caracas'. He agrees that the appeal 'should have been discussed more widely and more openly before being finalised' (Sen 2006, cited in Waterman 2006) and thus 'issued *for discussion* in the wider community of social movements and critical intellectuals worldwide' (Waterman 2006).

The perception that the forum has fulfilled its 'historical function' as a space for global civil society to meet and formulate alternatives and is now at a crossroads at which it should consider giving way to 'new modes of global organization of resistance and transformation' (Bello 2007) is reflected in the drawing up of both documents and, in this context, the presence of the ASM at the WPCCC may be indicative of a substantive strategy on the part of social movements associated with the ASM. On the other hand, the forum has never been the only mode of contestation. As stated in the WSF Charter of Principles, the forum does not 'intend to constitute the only option for interrelation and action by the organizations and movements that participate in it' (WSF 2002a). A number of organizations are both members of the WSF International Council and signed 'partners' to the call for a World People's Conference on Climate Change and the Rights of Mother Earth.[14]

Meanwhile, when asked whether, given the dramatic nature of climate change, the forum may be obliged to change its priorities and central themes, Santos, a key intellectual associated with the forum process, answered:

> Without a doubt. What's important is that the WSF should not deal with the topic in the style of Al Gore—that is, as a problem that has nothing to do with global capitalism, with indigenous and peasant movements, with the issues of land and water, with discrimination against women.
>
> (IPS 2008)

Further links have been established between individuals and movements that are concerned with climate change. In advance of the WPCCC, Bolivia's (now former) Ambassador to the United Nations Pablo Solón attended the Ten Years Social Forum in Porto Alegre where he met with climate justice activists and movements (Aguiton and Bullard 2010). Solón was also in attendance at the 2011 Dakar WSF in Senegal, where he participated in various events promoting the Cochabamba Agreement (ibid.) and at the more recent Thematic Social Forum in Porto Alegre in January 2012 where discussion centred on preparation for a People's Summit for social and environmental justice to be held alongside the UN Conference on Sustainable Development (UNCSD, Rio+20) in Rio de Janeiro, Brazil on 20–22 June 2012.[15] A Brazilian Civil Society Facilitating Committee (CFSC) for Rio+20, was formed during the 2011 Dakar WSF which worked with an International Coordination Group in preparation for the People's Summit. The CFSC includes movements which are also involved in the forum process, for example the United Workers Confederation (CUT), Brazilian Association of Non-governmental Organizations (ABONG), Via Campesina, WMW and the Group for Reflection and Support for the WSF Process (GRAP). The latter emerged from the Dakar forum to bring together some of the original Brazilian founders of the WSF and others in advance of Rio+20 which, according to its website, are concerned with the collective elaboration of a new paradigm in defence of life and common goods. Held in Aterro de Flamengo, Rio de Janeiro, the People's Summit produced a final declaration summarizing the main points discussed during plenary sessions and identifying the main axes of future struggles and convergence (Cúpula dos Povos 2012b).

Meanwhile in 2010, the People's Agreement was produced at the site of the Universidad de Valle campus in Tiquipaya, Cochabamba, through a process of deliberation, articulation of alternatives between northern- and southern-based social movements and 'movement building' (Blynn 2010b). Clearly, the role of states and governments in the WPCCC process appears to conflict with the 'open space' position and constraint put forward in the WSF Charter of Principles that the forum is a 'non-confessional, non-party context' (WSF 2002a). However, in reality, as continued links and frequent attendance of state representatives, particularly presidents of the Latin American Left at the forum shows, this has always been an ambiguous Charter-based feature of forums.[16] There has been some discussion on enabling a closer relationship between social movements and political parties (Smith *et al.* 2008).[17] Nonetheless, and possibly more indicative of the recent development of the WSF process, the WPCCC contrasts with the People's Summit held in Flamengo Park, Rio de Janeiro, which is conceived as an autonomous people's space that is free from corporations and government influence (Cúpula dos Povos 2012a).

Conclusions: global symbols, metaphors and resistance

The WSF and WPCCC are both positioned as symbolic challenges to hegemonic modes of thought and action through their respective provisions of an open space for 'global civil society' and proposals for closer engagement between humanity and nature through 'Mother Earth'. It is considered that the forum 'not only challenges dominant political theories and the various disciplines of the conventional social sciences, but challenges as well scientific knowledge as sole producer of social and political rationality' (Santos 2007).[18] The issue of utopian will is raised in its slogan 'another world is possible' and symbolic reference to 'emancipatory global civil society' in relation to the forum (ibid.; Santos 2006a). The World People's Conference on Climate Change and the Rights of Mother Earth, in similar terms, raises the spectre of the symbolic universal concept, Mother Earth, as an agent of change.

The issue that I raise here is not to argue that the intentions behind global contestation and the rights of Mother Earth are mistaken or to deny the necessity of change from a paradigm of excessive growth and instrumental rationality. It is, however, to caution against privileging analytical thought—in this case the symbolic concept, such that a symbol (global civil society, Mother Earth) is spontaneously identified with reality—in explanations of change. It is to remain cognisant of cultural and historical differentiation in the search for new paradigms of 'universal' knowledge. More precisely, theoretical reflexivity avoids the production of a mechanical formula for translating symbols or metaphors of resistance into action strategies and may instead contribute to a common position of effective resistance that is also diverse and promotes mutual respect:

> C'est un simple début de réflexion, sans prétention d'imposer un cadre de pensée sur ce problème, qui vise à ouvrir la discussion pour arriver à des

solutions permettant une lutte commune dans la diversité et le respect mutuel.

(Houtart 2010)

In the case of 'global civil society' as a metaphor for resistance, intimations of counter-hegemony have sought to bring together a 'multiplicity of antagonisms' in an appropriately global, cohesive, historical bloc (Bond 2006). The value of this type of counter-hegemony is asserted to be its diversity. The key distinguishing factor in the so-called 'teamster and turtle' 'battle of Seattle' and its later translation into the site of the World Social Forum is considered to be in its capacity to provide an 'open space' for the diverse constituents of global civil society—social movements, labour organizations, activists, civil societal organizations, indigenous groups, cultural groups, anarchists and so on. As developed further in Chapter 5, the strategy of 'convergence', linked to achieving consensus and synthesis between movements of global civil society, has characterized WSF strategy to date. This is related to the recent emphasis on 'new universality' or convening of 'an assembly of assemblies' on the final day of the forum to generate 'opportunities for exchange and collaboration that could constitute both the elaboration and the implementation of a new universality' (Caruso 2010a, 2010b).

However, the principle of convergence has endured beyond the 10-year anniversary of the WSF with little reassuring evidence of how an effective strategy of resistance can be formulated directly through it. It is not clear how the symbolic metaphor of resistance—global civil society/new universality—translates into a coherent strategy. What emerge are superficial metaphors for contestation which lack tangibility and recognition of the failures of 'global contestation' to (re)negotiate the tensions between and within movements of global civil society as they are concretely located in the global political economy. The continued failure to address ideological diversity dilutes and proves a serious barrier to achieving transformative change (Worth and Buckley 2009). Substantive analysis of global civil society and equally of 'Mother Earth', requires further conceptual development because, as discussed in Chapter 2, while analogies, metaphors, images and symbols contribute to conceptualization, their application to the dialectics of concept and reality calls for much further attention to their concrete modes of social relation in and towards the global political economy. Global civil society and Mother Earth potentially represent alternative politico-ethical worldviews, rooted in historical consciousness, which contrast with the instrumental rationality of current formulations. However, their full conceptual potentials are not realized in their current formulations. The result is that, rather than facilitating a strategy for resistance, metaphorical frameworks are imposed that may ultimately muddy the waters of resistance and give greater fuel to the re-imposition of an inside/outside divide in how we conceptualize 'global' resistance. Alternatively, as the next chapter explores further, the interstices of transversal hegemony are found in the broad dialectical relationship between consciousness and being at the centres and peripheries of contestation (cf. Neufeld 2002: 3; Thompson 1978: 225), which potentially realizes processes of engagement between human knowledge, consciousness and action (Gill 1993).

Notes

1 For assessments of events at COP15 in Copenhagen see, for example: Bond (2011), Dimitrov (2010), Fisher (2010), Death (2011).
2 While much of this discussion draws on the People's Agreement, referred to simply as 'the agreement', the texts of the various Working Groups that were involved in producing working drafts of the agreement are also used to add further insight to the content of the discussions at Cochabamba.
3 For discussions on the development of the climate justice network see, for example: Bond and Dorsey (2010), Pearse (2010), and Goodman (2009).
4 The Building Bridges Collective is composed of eight individuals: Yamine Brien, Jeremy Crowle Smith, Joanna Cabello, Alice Cutler, Mooness Davarian, Merel de Buck, Chris Kitchen and Bertie Russell. They are involved with various groups and networks including Rising Tide, No Borders, Climate Justice Action, Camp for Climate Action, Carbon Trade Watch, Somos Sur and Trapese Popular Education Collective. They participated in their individual capacities (not representing the groups mentioned above) in the WPCCC working groups on 'Action Strategies', 'Migration', 'Forests' and 'Structural Causes'.
5 As previously discussed, prior to the meeting, political-strategic assessments of the WSF process, the anti-globalization movement, and the international context from movements, organizations and International Council (IC) members were circulated: 51 general texts and interviews, 19 contributions from IC members, five from Global Day of Action (GDA) participants, and one from the commissions and workgroups. During the meeting five working groups discussed the strategic future of the WSF.
6 One such example of a follow-on event is the Cochabamba+1 conference that was held in Montreal in April 2011 and was organized by Alternatives and *Canadian Dimension* magazine. For further details see: www.alternatives.ca/en/agenda/cochabamba1-climate-justice-and-ecological-alternatives.
7 For the Bolivian submission see: pwccc.wordpress.com/2010/04/28/submission-by-the-plurinational-state-of-bolivia/; and for the text to facilitate negotiation between the parties see: unfccc.int/resource/docs/2010/awglca10/eng/06.pdf.
8 Movements include Via Campesina, Friends of the Earth, Third World Network, 350.org, the Indigenous Environmental Network, the Hemispheric Social Alliance and the Blue Planet Project. See: Blynn (2010a, 2010b).
9 The Bolivarian Alliance for the Peoples of the Americas/Alianza Bolivariana para los Pueblos de Nuestra América (ALBA) comprises Venezuela, Cuba, Bolivia, Nicaragua, Dominica, Saint Vincent and the Grenadines, Ecuador, Antigua and Barbuda. The Union of South American Nations/Unión de Naciones Sudamer-icanas (UNASUR) brings together Mercosur and the Andean Community, Chile, Guyana and Suriname.
10 An invitation to the ASM was issued in advance of the WPCCC on behalf of the following organizations: Alianza Social Continental, Friends of the Earth Latin America (ATALC), Centro Brasileiro de Solidariedade aos Povos e Luta pela Paz (Cebrapaz), Central Sindical de las Américas, Climate Justice Now!, Latin American Coordination of Rural Organizations/Via Campesina (CLOC), Convergencia de los Movimentos de los Pueblos de las Américas (COMPA), Federación Democrática Internacional de Mujeres (FDIM), World March of Women (WMW), Organización

Continental Latinoamérica y Caribeña de Estudiantes (OCLAE), Committee for the Cancellation of Third World Debt-Abya Yala Nuestra América Network (CADTM-AYNA), and Via Campesina (Via Campesina 2010a).

11 For more on the open space/social movements positions see: Grzybowski (2006), Sen (2009), Andreotti (2005), Wallerstein (2004), CEOS (2010), Keraghel and Sen (2004), Osterweil (2004a), Patomäki and Teivainen (2004a).

12 The text of both documents, and some published responses, is available online through the Open Space Forum at: www.openspaceforum.net/twiki/tiki-view_articles. php?type=Article&topic=12 and also at: www.cacim.net/bareader/home.html. For reference to models of charter development and their relationship to both documents see Waterman (2006).

13 More broadly, the Bamako Appeal is an initiative of the Forum du Tiers Monde/ Third World Forum, the World Forum of Alternatives, the Tricontinental Centre, Louvain-la-Neuve, Belgium, the Malian Social Forum and Environmental Development Action in the Third World (ENDA).

14 These include, for example, the Africa Trade Network, Amigos de la Tierra (Spain), the Brazilian Institute of Social and Economic Analysis (IBASE), Central de Trabajadores de la Argentina, Global Exchange, International Forum on Globalization, Jubilee 2000, Third World Network.

15 Rio+20 marked the 20th anniversary of the 1992 United Nations Conference on Environment and Development (UNCED) and the 10th anniversary of the 2002 World Summit on Sustainable Development (WSSD) in Johannesburg. For more on the People's Summit see: cupuladospovos.org.br/en/.

16 These receptions do vary. While President Luiz Inácio Lula da Silva of Brazil made an appearance before 100,000 people at the 2003 WSF in Porto Alegre, he was much less warmly received in 2005. Meanwhile, the warm reception President Hugo Chávez of Venezuela received in 2005 contrasted to the low-key nature of his appearance two years previously (Smith *et al.* 2008).

17 See, for example: Smith *et al.* (2008).

18 It is particularly in discussions of global climate change that knowledge has emerged as a salient theme. See introduction by Peet *et al.* (2011) and Jasanoff and Martello (2004) for their discussion on how 'global science' is nonetheless reflective of a situated knowledge with respect to power and local knowledge-power formations.

7   Transversal hegemony

In this chapter, the main features of a dialectical re-conceptualization of global civil society (GCS) are outlined while attention also turns to a consideration of the capacity of 'transversal hegemony' to engage in wider theoretical crossovers with potential benefits for the politics of resistance. As suggested in the introduction to this book, transversal hegemony is a confluence of meanings which prompts a reconsideration of the analytical consequences of demarcated structural and post-structural approaches most clearly seen in rapprochements between Gramsci and Foucault. Potentially, this points towards a new way of thinking which refutes the apparently antithetical nature of largely solitary enterprises and opens towards frank dialogue or conversation between approaches. Increasingly, the study of world politics and Global Political Economy (GPE) implicitly recognizes the necessity of, and potential benefits to be derived from, such fields of enquiry. It might no longer be the case that there is a lack of analytical instruments and sufficient understanding of collective actors involved in global contestation, but sustained reflexivity is required to conceptualize civil society and hegemony in the contemporary global political economy.

A critical conceptualization of global civil society which is facilitated through the dialectics of concept and reality is further understood through focusing on categories of research. Despite recent advances, social sciences are more amenable to exploratory forms of conceptualization than a focus on analogies, myths, stories, images and/or metaphors. Since conceptualization is nonetheless susceptible to a lengthening of correspondence between concept and reality, introducing the dialectic is an explicit attempt to overcome this. This is not to say, however, that analogies, myths, stories, images, transcripts, metaphors and so on are not significant—they have a striking capacity to encompass an appreciation of 'the real' and in their application to the social sciences also need further translation. Thus, for example, metaphorical allusion to the post-modern prince demands further means of translation to facilitate more tangible association to the forms, formats and conflicts inherent to resistance movements. The potential for aesthetic approaches to be included in a broadened range of legitimate approaches to studying world politics is the focus of recent work on using painting, music, poetry, photography and film to 'highlight how we understand and construct the world we live in' (Bleiker 2009: 8).[1] This may, for example, work to reduce the gap between scholarly discussion and the actual lives of indigenous people which was a clear issue in the production of the People's Agreement at the World People's Conference on Climate Change in Cochabamba, discussed in the previous chapter.

At the same time that the merit of further conceptualization can be posited, the denomination of the contemporary concept of global civil society as 'an analytical mirage'—as at once too broad and too narrow 'to provide an accurate picture of the changing political sociology of the contemporary world' (Cerny 2006: 96–97)—clearly points to its failure to correspond to the 'real'. Its location as exogenous to economic and political processes deceptively underestimates 'the extent to which individual and group actors are themselves embedded in economic and political-institutional contexts' (ibid.). Indeed, much of the literature on global civil society examined in this book gives credence to scepticism that an inherently benevolent global civil society is creating a new normative world order through operating tactically and strategically across a variety of levels unavailable to normal state and market actors (ibid.). What might be suggested, nevertheless, is that the analysis of global civil society in this book bears a relation to and potentially changes our understanding on Gramscian hegemony so that the form of transversal hegemony might be further considered. My focus on Gramsci and Foucault, in this account, takes its cue from existing studies which consider the theoretical potential of post-structuralism (e.g. de Goede 2006; Eschle and Maiguashca 2005; Maiguashca 2006) and existing integration of Foucault into Gramscian-influenced approaches (e.g. Gill 2008; Jessop and Sum 2006; Sum 2009). Global civil society potentially captures the accumulated meanings and contributions of alter-globalization movements, the post-modern prince, global social movements, and associated dynamics of change and contestation which are broad, contested and mediated by relations of inclusion and exclusion.

The nature of critique: voluntarism and mechanical categories of research

Many of the studies that have been referred to in this book provide and elaborate responses to the problems of governance and world order through outlining the nature of hegemony in a framework of global governance. In contrast, global civil society, whether substantially or metaphorically integrated into such accounts, is significant for the purpose of this book, less for what it tells us about the processes and workings of globalization and contestation, for it does so poorly, and more for how vying conceptualizations reveal, first, the limited nature of critique itself and, second, calls for further attention to be given to hegemony. The limited nature of critique is to be found in the prevalence of narrow instrumental, and broader contrasting, voluntarist conceptualizations of civil society, which in their respective, although not strictly delineated governance and activist representations, ultimately serve to

limit the conceptual usefulness of global civil society. Some of these representations appear to lend credence to the suggestion that its invocation signals
a retreat from politics or, even more seriously, that it is a reactionary response
to hollow hegemony or the weakening of national hegemony (Chandler
2004a, 2009a). In this section, I focus on how a critical political economy
conceptualization, drawing particularly on the Gramscian reference to categories
of research—bound in the dialectical nexus with categories of movement—
questions these assumptions and affirms the emancipative potential of global
civil society in global contestation (see Box 2.1 in Chapter 2; Gramsci 1971).

The emancipative potential of global civil society is not, however, axiomatically
assured. At its inception, the World Social Forum was considered to represent
the globalization protest movements of the 1990s and, more recently, the
global democratization movements of the twenty-first century (Teivainen
2007). Additionally, a recent collection on *Global Democracy and the World
Social Forums* considers it a laboratory for global democracy (Smith *et al.*
2008: xii). Elsewhere, the nature of its informal organizational structures and
decentralized forms of authority are considered to 'make it one of the most
promising civil society processes that may both contribute significantly to
global democratization initiatives and work to constitute such an initiative
in itself' (Byrd 2005: 158). Resistance movements, from multitude to the post-
modern prince, are also intertwined with theories of transnational and
global democracy. The principal stated aim of *Multitude* is to find a new
conceptualization of democracy and possibility for politics as the old choice
between sovereignty or anarchy is replaced by the 'power of the multitude to
create social relationships in common' (Hardt and Negri 2005: xvii, 336). Just
as multitude is considered to lie somewhere between war and democracy
(while moving in the direction towards a new form of democracy), resistance
movements are often implicitly characterized as occupying a similar space so that
the most frequent outcome or benefit is presented in terms of democratization
and, increasingly, new possibilities beyond territorial politics. However,
democratic possibilities must be actively nurtured so that civil society does
not detract from democracy (Scholte 2002: 281). This recalls the democratic
challenges presented by civil society and the wider issues of elitism, funding,
convergence, power and strategy which are examined in relation to global
governance and the World Social Forum in Chapters 4 and 5.

Clearly a positive initiative according to many accounts, it is less well
recognized that the WSF exerts a presence on the complex terrain of the
global political economy and its participants engage in various modes of
social relation in and towards it. The post-modern prince, multitude and/or
dominant representations of global civil society are shaped in response to and
because of this presence. Additionally, interactions between civil society and
international institutions associated with global governance, coupled with the
methods through which analysis emerges, are productive of, and significant
in, the 'making' of global civil society. The categorization of research, in
contrast, reflects a tendency towards instrumental and functional accounting

for global civil society or contrasting voluntarist methods of analysis. The absence of a dialectical nexus within and between categories of research, and indeed movement, presents an obstacle to furthering new thinking on the politics of resistance. In a wider and originally disciplinary sense a primary concern with the 'global accountability problem' (Scholte 2004: 233) has implications for the politics of resistance in denoting spheres of meaning to global civil society and related demands. The simple re-articulation of demands in the absence of ideological struggle, for example, can leave in place the dominant ideology and material inequalities (Maiguashca 2006), thus only succeeding in alleviating or smoothing over the global accountability problem.[2] Studies of global civil societal modes of relation to the global political economy, whether civic-consensual, unitary, or in other form, potentially examine not only the re-articulation of demands—or the move from protest to articulation of democratic alternatives to neoliberalism in the case of the World Social Forum—but also significant material and ideological aspects of contestation. Equally, a focus on instrumental and/or voluntarist categorizations, in the absence of a critical conceptualization of an emancipatory global civil society, dissociates global civil society from state and market agency.

The analytical contributions of global civil society are significant not when global civil society is adapted to 'fit' explanations of global governance, but rather when the varied insights or 'conceptual baggage' that it brings to modes of social relation are closely integrated. Studies on the historico-political accumulation of meanings related to global civil society intervene in the dialectical nexus to give form and voice to the constituents of resistance (Chase-Dunn 2011; Chase-Dunn and Gills 2005; Drainville 2004, 2012; Gills and Gray 2012; Thompson 1963). The precedents of alter-globalization movements can be traced through historical parallels and contrasts that are neither spontaneous nor new and much can be learned from 'the various strategic and tactical insights that incorporating history affords' (Broad and Heckscher 2003: 726). These strategic and tactical insights disrupt decontextualized and non-historicized interpretations of global civil society and emphasize instead an historicized, diachronic, format of thought (cf. Cox 2002). The possibilities of global civil society in diachronic time are more clearly understood through categories of research. This framework recognizes that in the absence of ideological struggle, material and ideological demands may simply be rearticulated towards functional and procedural resolutions. The dialectical balance, therefore, between Scholte's (2002) account of civil society and neo-Polanyian accounts of global civil society is the issue here. An extract from Gramsci's discussion on organic and conjunctural movements, examined in more detail below, may be adapted to illustrate this balance: 'In the first case there is an overestimation of mechanical causes, in the second an exaggeration of the voluntarist and individual element' (Gramsci 1971: 178). A dialectical balance or category of research contributes to conceptualizing global civil society.

The concept of global civil society and its application to the politics of resistance can be considered and contrasted with the framework to conceptualize resistance developed by Chin and Mittelman (1997). The principal objective of this framework was, through the 'Gramsci-Polanyi-Scott triad', to link different levels of analysis from the local to the global. As avenues for further research, the authors suggest further explorations of the forms, agents, sites and strategies of resistance from the perspective of multi-level analysis. Each part of the Gramsci-Polanyi-Scott triad targets differing objects of resistance. These include counter-hegemony targeting the state apparatuses, counter-movements targeting market forces, and counter-discourses concerning ideologies or public transcripts. Each element contributes important points of analysis to the global politics of resistance: The Gramscian critical consciousness of subaltern groups; Polanyian counter-movements as forms of resistance; and Scott's portrayal of the changing meaning of politics and resistance and infrapolitical or everyday forms of resistance. Each element of the triad also presents challenges such as incorporating new actors and spaces for counter-hegemonic consciousness; implied meanings of collectivity, hierarchy and united fronts within counter-movements; and the unidimensional class-focused nature of counter-discourses (ibid.).

The framework developed by Chin and Mittelman offers insight to the levels of analysis implicit in the politics of resistance from the perspective of Global Political Economy. It clearly identifies the contributions and challenges presented by each element of the triad and responds to the disciplinary-led certainty of theoretical clarity. There is, however, further potential considering, for example, the case of 'neo-Polanyian' optimism which, as I have considered in Chapter 2, converges towards accounts emphasizing: a) global civil society conceptualization through an over-reliance on spontaneous, axiomatic and often simplified dichotomies of globalization and resistance; b) a need for further conceptual and analytical clarity, theoretical development and dialectical relation to tangible qualities of contestation; and c) highlighting of unity or solidarity at the expense of difference, inequality and fragmentation. While the focus of analysis by Chin and Mittelman is primarily on these three levels of analysis, my focus differs in not carrying forward these distinctions; I do not consider that counter-hegemony is primarily state-oriented or counter-movements market-based, although this distinction does account for the tendency by Gramscian approaches to conflate counter-hegemony and the counter-movement (see Chapter 2). Rather, I start with global civil society as an essential tool of analysis to bring greater coherency to analysis of the modes of relation between forms of globalization and contestation and facilitate greater understanding on global agents, sites and strategies of resistance.

Global civil society, by its designation as 'global' alone but also in the way it is often conceptualized, is suggestive of a new form of politics. However, as shown in previous chapters, global civil society and its invocation at the World Social Forum is constitutive of the reproduction of the old patterns and modes of resistance of pluralist politics and often fails to produce substantive new analysis. Equally, the study by O'Brien *et al.* (2000) of *Contesting Global Governance* concludes with a disconcerting long-term prediction of the pluralization of governing structures within a system of 'complex multi-lateralism' despite the evidence of limited civil societal interaction with international financial institutions presented in the course of the study. Many current conceptualizations of global civil society are indicative not just of limited critique but also of diversions in the nature of critique itself, such as exemplified in the prospect of a neo-Gramscian diversion to liberal pluralism (Morton 2007a). 'For lack of theorizing', therefore, 'what we find might be considered counter-hegemonical … a residual category … that has unity only by default' (Drainville 2005: 900).

Establishing a more open dialogue between ideas potentially encourages new concepts to emerge and further development of key conceptual tools. In Gramscian influenced studies, lines are clearly drawn around a transnational capitalist class engaged in historically bound elaborations of hegemony or *blocco historico* and increasingly around the emergence of counter-hegemonic forces, rarely referred to as global civil society, in response to, for example, the structural crises of over-accumulation, social polarization, and a crisis of legitimacy and authority (Robinson 2005). Further attention has been given to hegemony as it is seen to move from a statist to a transnational or global conception (ibid.). This reverts to 'a more "pure" Gramscian view of hegemony as a form of social domination exercised not by states but by social groups and classes operating through states and other institutions' (Robinson 2005: 3). This focus facilitates further discussion on transnational capitalist class formation and a corresponding discussion on counter-hegemony. It identifies three sectors within counter-hegemony to comprise: an anti-globalist Far Right; progressive elites and nationalist groups in Third World countries; and popular sectors worldwide as represented by the global justice movement (ibid.: 571). Global civil society, as I conceive it in this book, does not adopt a similar sectoral approach, but is considered part of an inclusive ontology which does not differentiate between the worlds of world politics and social movements. This is in agreement with Walker who refutes the insistence by the 'canonical traditions of modern political theory' that 'a serious politics requires that temporality and movement must be tamed upon the certain ground of spatial form' (Walker 1994: 143). Furthering this, and reflecting my concern with hegemony, is a parallel critique of statist conceptions of hegemony which are borne out in the transnational class school of thought but which all too often represent an end point of analysis leaving to the side much of the hard work on conceptualizing counter-hegemony (cf. Peet 2007). From the viewpoint of the politics of resistance, global civil society offers insight to modes of social relation towards the global political economy and is configured close to a conception of transversal hegemony upon which the challenges of spatial form are placed. This nature of critique calls attention to the potential contributions of Foucault to a critical Global Political Economy perspective on transversal hegemony.

Transversal hegemony: dialogue and knowledge

Alongside the proliferation of concepts and approaches that have emerged in recent times, the continued relevance of Gramscian Marxism is reaffirmed in this section through exploring the capacity of critical theory to draw on broad influences in an elaboration of thought that is open to intellectual and cross-disciplinary influences. This is centred on the proposition that the provisional and approximate nature of knowledge formation lays claim to silences (Thompson 1978: 235). This is the case both for post-structural silences on Marx and capital (Laffey 2010) and Gramscian silences on knowledge and power in relation to hegemony and civil society. In response to the 'impoverishment of political imagination' (Ashley 1984: 296) which affects contemporary conceptualizations of global civil society and hegemony, a more open form of investigation and critique acknowledges the principle of 'developing knowledge' and attempts to 'interrogate the real silences, through the dialogue of knowledge' (Thompson 1978: 380, 242, 359).

This form of dialogue co-exists with earlier conversations between traditional Marxism and historical materialism and the later emergence of a series of (neo-)Gramscian approaches. 'Open Marxism', for example, continues to exist in dialogue with traditional forms of Marxism and, in this sense, continues to play a role in eschewing reductionism, economism and ahistoricism whilst, to varying degrees, retaining Marxist insights and traditions (cf. Drainville 1994). Meanwhile, critical research acknowledges the significance of Foucault's concept of power (e.g. Gill 1993, 1995, 2008; de Goede 2003, 2006). Certain insights on hegemony from authors such as Stuart Hall and Ernesto Laclau (in addition to focusing on Gramscian concepts such as Caesarism and *trasformismo*) have also been used to transcend what is considered to be the narrow Coxian methodological framework (Worth 2008). Gill uses certain ideas from Foucault 'but repositions them within an historical materialist framework to sketch a model of power that is able to account for those who are included and those who are excluded or marginalized in the global political economy' (Gill 2003: 122). Many of these dialogues are useful towards considering further conceptual and concrete applications of civil society and hegemony.

It is increasingly apparent that critical Global Political Economy perspectives have much to learn from dialogue with recent post-structural interventions on rethinking the politics of dissent that have been described as 'perhaps the most controversial, but perhaps also the most promising, poststructural intervention[s] in the study of the global political economy' (de Goede 2006: 11). Considered in this section in further detail below, there is an openness towards considering post-structural avenues where certain points of juncture are sought through focusing on shared concerns with 'power, knowledge, and the construction of the subject' (Eschle 2005) and on the particular contributions of Foucault to reinvigorate critical conceptualization (Amoore and Langley 2004; Amoore 2005; Jessop and Sum 2006). This discussion takes places amidst recognition of points of disjuncture between Gramscian and post-structural approaches and clear signals of the presence of 'alternative and incompatible traditions' therein (Thompson 1978: 357). However, as the advancements that resulted from earlier dialogue within Marxism and, specifically, the polemic between 'scientific structural' and 'humanist' Marxism has shown (e.g. Thompson 1978), opening discussion between structural Gramscian and post-structural approaches may have potentially progressive analytical consequences. The remainder of this chapter follows an exploratory path in considering Foucault's concern with power alongside Gramscian 'transversal' hegemony. Through the dialogue of knowledge, analytical advances and tensions are considered to contribute to a critical interrogation of the 'settled boundaries and concepts of Global Political Economy' (de Goede 2006), while also reinvigorating a critical Gramscian approach.

Crossovers: power and global civil society

Positive areas of crossover coexist with clear points of disjuncture between approaches. Prominent among disjuncture is the often juxtaposed emphasis on discourse, identity, culture and diffused power on the one hand, and the study of real material inequality and global capitalism on the other hand (de Goede 2006). Thus, it is sometimes suggested that 'surely it is time for postmodern and poststructural thinkers to "get real", to accept the bare materiality at the centre of serious political life, and to assign discourse its proper place in the realm that is "ideal", or "merely cultural"' (Amoore 2006: 258).[3] Each form of scholarship has its own sets of conventions, norms and commonsense understandings that enable self-identification and reproduction but these can also be disabling in setting restrictions and incurring silences. Laffey, for example, refers to the restricting influence of 'protocols, inheritances and exemplars … [on] what can be thought about and how' (Laffey 2010: 100). While these lines are not always clearly demarcated, the lack of substantial dialogue between approaches and their tendency towards opposition, does not easily facilitate a dialogue of knowledge. Thus, examples where this has occurred are illustrative and, in some cases, similarities between approaches can also be pointed towards. One example, expanded upon in this section in relation to their application of Foucault, is Amoore and Langley's (2004, 2005) discussion on the ambiguities of global civil society. Partly, this makes Gramscian accounts conspicuous for their persistent silences and lack of analysis on global civil society. When considered within the dialectical nexus, their interrogation of the silences of Gramscian GPE adds substance to the presence and absence of subjects within global civil society in addition to its subjective constitution. However, the ambiguities of global civil society, situated in an analytics of power, are nonetheless problematic for Gramscian Marxism.

Underwriting the politics of dissent is the tenet that where there is power there is resistance and that power has positive effects in constituting subjects (Poster 2001): 'In the relations of power, there is necessarily the possibility of resistance, for if there were no possibility of resistance ... there would be no relations of power' (Foucault 1987: 12). If this is often the starting point of the politics of dissent, power is further considered as a process: 'power is not an institution, and not a structure; neither is it a certain strength we are endowed with; it is the name that one attributes to a complex strategical situation in a particular society' (Foucault 1980: 93, cited in Flyvbjerg 2001: 117). Civil society cannot then simply rise up and challenge because it is itself inscribed with the same relations of power that run though states, organizations and markets. So while, for example, the success of women's movements to effect political transformation in former communist Europe is noted, so also is the later displacement of risk onto women and migrant workers (Amoore and Langley 2005: 152). This is close to Foucault's consideration that 'power comes from below and does not contain a general ordering principle: "both the dominant and dominated enter into relations of power which none of them control in a simple, absolute way"' (Flyvbjerg 2001: 121).

The contradictory nature of both the discourse and practices of global civil society is also highlighted: 'that is, they simultaneously exclude, control and discipline, even as they hold out the potential for resistance' (Amoore and Langley 2005: 138). Global civil society is recognized as an ambiguous, contradictory and contestable site of governance and power. Consequently, claims to speak on behalf of a collective 'we' are critiqued for ignoring workers on the margins of the global political economy and other more 'silent resistances' or the existence even of multiple global civil societies (Amoore 2006). Amoore and Langley (2005), in particular, critically address the presentation of social movements as somehow outside or below power—as intrinsically counter-hegemonic or emancipatory or part of a power-free global civil society that is unconcerned with its claim on power. As a result, within power-free global civil society, strategies to determine who is being included and excluded are neglected (Eschle 2005: 23). This has led poststructuralists to highlight the differentiated 'politics of power' in global civil society, that is its inherent inequalities and conflict or power relations: 'We wish to bring our concerns with power relations to front and centre by reconsidering GCS as precisely a site of government—as a place where the global political economy is shaped, regulated or deregulated, disciplined or sustained' (Amoore and Langley 2005: 147). As a site of government, however, global civil society is not bound by 'clearly defined structures of power' and may play an ambiguous role in economic change and forms of governance. Foucault, for example, emphasized the importance of process over structure: 'power must be understood as a multiplicity of force relations ... power is the process, which via struggles and confrontations transforms, supports, or reverses these force relations' (Flyvbjerg 2001: 120). Expanding on their observations, Amoore and Langley borrow Foucault's notion of governmentality or 'governance from a distance' which acts to re-politicize private decisions. While governmentality moves towards re-politicization this does not mean 'that GCS is simply synonymous with the governing of the latest (neo-liberal, global) stage of bourgeois capitalism, far from it. Rather, spaces of GCS would be treated as ambiguous, open to contestation and often contradictory' (Amoore and Langley 2005: 148).

In their application of Foucauldian power to global civil society and resistance, Amoore and Langley attempt to move beyond limited forms of critique through seeking to 'reopen areas of the GCS debate that ... have been prematurely closed down' (Amoore and Langley 2004: 90; Amoore and Langley 2005). Their succinct post-structural interpretation of global civil society in relation to power is instructive for studies on global contestation not only because it serves to reopen areas of debate but also because it does not assume the analytical distinctiveness of resistance, power and global order (cf. Coleman and Tucker 2011: 400). From this point of view, these authors respond to conceptual and disciplinary silences on the all too often taken-for-granted nature of civil society, power and counter-power and also confront their implicit ambiguities. For Gramscian Marxism, however, this presents the dual challenge of considering areas for debate that have been prematurely closed down while maintaining conceptual relevance.

This is not without some manner of instruction from post-structuralism. In view of the binary tendency of some more mechanical applications of hegemony and counter-hegemony, the problematization by Foucault of 'a clear and unambiguous divide between domination and resistance' is helpful towards considering not just a conceptualization of the 'Great Refusal' but, in addition, the 'plurality of resistances' (cf. Amoore 2005: 14). The post-structural emphasis on difference or diversity clearly contrasts with the radical Left's strategic preoccupation with achieving unity among social forces. Sanbonmatsu (2004) suggests that the 'expressivist bias' in post-structural thought has led to the 'mystification of actual social relations' to the detriment of political strategy. Michel Foucault is named as the 'poststructuralist critic whose broad attack on all varieties of strategic political thought ... has done the most damage to the radical tradition' (ibid.: 15). The degree of impairment to the 'radical tradition', however, is somewhat overstated. There are, for example, clear problems with a Gramscian focus on the contemporary possibility of a unified counter-hegemonic global civil society to engage in a sustained war of position. In relation to the World Social Forum, as discussed in Chapter 5, the strategy of 'convergence' presents clear difficulties by facilitating forms of elitism, silencing absent or less obtrusive voices, and 'giving imaginary coherence to practices of resistance' (Drainville 2005: 900). Enabling the cultivation of appropriate conditions for political agency rests on dealing with diversity and recognizing the 'gridding' of ambiguities (Drainville 2004) as a common response, often seen, for example, in civic-consensual and other modes of social relation in and towards the global political economy. Amoore (2006) is centrally concerned with the ways in which ambiguities are 'gridded' and delineated in normal discourse and is critical of attempts to drown out marginal voices. Instead, more meaning is found in the 'out of place' or 'least obtrusive moments of dissent' (Amoore 2006: 260).[4] However, a focus on dissent also makes more apparent the tension between this approach and that concerned with modes of social relation. Contestation at the World Social Forum is gridded through a much more integral notion of modes of social relation, not least discursive and less obtrusive, but also in a structural and historical 'placed' context. The strategy of convergence, in this context, in addition to 'open space' and 'movement', does not negotiate the construction and position of global civil society at the site of the World Social Forum.

This discussion brings into focus an important consideration: that actors in global civil society may come together and act in common at moments of contestation, but 'this doesn't mean that their interests are really similar, that they could survive a series of divisive tactical concessions, or that they could agree on a concrete, positive political program towards global democracy' (Brown and Szeman 2005: 377). Thus, even if global civil society represents a sphere of 'willed action' in contrast to arenas of unwilled non-purposive inaction (Baker 2002b: 6; see Chapter 3), this does not suggest that a unified, strategic and purposive form of contestation is in evidence. Hardt and Negri are less convinced of the need for forces of resistance to unite and stress instead 'the ability [of multitude] to act in common without unification', which is summed up in the definition of multitude as 'singularities that act in common' (Hardt and Negri 2005: 379, 105). While this representation brings into view the 'underlying reality of fragmentation and inequality' to which Walker (1988: 104) refers, it nevertheless tends to simplify tendencies towards unity (Laclau 2005: 243, cited in Munck 2007: 134–35) and is not mindful of the processes of negotiation and renegotiation within transversal hegemony. Hardt and Negri neglect to present relations of social power at work in the global political economy as historical and subjective processes—in contra-distinction to automatic and self-sustaining relations—which are fraught with tension and possibilities for change and conflict (Rupert and Solomon 2006: 55–56). Furthermore, in a wider critique of Hardt and Negri's arguments, Laclau (2005: 242) suggests that they mistakenly privilege tactics over strategy, making tactical interventions 'the only game in town' and thus eclipsing politics. This brings into focus the following discussion on 'hegemony, tactics and strategy' and counterpoises the Gramscian emphasis on the inter-action and multiplicity of levels, moments and relations of force to the more static and one-sided privileging of tactics by Hardt and Negri.[5]

Hegemony, tactics and strategy

Transversal hegemony has a quality of reverberation in its incorporation of new areas for debate, relation to the global political imagination, and potential capacity to move from the tendency to 'remain wedded to a rather traditional, state-centric view of class hegemony and domination' and more fully develop 'the full implications of Gramsci's concern with civil society and its role in constituting power and hegemony' (Jessop and Sum 2006: 161). Accordingly, fixed historical periods are not defined by a set configuration of hegemonic and non-hegemonic forces but:

> hegemony comprises of [sic] a multiple set of cultural, social and economic agents that are often complex and contradictory in nature, which serve to construct certain positions and practices in order that they can make consensual 'common sense' of the ideological constraints which characterise hegemony as a whole ([Stuart Hall] 1988: 142, 198–171). In turn these agents move to shape and re-shape the dominant ideology on which a hegemonic relationship is based.
>
> (Worth 2008: 644)

Despite the apparent fluidity of hegemony and its potential to combine influences, ideas, identities, values and interests, hegemonic projects can tend towards exclusivity and are not necessarily representative of class, gender, ethnicity or race (Rupert 2003):

> The gaps between discourses and practices at the microlevel open up spaces for alternative conceptions of society and counter hegemonic subjectivities. Likewise, at the macrolevel, the very selectivity of hegemonic projects means that some identities and interests are excluded and suppressed.
>
> (Jessop and Sum 2006: 170)

An extension of this recognition can be achieved through consideration of Gramscian power within relations of coercion and consent and the formation and negotiation of hegemony throughout civil society, educational systems, families and in the practices of everyday life (Holab 1992: 197). Gramsci's concept of hegemony, thus understood, 'attempts to grasp the power relations in the interstices of everyday life' and lends itself to 'probing relations of domination' (ibid.). If Gramsci was capable of 'forgetting ... one of his own powerful analytical tools in the demystification of power: the ubiquitous operations of hegemony' (ibid.), (neo-)Gramscians might stand so accused. In the realm of an uneasy dialogue between structural and post-structural understandings on power, our analytical tools for understanding hegemony are sharpened through openness to transversality.

A further example demonstrates how broader deference to post-structuralism more generally can work to bring interaction back to Gramsci in a way that reveals and builds on the intricacies, inter-linkages and inter-textual nature of hegemony. This can be seen in relation to *The Practice of Everyday Life* (de Certeau 2002), which puts forward a theory of strategy and tactics (Jessop and Sum 2006: 171). Strategy, in this case, is operated continuously and legitimately by dominant social forces. Tactics, meanwhile, take place on the 'outside', in the practice of everyday life looking for weak points to secure transient victories. It is suggested that this theory can help to reveal the tension across hegemonic and counter-hegemonic power: 'Hegemony is necessarily produced and reproduced in everyday transactions. Their production and reproduction depend on complex interlinkages and intertextualities across different sites and scales of economic, political, and social organization' (Jessop and Sum 2006: 173). A close examination of Gramsci's writing, which follows, reveals a similar construction of strategy and tactics.

Thus, Gramsci's elaboration of the three relations of force (social, political and military) in conjunction with temporal distinctions reveals comparable aspects of strategy and tactics (Gramsci 1971: 180–84). In Gramsci's text, 'situation' relates to strategy and more permanent organic movements, while conjuncture relates to 'tactics' and more immediate conjunctural movements. Gramsci makes clear that any rupture in the equilibrium of forces is in response to oscillation between these relations of force on the basis of conflict, not merely on the economic or more immediate plane, but on higher planes of conflict such as may relate to power, autonomy or independence. Continual movement between the three relations is placed by Gramsci as an analysis primarily of 'situation' that relates to strategy. Strategy is counterpoised to the study of conjuncture that 'is more closely linked to immediate politics, to "tactics" and agitation' (ibid.: 177, note 79). In parallel, Gramsci's consideration of more permanent organic movements and immediate conjunctural movements suggests that he recognized the existence of a variety of levels and degrees of intensity: 'various moments and levels' (ibid.: 180). Organic movements, for example, contrast with the 'incessant and persistent' efforts of the conjunctural opposition (ibid.: 178). They are composed of 'wider social groupings', give rise to 'socio-historical criticism' and have long-lasting historical significance (ibid.). Nonetheless, despite appearances, '[t]he dialectical nexus between the two categories of movement, and therefore of research, is hard to establish precisely' and a 'common error in historico-political analysis consists in an inability to find the correct relation between what is organic and what is conjunctural' (ibid.). This account provides further understanding on modes of social relation within a temporal, historical and transversal hegemony. It is here also that the balance between Scholte's account of civil society and neo-Polanyian accounts is separated by two methodological poles—one which overestimates mechanical causes and another which exaggerates the voluntarist and individual element, but each of which shapes the concept of global civil society.

> [T]he second wave of critical approaches toward globalisation makes an important contribution to our understanding of globalization firstly by challenging some of the prevalent myths about it and, second, in emphasising the role of human agency in producing and resisting it.
>
> (Marchand and Runyan 2000: 7)

The prevalent myths referred to in this extract often serve to restrict agency through, for example, the myths that globalization is primarily an economic process and predetermined logic within which human agency has been eliminated. While Gramscian approaches certainly address the question of agency by referring to the emergence of a self-conscious agent in the making of history, the nature of a self-conscious active resistance can be overwhelmed by neo-Polanyian influences. Returning the focus to hegemony, tactics and strategy demystifies modes of social relation and more clearly allows for an assessment of concrete strategic difficulties. Amoore and Langley (2004), returning to the above point from a conceptual viewpoint, indicate the 'silences' of Gramscian approaches but also underline the ambiguities, tensions and contradictions within dominant conceptualizations and representations of 'global civil society'. Doing so does not seek to muddy the waters of counter-hegemonic formations with stories of fragmentation and micro-resistances but, rather, can be considered to move Gramscian approaches from a priori assumptions of 'willed action' towards a conceptual grounding that deals with the formation, negotiation and re-negotiation of *transversal* hegemony *and* the significant role of historical subjects therein. This recovers the notion of the historical subject or human agency, rejects neo-Gramscian tendencies towards privileging unity and the automatic rise of agency, and stresses 'history as process' whereby 'every choice and every institution is still to be made' (Thompson 1978: 354). A dialectical understanding of self-conscious agency in the making of history, thus, precedes celebrations of an instrumental or emancipatory global civil society, or even allusions to 'a collegial coordination of different groups spanning international civil society' (Breiner 2006: 171).[6]

However, recent post-structural and critical interventions in GPE, such as the suggestion that more attention should be paid to political agency (Eschle and Maiguashca 2007), contribute to a reformulated perspective on civil societal modes of relation to the global political economy. This argument leaves aside the above discussion on resistance as unified or fragmented and underlines, instead, continual processes of negotiation and renegotiation within transversal forms of hegemony. This moves discussion from primarily instrumental considerations of the form, potential and size of resistance movements—such as the continually re-emphasized exponential growth of the World Social Forum by forum organizers—towards a consideration of the existence of a multiplicity of levels and relations of force (Gramsci 1971).[7] The meaning of hegemony is renegotiated in response to the perception supported by neorealist and critical theorists alike that hegemony is a 'top-down relation imposed on subordinate states, classes or groups' (Davies 1999: 3), as explained further in the following extract:

Such approaches [neorealist and critical] cannot explain the variety of political and cultural responses to international relations on the part of subaltern groups, and thus do not properly examine the conditions for hegemony or its dissolution: do not properly understand hegemony to be a form of struggle.

(Davies 1999: 3)

This further confirms the assertion by 'cultural' political economists Jessop and Sum (2006: 161) that the Italian School fails to develop the full implications of Gramsci's concern with civil society—especially as it relates to hegemony and gives greater meaning to examining the nexus of social relations between globalization and contestation, rather than privileging top-down or bottom-up perspectives (cf. Drainville 2004).

The dialectical interaction of concept and reality, such as demonstrated through an emphasis on 'constituting global civil society', can benefit from the more explicit integration of insights from Gramsci and Foucault. Conceptually, an approach suggested by Sum (2009) indicates that Foucault may be used by Gramscian approaches as an *'entrypoint* for understanding discursive aspects of subject formation and techniques of subjectivation', while retaining the importance of social, and material, relations. In return, deference to structural historical materialism provokes more intense connection to the 'unsuspected complexities' and strands, events, persons, ideas, contexts and circumstances that have an effect on developing political consciousness (Thompson 1963: 73). Theory adapts to reflect changing realities so that social structure and agency can be integral.

Place and positionality

Further to the above focus on transversal hegemony, understanding global politics as 'placed politics' facilitates dialogue between Foucauldian power and Gramscian hegemony in order to bring the nebulous practices of power to rest on placed locations in the global political economy. Focusing on 'situated practices' allows for consideration of the making of transnational subjects and encourages openness towards the prospects for more radical possibilities to emerge from transversal hegemony. This is related to the 'dialectics of presence' and works that 'look critically into global power as a relational, contingent and situated arrangement' (Drainville 2004: 32). From a critical feminist perspective, but in common with this approach, Marchand (2003: 149; Marchand 2000) contributes to the globalization-contestation nexus through the 'politics of location' and the notion of 'positionality' to enable recognition of not only 'the contextual and embedded nature of ... resistances' but also of the fluctuating positionality of men and women in the global economy as key factors in informing resistance practices. Counter-hegemony is constantly negotiated and re-negotiated according to this perspective: 'resistances are as much structured by global restructuring as resistance are structuring global restructuring' (ibid.).

The spatial qualities of Gramsci's philosophy of praxis can also be considered in relation to the notion of positionality that is put forward here. While the particular 'spatio-temporal' approach that Gramsci adopted is clear in many of his key concepts (historical bloc, hegemonic bloc), his 'interest in place, space and scale' is also apparent in the analysis of uneven development between North and South (Jessop 2005: 424). The bounded site of space is where interactions among social forces take place. This site has 'temporal depth' so that in addition to its contemporary relevance to everyday life, it is also bound up with collective memories and social identities. The constraints of the boundaries of space are present in the privileging of some identities and interests over others, but these boundaries are also beneficial in facilitating wider connections. Taking the above points into account, 'the naming, delimitation and meaning of places are always contested and changeable and the coordinates of any given physical space can be connected to a multiplicity of places with different identities, spatio-temporal boundaries and social significance' (ibid.: 424). This does not detract, however, from the concrete positioning of contestation on the terrain of the global political economy as indicated by the studies of the World Social Forum and World People's Conference on Climate Change.

In the context of this book, positionality interacts with boundary (re)negotiations and can be conceptualized as a way to overcome the contradictory strategies of 'gridding' and recontextualization through opening the way towards dialogue on transversal hegemony and the boundaries between globalization and contestation, local and global, public and private and also to the recognition of the variety of levels and degrees of force through which resistance acts: 'It is exactly around the rearticulations and negotiations of these boundaries as well as at their interstices that resistances occur' (Marchand 2003: 149). This further emphasizes the relational, contingent and situated nature of global power. When the politics of location is applied to the World Social Forum, encouragement towards the convergence of social movements and the principle 'defining' debates conducted and fuelled by key WSF actors and convenors, as examined in Chapter 5, suggest a 'gridding' or delimiting of space in both physical and virtual terms. Thus, protests and demonstrations at the Nairobi WSF circled the enclosed space of the Moi International Sports Centre in Kasarani on the outskirts of Nairobi while opposition was contained within the 'alternative' forum held by the People's Parliament in Jeevanjee Gardens in Nairobi 15 kilometres away. Meanwhile, manifestos and appeals circulate through electronic mailing lists.[8] There is a continuing dialectics between the concept and reality of global civil society and the potential for finding the more radical possibilities that can emerge from a concrete interrogation of real lived experience and modes of social relations alongside the dialogue of knowledge.

Considering the above, a dialogue of knowledge that is concerned with positioning might be located outside the sameness/difference binary (Western/ non-Western) and within 'conversations between multiple, fractured self-identities, which acknowledge the imperfect and provisional nature of the insights that they generate' (Hutchings 2011: 647). Otherwise what is likely to result is the 'geopolitical relocation of a disciplinary hegemony' (ibid.) that might, for example, privilege a Southern, Latin American perspective on contestation. Global civil society, although critiqued as a Western construct, is implicated in models for dialogue with non-Western voices as 'Mother

Earth' and '*buen vivir*' enter the discourse of global contestation. Even if this is not yet the case, it does point to specific engagement between differing ways of thinking on various issues. In this way, emphasis is placed on including excluded voices rather than ensuring that Latin American voices are included. In the context of global contestation and the World Social Forum, in any form of move towards a 'new politics' the voices of the academy might be seen as 'participants in dialogic exchange oriented towards the expansive transformation of disciplinary imaginaries' (ibid.; Smith *et al.* 2008).

Conclusions

The 'telling silence' of dissident scholarship for neglecting capital and Marx, despite the presence of both in the otherwise formative writings of Richard Ashley and Michel Foucault, has been recently considered (Laffey 2010: 997). Thus, the production of post-structural silences in the 1980s has had negative impacts for dissident scholarship. My concern, meanwhile, is with the possibilities of recent post-structural interventions in GPE to shed light onto the silences of Gramscian scholarship. Through their aim to provide a critical interrogation of disciplinary boundaries and concepts, recent interventions impinge on Gramscian scholarship to make it more aware of its own silences, particularly concerning the politics of resistance. Initiating a dialogue of knowledge between approaches serves to emphasize the developing and provisional nature of knowledge construction from wherein the real silences of theory emerge. Their production makes it difficult for analysis of the 'worlding of theory, the ways in which theory is not only in the world but in important ways is also constitutive of it' (Laffey 2010: 991).

Global civil society, when placed within the dialogue of knowledge, negotiates the boundaries between 'mechanical' and 'voluntarist', 'empirical' and 'normative' (Gramsci 1971; Helleiner 2001). Drawing attention to conceptualizations of agency, power and place, addresses some key criticisms of Gramscian approaches for distinguishing between material and ideological modes of power but then going on to privilege the former (Maiguashca 2006: 251). Global civil society might then be understood to be one of many sites within which 'struggles over wealth, power, and knowledge are taking place' (cf. Murphy 2000: 799).[9] It is a primary political site which is permeated by relations of inequality, power and conflict. It is also open to contestation at a variety of temporal levels from the permanent to the immediate, and at a variety of relations of force, which oscillate between the social, political and military.

In critically locating silences the aim of this chapter has a negative undertone but, in the spirit of Ashley's attack on 'the poverty of neorealism', my argument has a positive aspect 'in its implications for an approach that would be better' (Ashley 1984: 228). In this spirit, I examine the prospects for a critical interrogation of the silences surrounding the dialogue between material and ideational knowledge. This raises again the 'spectre of Althusserian structural

Marxism' (Drainville 1994: 108; Laffey 2004: 466) and seeks to focus on, for the benefit of further contemporary analysis on the politics of resistance, a conversation on structuralism and post-structuralism in Global Political Economy. Deference to the vocabulary we use incorporates its dialectical meaning so that even in its 'sense as ideology' it is understood to be born from the 'pressure of real experience' (Thompson 1978; Chapter 2 in this book). Instituting a dialogue of knowledge is not an attempt to achieve a synthesis between Gramscian material and post-structural ideational knowledge construction. Rather, it reflects a call for reflexivity and much deeper attention to the usage of vocabularies with which to further theory and practice in Global Political Economy.

Notes

1 See the fourth section of Amoore (2005), which focuses on cultures of resistance, including a piece by Bleiker. See also, Worth and Kuhling (2004), who draw on Gramsci and Laclau and Mouffe to put forward an examination of culture and resistance movements in IPE.

2 Maiguashca (2006: 250) makes this point in relation to the re-articulation of women's reproductive rights through global United Nations forums—the absence of an ideological struggle ensures the continued prevailing of the neo-Malthusian population paradigm that focuses on top-down, donor-imposed models of family planning in an effort to bring down population levels as demonstrated in the failure to consider issues such as women's right to abortion, social and economic inequalities, neoliberal market-oriented programmes, or to redirect funds from traditional family planning services focusing on contraceptives and sterilization to AIDS, sexual health and education.

3 Laclau and Mouffe, on the other hand, do not see any reason for incompatibility between both approaches, and argue that in fact post-modernism achieves the emancipatory potential of Marxism by moving from a totalizing vision and recognizing both the limitations and contributions of emancipatory action (Amoore 2006; Daly 1999).

4 This reflects a concern with avoiding the reproduction of a discourse of them/us, a process Amoore (2006) finds reflected in the reproduction of the 'with or without us' discourse by the 'great refusal' of the globalizing post-9/11 world to recognize marginal voices.

5 Sanbonmatsu (2009), for example, critiques the wider Left for confusing tactics for strategy.

6 Breiner (2006) refers here to the post-modern prince, or 'coalescence of the "different" movements' posited by Sanbonmatsu (2004: 19).

7 This approach has much in common with the objective of Marchand (2000) to focus on boundary (re)negotiation between the 'state and market, global and local, national and international, public/semipublic/private/semi-private spheres or spaces'.

8 These mailing lists include, for example, WSFDiscuss (see www.openspaceforum. net/mailman/listinfo/worldsocialforum-discuss_openspaceforum.net) and Critical Engagement with Open Space (CEOS) (see www.openspaceforum.net/twiki/tiki-index.php?page=CEOSProcessIntroLetter).

9 It should be noted that Murphy (2000) is here referring to global governance rather than global civil society.

8 Conclusions

Global civil society and the global political imagination

In this book, I have argued for a re-conceptualization of global civil society which, through the dialectics of concept and reality, comes to terms with the deep-rooted challenges invoked by global transformation. The four principal strands of this argument rest on a sequence of chapters focusing on alter-globalization, contesting global governance, the World Social Forum (WSF) and the World People's Conference on Climate Change (WPCCC), each of which demonstrates how contemporary conceptual challenges relate to global civil society and transversal hegemony. In the case of the World Social Forum, for example, I combined critical literature evaluation and observer participation at the Nairobi WSF in 2007 to point towards the conceptual neglect of global civil society as scholars, activists and its varied constituents move between rejecting its conceptual usefulness and celebrating its instrumental, transformative and emancipative potential. Most importantly, these studies draw attention to the making of global civil society by scholars, policy makers, officials and activists through their definitions, analogies, metaphors, images and conceptualizations. These studies also situate global civil society in concrete, substantive locations at the WSF and WPCCC which are visualized as terrains from which participants engage in various modes of social relations in and towards the global political economy. This disrupts the dual characterization of hegemony which automatically centres hegemony 'on a logic of replication and passive revolution' such as associated with the World Economic Forum, and counter-hegemony 'on a logic of prefiguration and transformation' such as associated with the World Social Forum (Carroll 2007: 36). I highlight the continual negotiation and renegotiation of the boundaries, interactions and interstices within 'transversal' hegemony at the World Social Forum so that contestation is not reified to predominant logics of prefiguration and transformation. The dialectical nexus between concept and reality, in turn, reconfigures contemporary conceptualizations of global civil society while drawing on critical Global Political Economy and more fully integrating insights from, amongst others, Gramsci (1971), Cox (1999, 2002), Thompson (1963, 1978) and Drainville (2004, 2012). The dialectical nexus potentially enables critical re-conceptualizations of civil society and hegemony and responds to the changing realities under contestation in the global political economy. In this final chapter, I will briefly summarize and indicate the main contributions of this study on global civil society and transversal hegemony.

Reluctance to conceptualize Gramscian civil society more fully and extend its application in Global Political Economy can partly be attributed to the inconsistent and varying nature of references to civil society in the *Prison Notebooks* (Gramsci 1971). An early and formative contribution by Germain and Kenny (1998) which disputed the possibility of 'internationalizing' civil society has left its imprint on the development of Gramscian GPE. A conceptual analysis of the history of civil society in Chapter 3 found that many applications downplay central insights on its position as a political and ideological realm. Gramsci's civil society, for example, takes on a 'prophetic quality' as the antithesis to the despotic communist state. Reduced to a sphere of 'unwilled action' (Pearce 1997), this weak attribution of agency to Gramscian civil society continues to evade the realm of politics in favour of a 'third sector' position in contradistinction to the state and market. Further applications, drawing on Cox (1999) and Gill (2008), more specifically underline its dual role in stabilizing and reproducing existing social orders and as a potential agent of transformation. The dialectics of concept and reality (Cox 1999), in its application to the dialectical nexus proposed by Gramsci (1971) and to the conceptualization of global civil society in this book, seeks to draw on neo-Gramscian 'sensitivity to the importance of morals, values and ideas ... by elevating consciousness and the formation of subjectivity to the status of a major analytical concern' (Kenny and Germain 2005: 7). However, it also seeks to extend our contemporary understanding of global civil society as it engages in creative modes of social relation in and towards the global political economy.

There is, then, a lacuna in critical Gramscian approaches to resistance in Global Political Economy—civil society and hegemony have thus far been poorly adjusted to the changing political realities of change and contestation in the global political economy—but this does not preclude the potential of further conceptual inquiry. The critical political economy of resistance in this book draws on the analytical potential of civil society and hegemony to narrow the gap between the 'normative promise' of studies on contestation and the 'empirical realities' experienced by civil society on the terrain of the global political economy (cf. Helleiner 2001). Drawing on wider developments in social science, the isolation of some key features of critical globalization studies (Mittelman 2005) and innovations in international studies (Gill and Mittelman 1997)—including reflexivity, rigorous historical thinking, decentring, crossovers and strategic transformations—is partly instructive. These enable a more effective analysis of the shortcomings and merits of conceptualizations of global civil society, and reflection on Gramscian usages of the term and avenues for its wider usefulness beyond the realm of prophecy or interregnum. Absolute historicism, additionally, returns to the Gramscian text and time to reconsider the dialectical nexus in an era of globalization and contestation within which global civil society is deeply embedded. This signals a shift from an almost exclusive focus on elite-driven hegemony and counter-hegemony 'from below', to consideration of key processes involved in the negotiation and renegotiation of a transversal interpretation of hegemony. This leads me to take up the post-structural and wider critical theoretical concern with the language of binaries and dissatisfaction with exemplars such as globalization/ contestation and hegemony/counter-hegemony. My approach differs in consolidating the potential of the dialectical nexus to locate more sufficiently the substantive materiality of modes of social relation in the global political economy. Recognizing the evident global complexity of overlapping and coinciding connections and layered temporalities and levels of relations of force does not serve merely to add up to contrasting movements of hegemony and counter-hegemony. Rather, it points to real existing social forces engaging in modes of social relation in and towards the global political economy that are not understood apart from intervening stories, myths, analogies, transcripts, images and concepts.

An accumulation of meanings is implicit in conceptualizations of global civil society—discursive, literary, academic, policy oriented—which reflect the subjective interests of those engaged in its construction. The presentation of contrasting academic and, in some cases, scholar activist conceptualizations of global civil society in this book gives some insight into the resulting, conflict-ridden, conceptual terrain occupied by the concept as it is put to a range of instrumental and normative uses. Practices of definition and usage, which might be extended to include the above-mentioned stories, myths, analogies, transcripts and images, contribute to conceptualizations of global civil society and condition possibilities of thought, action and political imagination (cf. Baker 2002b). From a scholarly or academic viewpoint, that to which I am closest, this affirms that 'we have no monopoly on "truth" creation', but should, nonetheless, continue to ask 'ourselves honest questions about our role as knowledge constructors' (Amoore *et al.* 2000: 67). The ambiguities of knowledge construction and clear tensions between empirical reality and academic intent were most clear in Chapter 4 on global governance and constituting global civil society. Civic-consensual and unitary modes of relation, borrowing from Drainville (2004, 2012), give further definition and clarity to processes of knowledge construction in studies on contesting global governance and further underline how knowledge and interests are constitutive of global civil society. Comparable reflections on the socio-political formation and maintenance of 'common sense' as a political arena of struggle have been put forward to illustrate more clearly the boundaries of thought and action (cf. Rupert 2003; Smith 1996). The wider applicability of these concerns is reflected in transdisciplinary debates on the Anglo-American construction of knowledge in varied disciplines from Political Geography (e.g. Power 2010), Sociology (e.g. Connell 2007), to International Relations (e.g. Bilgin 2008).

Just as civil society is delineated, categorized and circumscribed within formal institutions of global governance, it is also drawn as a transformative and emancipative force through neo-Polanyian optimism. Attributing to global civil society an inherently but also overtly normative role reflects an alternative avenue in the history of the concept that diverts somewhat from more functional 'third sector' formulations and emphasizes, instead, the beneficial contributions it can make towards constructing a new world order. However, particularly in the case of the World Social Forum, neo-Polanyian optimism gives insufficient attention to the challenges within modes of contestation such as co-option, hierarchy, inequality, power and strategy. It aligns too easily with representations of spontaneous, axiomatic and often simplified resistance forms and fails to respond to calls for further conceptual clarity, theoretical development and relation to more tangible or substantial aspects of contestation. It highlights collectivity and solidarity but excludes sufficient attention to issues of difference, inequality and fragmentation within global civil society or its constituents. This is not to dispute the many positive insights that Polanyi (1944) offers, but rather to suggest that resistance modes, structures and processes might be considered central rather than ancillary. Thus, the 'analytical triangle' of state, market and civil society is linked to 'our ability to reconstruct, or create, social solidarity, trust and political legitimacy' (Devetak and Higgott 1999: 490).

From this point of view, focusing on global civil society facilitates a broader analysis of hegemony and contestation in the global political economy than global social movements, critical social movements, or the post-modern prince alone. A key benefit of adopting the concept of global civil society is reflected in the broad nature of the term and its capacity to encompass a range of perspectives, actors and processes wherein the nexus between co-option and (re)negotiation might be more fully understood. This brought the focus, in this book, to the interaction between 'global social movements', civil society organizations, non-governmental organizations and international organizations, and to the similarly broad constituents of global civil society at the World Social Forum and World People's Conference on Climate Change. Adopting the concept of global civil society in these disparate contexts drew together a range of competing perspectives and ideas and in doing so facilitated a greater understanding of, for example, processes of *trasformismo* and co-option. Such processes are clarified where global civil society engages in a variety of modes of social relation, from unitary to civic-consensual, in and towards the global political economy.

Emphasizing global social relations through examining modes of social relations engages in a more critical conceptualization of global civil society which perturbs the certainty that counter-hegemony will spontaneously produce an alternative hegemonic model. Thus, representations of the World Social Forum as an articulation of resistance by global civil society does not assure the position of global civil society as an agent for change or assure its capacity to construct or constitute an alternative to neoliberal globalization (see also Worth 2013). Rather, the WSF plays an ambiguous role in contesting globalization. It has an uncertain relationship with both the state and economy, and remains stratified in terms of objectives and composition.

These challenges have manifested themselves through the WSF International Council debates, the unresolved issues of sponsorship and funding, and recent proposals for political programmes to guide the actions of the forum. As demonstrated throughout this book, 'all good things put together do not necessarily add up to [hegemony because] there is no preordained outcome to the politics of hegemony' (Nederveen Pieterse 2001: 78). Thus, the space/ movement debate gives expression to *trasformismo* or to the assimilation of counter-hegemony into dominant conservative or left-oriented objectives, which consequently impacts on emerging forms of contestation. Reference to modes of social relation underlines the need to unsettle assumptions on global civil society and hegemony so that the sum of the varied parts of the WSF cannot be considered to add up to a counter-hegemonic whole.

The challenges that are associated with approaching contestation through conceptualizing global civil society must be clearly acknowledged in a book such as this that argues for continued discussion and re-conceptualization in the context of the dialectical nexus. Some of these challenges relate to delimiting conceptualizations of global civil society which automatically confer it with democratic, transformative, non-state and non-commercial properties. The consequent 'common sense' attributes uncritical and unconscious perceptions and understandings to global civil society and lacks adequate conceptualization. In summary, three main avenues of existing analysis can be delineated: a broad convergence in supporting the transformative capacity of global civil society; other more functional and procedural analyses which emphasize the instrumental usages of global civil society; and lastly, analyses that largely dispute the analytical usefulness of global civil society. The task of a critical perspective on global civil society, in this book, has been to navigate between exaggerated voluntarist and overestimated mechanical accounts while avoiding the shortcomings of both (cf. Gramsci 1971: 178).

I situate this account within calls for an historicist turn and new International Political Economy (NIPE) (Amoore *et al.* 2000; Gills 2000, 2001; Murphy and Tooze 1991), but it is also located within a more prevalent and intensifying critique of the contemporary world order and recognition that while the vocabulary with which to understand continuity and change is proliferating, more needs to be done to capture the dialectical nexus between concept and reality. Partly, this can be achieved through more open consideration of the contributions of other perspectives including post-structuralism and disciplines across the social sciences, while retaining a critical disposition and effectively building on concepts like civil society and hegemony. Thus, a re-conceptualized global civil society is deeply embedded in the economy and society while it is mediated by vying configurations of power. Its 'embeddedness' denotes spatial attributes to global civil society as it moves within the politics of space which threatens to 'grid' its ambiguities. Placing or locating contestation in concrete spaces such as in global civil society and in the World Social Forum enables an examination of limitations and constraints implicit in processes of global restructuring. In addition, evaluating the WSF through a critical conceptualization of global civil society underlines the tenacity of relations of power, inequality and competition. This does not indicate that the focus of analysis is on materiality at the expense of conceptualization. Rather, it is undertaken with a commitment to reflexivity that, broadly explained, combines three dimensions of 'relational thinking':

> This involves understanding the world 'out there' (practices, institutions, structures of social re/production), how we think (meaning systems, ideologies, paradigms), and who we are (subjectivity, agency, self and collective identities) as interacting dimensions of social reality.
>
> (Peterson 1997: 185, cited in Marchand and Runyan 2000: 9)

In attempting to combine the three dimensions of relational thinking in this book, I cannot claim to have captured completely the full potential of how global civil society contributes to our understanding of the world 'out there', how we think and who we are as interacting parts of social reality. Meta-theoretical concern with the motivations and dynamics of contemporary conceptualizations of global civil society are integrated with praxis through studies on contesting global governance, the WSF and WPCCC.

It can be concluded that the literature which deals with contestation to globalization, in its various guises, requires further development. In pointing towards the discontinuity between normative conceptualizations and empirical realities associated with each, the potential of the dialectical nexus can be proposed. Many of the principal themes that have been addressed in this book, such as the critique of neo-Polanyian optimism, are eminently of a conceptual and normative nature. I began by noting that in relation to the question of contestation to globalization, scholars of Global Political Economy notably have neglected to demonstrate the potential conceptual contributions of global civil society. This was confirmed through a conceptual evaluation of studies on global contestation. In relation to the World Social Forum, prevailing forms of neo-Polanyian optimism lead to insufficient responses to the significant organizational and strategic challenges that confront the forum. This precludes an accurate understanding of contestation and the complexities of transversal hegemony. Normative, voluntarist accounts of global civil society avoid 'the empirical difficulties of substantiating the existence and influence of an "actually existing" global civil society' (Chandler 2007: 291), and also negate the 'dialectics of presence' (Drainville 2004). Similarly, however, instrumental, mechanical accounts, in their search for functional efficiency and close reliance on immediate contextual factors, are abstracted from modes of social relation in the global political economy. It can be concluded that normative and instrumental accounts of global civil society serve to abstract civil society from relations of hegemony and limit its usefulness as an analytical instrument with which to discern the global political economy of resistance.

In response to these shortcomings, I sought to put forward a critical per-spective on the global political economy of resistance to demonstrate the strong analytical potential of global civil society, when re-conceptualized, to improve understandings of material, political and ideological change in the global political economy. In seeking to extend a prevailing focus on traditional Gramscian hegemony and counter-hegemony, the concept of transversal hegemony is used to recover the full complexity of its inherent modes of social relation. Within movements of hegemony occurs the 'dialectical nexus' between organic and conjunctural movements, strategy and tactics, and through the concept of transversal hegemony, an ability to locate the inter-linkages and inter-relations of hegemony across temporal and spatial levels, from local to global, and across economic, political and military relations of force. In summary, therefore, replacing the broad dichotomy of hegemony and counter-hegemony with transversal hegemony has a number of positive effects. It demonstrates the complexities of hegemony—its interstices, (re)negotiations and (re)articulations—and resists the 'making' of global civil society as a 'static category' (cf. Thompson 1978: 238) or consensual counter-hegemonic force. It lays bare the exclusivity of certain projects of 'hegemony' and 'counter-hegemony' and, furthermore, counters the continuing 'rationalization of global politics' (Ashley 1984: 228). Lastly, transversal hegemony constitutes a key analytical tool through which modes of social relation within the globalization-contestation nexus are examined.

The positing of a 'nexus' between globalization and contestation acknowledges plural forms of each and places an emphasis on the fragility and junction points between boundaries. From a conceptual viewpoint, the nexus identifies congruent points between traditions and/or points of disjuncture between 'alternative and incompatible traditions' (Thompson 1978: 357). The nexus also emphasizes the meeting points of varying modes of social relation. These may represent unique junctures or 'moment[s] of becoming, of alternative possibilities, of ascendant and descendant forces' (ibid.: 295). A reformulated Gramscian approach towards understanding the globalization-contestation nexus draws, methodologically, on what E.P. Thompson would describe as 'a total history of society in which all other sectoral histories are convened' (ibid.: 262) whose sectoral histories refer to economic, political, or intellectual history or history of labour. In attempting to avoid the 'vocabulary of [scientific] structuralism', broadly applied to identify its core elements across theoretical perspectives in this book, it is worth distinguishing between the apparent co-option and assimilation of reforms and the recognition that these processes are 'still the outcome of human choices and struggles' (ibid.: 265). Thus, from the critique of the structural stasis of fixed concepts and closed systems emerges 'the most profound characteristic of the Marxist dialectic', which underlines 'history as *process*, as open-ended and indeterminate eventuation … in which categories are defined in particular contexts but are continually undergoing historical re-definition, and whose structure is not pre-given but protean, continually changing in form and in articulation' (ibid.: 275–76). A critical global political economy of resistance, drawing on global civil society, counters both uncritical celebrations of its emancipative and instrumental potential and rejections of its conceptual usefulness. The dialectical interactions between the theory and reality of global civil society have a formative and constitutive effect on its making. Our observations, experiences, perceptions and conceptualizations retain a formative influence in the realization of appropriate analytical tools through which to explore the transversal nature of hegemony, the nexus between globalization and contestation, or the 'limits and possibilities of global social relations' (Drainville 2004: 9). This narrows the perceived gap between neo-Polanyian conceptual promise and explicit empirical realities and draws on a normative emphasis on elucidating points of change, or as Gramsci would perhaps propose, on identifying points of rupture in the equilibrium of forces. The role of the analyst, activist or academic is part of this enterprise, a situation that is accurately described as follows: 'We ourselves choose to emphasize the importance and the possibility of *transformative moments* and *emancipatory moments* in social experience', in order to 'identify and understand *transformative conditions* in human history, as well as *emancipatory conditions*' (Amoore *et al.* 2000: 67, emphasis in original). An immense task, therefore, confronts scholars, activists and the varied constituents of the global political economy of resistance to conceptualize resistance in a manner that leads to an accurate explanation of the complexities of movements of transversal hegemony in the global political economy. Understanding the dialectical nexus between the concept and reality of global civil society is crucial towards accomplishing this task.

Bibliography

Abbott, J.P. and Worth, O. (eds) (2002) *Critical Perspectives on International Political Economy*, Basingstoke: Palgrave Macmillan.

Adorno, T.W. and Horkheimer, M. (1944) *Dialectic of Enlightenment*, New York: Continuum.

Agathangelou, A.M. (2012) 'The Living and Being of the Streets: Fanon and the Arab Uprisings', *Globalizations* 9(3): 451–66.

Aguiton, C. and Bullard, N. (2010) 'Defending Mother Earth in Cochabamba', 1 February, m-e-dium.net/articles/post/nico/2010/02/defending-mother-earth-in-cochabamba-by-christophe-aguiton-and-nicola-bullard/ (accessed 10 August 2012).

AIDOH (2007) 'World Social Forum Nairobi 2007: In the Name of God. In Memory of the Victims of Fundamentalism', Art in Defence of Humanism, www.aidoh.dk/new-struct/Happenings-and-Projects/2007/KE/GB-Leaflet.htm (accessed 31 March 2010).

Albert, M. (2011) 'We are the 99%?' *ZNet*, 21 November, www.zcommunications.org/we-are-the-99-by-michael-albert (accessed 10 August 2012).

Alloo, F., Kumar, C., Amin, S., Tandon, Y., Longwe, S., Caruso, G. and Whitaker, C. (2011) 'Another World is Possible: Reflections on the World Social Forum 2011, Dakar', *Development* 54(2): 217–31.

Althusser, L. (2006) *For Marx*, London: Verso.

Althusser, L. and Balibar, E. (2009) *Reading Capital*, London: Verso.

Amin, S. (2005) 'Empire and Multitude', *Monthly Review* 57(6): 4–12.

——(2007a) 'Towards a Fifth International?' in K. Sehm Patomäki and M. Ulvila (eds) *Global Political Parties*, London: Zed Books, 123–43.

——(2007b) 'WSF Nairobi: An Assessment', *Third World Forum*, www.forumtiersmonde.net/fren/index.php?option=com_content&view=article&id=58&Itemid=85 (accessed 10 August 2012).

——(2011) 'Evaluation of the WSF 2011 Dakar', 22 February, www.forumtiersmonde.net/fren/index.php?option=com_content&view=article&id=283:evaluation-of-the-wsf-2011-dakar&catid=64:meetings&Itemid=143 (accessed 10 August 2012).

Amoore, L. (ed.) (2005) *The Global Resistance Reader*, London: Routledge.

——(2006) '"There is no Great Refusal": The Ambivalent Politics of Resistance', in M. de Goede (ed.) *International Political Economy and Poststructural Politics*, London: Palgrave, 255–74.

Amoore, L., Dodgson, R., Germain, R.D., Gills, B.K., Langley, P. and Watson, I. (2000) 'Paths to a Historicized International Political Economy', *Review of International Political Economy* 7(1): 53–71.

Amoore, L., Dodgson, R., Gills, B., Langley, P., Marshall, D. and Watson, I. (1997) 'Overturning Globalisation: Resisting the Teleological, Reclaiming the Political', *New Political Economy* 2(1): 179–96.

Amoore, L. and Langley, P. (2002) 'Process, Project, and Practice? The Politics of Globalisation', in J. Abbott and O. Worth (eds) *Critical Perspectives on International Political Economy*, Basingstoke: Palgrave Macmillan, 58–81.

——(2004) 'Ambiguities of Global Civil Society', *Review of International Studies* 30 (1): 89–110.

——(2005) 'Global Civil Society and Global Governmentality', in R.D. Germain and M. Kenny (eds) *The Idea of Global Civil Society: Politics and Ethics in a Globalizing Era*, Oxfordshire: Routledge, 137–55.

Anand, N. (2004) 'Bound to Mobility: Identity and Purpose at the WSF', in J. Sen, A. Anand, A. Escobar and P. Waterman (eds) *World Social Forum: Challenging Empires*, New Delhi: The Viveka Foundation, 140–47.

Ancelovici, M. (2002) 'Organizing against Globalization: The Case of Attac in France', *Politics and Society* 30: 427–63.

Anderson, P. (1976) 'The Antinomies of Antonio Gramsci', *New Left Review* 100: 5–78.

Andreotti, V. (2005) 'The Other Worlds Educational Project and the Challenges and Possibilities of Open Spaces', *Ephemera: Theory and Politics in Organization* 5 (2): 102–15.

Anheier, H., Glasius, M. and Kaldor, M. (2001) 'Introducing Global Civil Society', in H. Anheier, M. Glasius and M. Kaldor (eds) *Global Civil Society 2001*, Oxford: Oxford University Press, 3–22.

Appelbaum, R.P. and Robinson, W.I. (eds) (2005) *Critical Globalization Studies*, New York: Routledge.

Armstrong, C. (2006) 'Global Civil Society and the Question of Global Citizenship', *Voluntas* 17: 349–57.

Armstrong, K. (2002) 'Rediscovering Civil Society: The European Union and the White Paper on Governance', *European Law Journal* 8: 105–26.

Ashley, R.K. (1984) 'The Poverty of Neorealism', *International Organization* 38 (2): 225–86.

Augelli, E. and Murphy, C. (1988) *America's Quest for Supremacy and the Third World: An Essay in Gramscian Analysis*, London: Pinter.

Axford, B. (2005) 'Critical Globalization Studies and a Network Perspective on Global Civil Society', in R.P. Appelbaum and W.I. Robinson (eds) *Critical Globalization Studies*, New York: Routledge, 187–95.

Ayya (2010) 'Thoughts and Analysis from Cochabamba and Beyond', ayya2cochabamba. wordpress.com/about/ (accessed 10 August 2012).

Baker, G. (1998) 'Civil Society and Democracy: The Gap Between Theory and Possibility', *Politics* 18(2): 81–87.

——(2002a) 'Problems in the Theorisation of Global Civil Society', *Political Studies* 50: 928–43.

——(2002b) *Civil Society and Democratic Theory*, London: Routledge.

Baker, G. and Chandler, D. (eds) (2005) *Global Civil Society: Contested Futures*, New York: Routledge.

Bartelson, J. (2000) 'Three Concepts of Globalization', *International Sociology* 15(2): 180–96.

——(2006) 'Making Sense of Global Civil Society', *European Journal of International Relations* 12(3): 371–95.

——(2011) 'What is Wrong with the World?' *Contemporary Political Theory* 10(2): 290–93.

BBC (2005) 'Fury at Kenya Shoot-to-kill Order', news.bbc.co.uk/2/hi/africa/4374649. stm (accessed 10 April 2010).

——(2006) 'In Pictures: Kenya Press Raid', news.bbc.co.uk/2/hi/in_pictures/4765728. stm (accessed 10 April 2010).

Bello, W. (2000) 'The Struggle for a Deglobalized World', www.corpwatch.org/article. php?id=322 (accessed 7 August 2008).

——(2007) 'The Forum at the Crossroads', *Foreign Policy in Focus*, 4 May, www.fpif. org/fpiftxt/4196 (accessed 10 April 2012).

Bernard, M. (1997) 'Ecology, Political Economy and the Counter-movement: Karl Polanyi and the Second Great Transformation', in S. Gill and J. Mittelman (eds) *Innovation and Transformation in International Studies*, United Kingdom: Cambridge University Press, 75–90.

Bieler, A. and Morton, A.D. (eds) (2001) *Social Forces in the Making of the New Europe: The Restructuring of European Social Forces in the Global Political Economy*, Basingstoke: Palgrave.

Bilgin, P. (2008) 'Thinking Beyond 'Western' IR?' *Third World Quarterly* 29(1): 5–23.

Birchfield, V. (1999) 'Contesting the Hegemony of Market Ideology: Gramsci's "Good Sense" and Polanyi's "Double Movement"', *Review of International Political Economy* 6(1): 27–54.

——(2005) 'José Bové and the Globalisation Countermovement in France and Beyond: A Polanyian Interpretation', *Review of International Studies* 31: 581–98.

Birchfield, V. and Freyberg-Inan, A. (2004) 'Constructing Opposition in an Age of Globalization: The Potential of Attac', *Globalizations* 1(2): 278–304.

——(2005) 'Organic Intellectuals and Counter-hegemonic Politics in the Age of Globalisation: The Case of Attac', in C. Eschle and B. Maiguashca (eds) *Critical Theories, International Relations and 'the Anti-Globalisation Movement'*, New York: Routledge, 154–73.

Bleiker, R. (2000) *Popular Dissent, Human Agency and Global Politics*, Cambridge: Cambridge University Press.

——(2009) *Aesthetics and World Politics*, London: Palgrave Macmillan.

Blynn, K. (2010a) 'Kelly Blynn of 350.org Talks to OneClimate Live from the People's Climate Summit', *350.org*, 22 April, www.350.org/en/about/blogs/video-updates-fresh-bolivia (accessed 10 August 2012).

——(2010b) 'Bolivia and Civil Society Allies Head to the UN, Cochabamba Accord in Hand', *350.0rg*, www.350.org/en/node/16713 (accessed 10 August 2012).

Böhm, S., Sullivan, S. and Reyes, O. (2005) 'The Organisation and Politics of Social Forums', *Ephemera: Theory and Politics in Organization* 5(2): 98–101.

Bond, P. (2005) 'Gramsci, Polanyi and Impressions from Africa on the Social Forum Phenomenon', *International Journal of Urban and Regional Research* 29(2): 433–40.

——(2006) 'Civil Society on Global Governance: Facing Up to Divergent Analysis, Strategy and Tactics', *Voluntas* 17(4): 357–69.

——(2010) 'The World Social Forum', in R. Taylor (ed.) *Third Sector Research*, New York: Springer, 327–36.

——(2011) 'From Copenhagen to Cancún to Durban: Moving Deckchairs on the Climate Titanic', *Capitalism Nature Socialism* 22(2): 3–26.

Bond, P. and Dorsey, M.K. (2010) 'Anatomies of Environmental Knowledge and Resistance: Diverse Climate Justice Movements and Waning Eco-neoliberalism', *Journal of Australian Political Economy* 66: 286–316.

Boucher, D. (1998) *Political Theories of International Relations*, Oxford: Oxford University Press.

Brasset, J. (2011) 'After Walker', *Contemporary Political Theory* 10(2): 291–93.

Brecher, J. (2011) 'The 99 Percent Organize Themselves', *The Nation*, 4 November, www.thenation.com (accessed 10 April 2012).

Breiner, P. (2006) 'Book review of "The Postmodern Prince: Critical Theory, Left Strategy, and the Making of a New Political Subject"', *Political Theory* 4(1): 170–71.

Brien, Y., Cutler, A. and Russell, B. (2010) 'Summit Difference', *New Internationalist* 433, www.newint.org/features/2010/06/01/cochabamba-climate-summit/ (accessed 10 August 2012).

Brincat, S. (2010) 'Towards a Social-relational Dialectic for World Politics', *European Journal of International Relations* 17(4): 679–703.

Broad, R. and Heckscher, Z. (2003) 'Before Seattle: The Historical Roots of the Current Movement Against Corporate-led Globalisation', *Third World Quarterly* 24(4): 713–28.

Bromley, S. (1995) 'Rethinking International Political Economy', in J. Macmillan and A. Linklater (eds) *Boundaries in Question: New Directions in International Relations*, London: Pinter, 228–43.

Brown, N. and Szeman, I. (2005) 'What is the Multitude? Questions for Michael Hardt and Antonio Negri', *Cultural Studies* 19(3): 372–87.

Buckley, K. (2013) 'Global Civil Society: The Dialectics of Concept and Reality', *Globalizations* 12(2).

Building Bridges Collective (2010) *Space for Movement? Reflections from Bolivia on Climate Justice, Social Movements, and the State*, Leeds, UK: Footprint Workers Co-op, spaceformovement.wordpress.com (accessed 10 August 2012).

Bullard, N. (2010) 'Intervention by Climate Justice Now! Members to the Opening Session of the ad hoc Working Group on the Kyoto Protocol', 1 June, climatjustice. files.wordpress.com/2010/06/intervention-cjn-ouverture-awg-kp.pdf (accessed 10 August 2012).

Burawoy, M. (2003) 'A Sociological Marxism: The Complementary Convergence of Antonio Gramsci and Karl Polanyi', *Politics and Society* 31(2): 193–261.

Burbach, R. (2001) *Globalization and Postmodern Politics: From Zapatistas to High-Tech Robber Barons*, London: Pluto Press.

Burns, A. (2002) 'Hegel (1770–1831)', in A. Edwards and J. Townshend (eds) *Interpreting Modern Political Philosophy: From Machiavelli to Marx*, Basingstoke: Palgrave, 162–79.

Buttigieg, J.A. (1995) 'Gramsci on Civil Society', *boundary 2* 22(3): 1–32.

Byrd, S.C. (2005) 'The Porto Alegre Consensus: Theorizing the Forum Movement', *Globalizations* 2(1): 151–63.

CACIM (2009a) 'Indigenous People: "Another World is Possible" only if …', A report on the seminar entitled 'The Politics, Potentials, and Meanings of the WSF in Belém', 29 January, www.choike.org/2009/eng/informes/4601.html (accessed 26 July 2009).

——(2009b) 'Opening up the WSF: Rediscovering its Spirit', A report on a seminar organised by CACIM at the WSF in Belém, Brazil, on 29 January on 'Critically engaging with the principles underlying the WSF', 12 June, cacim.net/twiki/tiki-download_file.php?fileId=46 (accessed 10 August 2012).

CACIM and CCS (2007) 'In Defence of Open Space', World Social Forum Session, Indian Institute for Critical Action: Centre in Movement (CACIM) and the University of KwaZulu-Natal Centre for Civil Society (CCS) Durban, South Africa, 23 January, Nairobi.

Calderón, F., Piscitelli, A. and Reyna, J.L. (1992) 'Social Movements: Actors, Theories, Expectations', in S. Alvarez and A. Escobar (eds) *The Making of Social Movements in Latin America: Identity, Strategy and Democracy*, Boulder: Westview Press.

Caritas (2007) '2003–7 Globalising Solidarity: Caritas Internationalis Activities Report', www.caritas.org/Upload/R/Report-FRA07.pdf (accessed 21 September 2007).

Carroll, W.K. (2007) 'Hegemony and Counter-hegemony in a Global Field', *Studies in Social Justice* 1(1): 36–66.

Caruso, G. (2007) 'Organising Global Civil Society: The World Social Forum 2004', unpublished thesis, University of London.

——(2010a) 'Road to Dakar: The WSF Towards a New Emancipatory Universality', 26 May, giuseppecaruso.wordpress.com/2010/05/26/road-to-dakar-the-wsf-towards-a-new-emancipatory-universality/ (accessed 10 August 2012).

——(2010b) 'Downwind Towards Dakar? World Social Forum International Council Meeting Dakar November 2010', 20 November, giuseppecaruso.wordpress.com/2010/11/20/downwind-towards-dakar-world-social-forum-international-council-meeting-dakar-november-2010/ (accessed 10 August 2012).

——(2011) 'Preliminary Notes on the World Social Forum 2011, Dakar', 22 February, giuseppecaruso.wordpress.com/2011/02/22/a-preliminary-assessment-of-the-world-social-forum-2011-dakar/ (accessed 10 August 2012).

CEOS (2010) 'Critical Engagement with Open Space', mail.openspaceforum.net/mailman/listinfo/ceos_openspaceforum.net (accessed 31 May 2010).

Cerny, P.G. (2004) 'Mapping Varieties of Neoliberalism', *IPEG papers in Global Political Economy* 12 (May).

——(2006) 'Plurality, Pluralism, and Power: Elements of Pluralist Analysis in an Age of Globalization', in R. Eisfeld (ed.) *Pluralism: Developments in the Theory and Practice of Democracy*, Opladen and Farmington Hills: Barbara Budrich Publishers, 81–111.

Chandler, D. (2004a) *Constructing Global Civil Society*, Basingstoke: Palgrave.

——(2004b) 'Building Global Civil Society "from Below"?' *Millennium: Journal of International Studies* 33(2): 313–39.

——(2005) 'Constructing Global Civil Society', in G. Baker and D. Chandler (eds) *Global Civil Society: Contested Futures*, New York: Routledge, 149–70.

——(2007) 'Deriving Norms from "Global Space": The Limits of Communicative Approaches to Global Civil Society Theorising', *Globalizations* 4(2): 283–98.

——(2009a) *Hollow Hegemony: Rethinking Global Politics, Power and Resistance*, New York: Pluto Press.

——(2009b) 'The Global Ideology: Rethinking the Politics of the "Global Turn" in IR', *International Relations* 23(4): 530–47.

Charnock, G., Purcell, T. and Ribera-Fumaz, R. (2012) '¡Indignate!: The 2011 Popular Protests and the Limits to Democracy in Spain', *Capital & Class* 36(3): 3–11.

Chase-Dunn, C. (2011) 'Continuities and Transformations in the Evolution of World Systems: Terminal Crisis or a New Systemic Cycle of Accumulation', IROWS Working Paper 70, irows.ucr.edu/papers/irows70/irows70.htm (accessed 10 August 2012).

Chase-Dunn, C. and Gills, B. (2005) 'Waves of Globalization and Resistance in the Capitalist World System: Social Movements and Critical Global Studies', in R.P. Appelbaum and W.I. Robinson (eds) *Critical Globalization Studies*, New York: Routledge, 45–54.

Chase-Dunn, C. and Reese, E. (2006) 'Global Party Formation in World Historical Perspective', paper presented at the annual meeting of the International Studies Association, San Diego, 22 March (available in K. Sehm Patomaki and M. Ulvila (eds) 'Democratic Politics Globally: Elements for a Dialogue on Global Political Party Formations', NIGD Working Paper 1/2006).

Chávez, F. (2010) 'Cochabamba Conference Proposes Climate Justice Tribunal to Tackle Climate Change', *Third World Resurgence* 236, April, Third World Network, www.twnside.org.sg/title2/resurgence/2010/236/cover06.htm (accessed 10 August 2012).

Chin, C. and Mittelman, J.H. (1997) 'Conceptualising Resistance to Globalisation', *New Political Economy* 2(1): 25–38 (reprinted in B. Gills (ed.) (2000) *Globalization and the Politics of Resistance*, Basingstoke: Palgrave, Macmillan, 12–28).

Choonara, J. (2005) 'Marx or the Multitude: A Review', *International Socialism* 105: 9 January.

Clarke, I. (1998) 'Beyond the Great Divide: Globalization and the Theory of International Relations', *Review of International Studies* 24(4): 479–98.

——(1999) *Globalization and International Relations Theory*, Oxford: Oxford University Press.

——(2011) *Hegemony in International Society*, London: Palgrave.

Cohen, J.L. and Arato, A. (1992) *Civil Society and Political Theory*, MIT Press: Cambridge.

Colás, A. (2002) *International Civil Society*, Malden, MA: Blackwell Publishers.

Coleman, L.M. and Tucker, K. (2011) 'Between Discipline and Dissent', *Globalizations* 8(4): 397–410.

Committee on Civil Society (2007) 'The Committee on Civil Society Research, Sweden', wsfprocess.net/organisations/the-committee-on-civil-society-research-sweden/folder_ listing (accessed 5 February 2007).

Connell, R. (2007) *Southern Theory: The Global Dynamics of Knowledge in Social Science*, Cambridge/Sydney: Polity/Allen & Unwin.

Conway, J. (2005) 'Social Forums, Social Movements and Social Change: A Response to Peter Marcuse on the Subject of the World Social Forum', *International Journal of Urban and Regional Research* 29(2): 425–28.

——(2011) 'Cosmopolitan or Colonial? The World Social Forum as "Contact Zone"', *Third World Quarterly* 32(2): 217–36.

——(2012a) *Edges of Global Justice: The World Social Forum and its 'Others'*, London: Routledge.

——(2012b) 'Transnational Feminisms Building Anti-globalization Solidarities', *Globalizations* 9(3): 379–93.

Cox, R.W. (1981) 'Social Forces, States and World Order: Beyond International Relations Theory', *Millennium: Journal of International Studies* 10(2): 126–55 (reprinted in R. O'Keohane (ed.) (1986) *Neorealism and Its Critics*, New York: Columbia University Press, 204–54).

——(1983) 'Gramsci, Hegemony and International Relations: An Essay in Method', *Millennium: Journal of International Studies* 12(2): 162–75 (reprinted in R.W. Cox with T. Sinclair (1996) *Approaches to World Order,* Cambridge: Cambridge University Press, 124–43; reprinted in L. Amoore (ed.) (2005) *The Global Resistance Reader*, London: Routledge, 35–47; and also in S. Gill (ed.) (1993) *Gramsci, Historical Materialism and International Relations*, New York: Cambridge University Press, 49–67).

——(1987) *Production, Power and World Order: Social Forces in the Making of History*, New York: Columbia University Press.

——(1995) 'Critical Political Economy', in B. Hettne (ed.) *International Political Economy. Understanding Global Disorder*, London: Zed Books, 31–45.

——(with Sinclair, T.) (1996) *Approaches to World Order*, Cambridge: Cambridge University Press.

——(1999) 'Civil Society at the Turn of the Millennium: Prospects for an Alternative World Order', *Review of International Studies* 25(1): 3–28.

——(with Schechter, M.G.) (2002) *The Political Economy of a Plural World: Critical Reflections on Power, Morals and Civilization*, London: Routledge.

Cox, W.S. and Turenne Sjolander, C. (eds) (1994) *Beyond Positivism. Critical Reflections on International Relations*, Boulder: Lynne Rienner.

Cúpula dos Povos (2012a) 'Guiding Document: Dynamic and Methodology of the People's Summit', 10 April, cupuladospovos.org.br/en/2012/04/guiding-document-dinamic-and-methodology-of-the-peoples-summit/ (accessed 10 August 2012).

——(2012b) 'Final Declaration of the People's Summit at Rio+20', 19 July, cupuladospovos.org.br/en/2012/07/final-declaration-of-the-peoples-summit-at-rio20/ (accessed 10 August 2012).

Daly, G. (1999) 'Marxism and Postmodernity', in A. Gamble, D. Marsh and T. Tant (eds) *Marxism and Social Science*, Basingstoke: Macmillan, 61–84.

Davies, M. (1999) *International Political Economy and Mass Communication in Chile: National Intellectuals and Transnational Hegemony*, Basingstoke: Macmillan.

——(2006) 'Everyday Life in the Global Political Economy', in M. de Goede (ed.) *International Political Economy and Poststructural Politics*, London: Palgrave, 219–37.

Day, R. (2005) *Gramsci is Dead: Anarchist Currents in the Newest Social Movements*, London: Pluto.

Death, C. (2011) 'Summit Theatre: Exemplary Governmentality and Environmental Diplomacy in Johannesburg and Copenhagen', *Environmental Politics* 20(1): 1–19.

de Certeau, M. (2002) *The Practice of Everyday Life*, Berkeley: University of California Press.

de Goede, M. (2003) 'Beyond Economism in IPE', *Review of International Studies* 29 (1): 79–97.

——(2006) 'Introduction: International Political Economy and the Promises of Poststructural Politics', in M. de Goede (ed.) *International Political Economy and Poststructural Politics*, London: Palgrave, 1–20.

The Democracy Center (2011) 'An Open Letter About the Current Situation in Bolivia', 28 September, Global Justice Ecology Project, climate-connections.org/2011/09/28/an-open-letter-about-the-current-situation-in-bolivia/ (accessed 10 August 2012).

de Schutter, O. (2002) 'Europe in Search of its Civil Society', *European Law Journal* 8: 200–21.

Development Dialogue (2007) 'Global Civil Society: More or Less Democracy?' *Development Dialogue* (special issue) 49, www.dhf.uu.se/pdffiler/DD2007_49_civ_soc/development_dialogue_49.pdf (accessed 16 Dec 2008).

Devetak, R. and Higgott, R. (1999) 'Justice Unbound? Globalisation, States and the Transformation of the Social Bond', *International Affairs* 75(3): 483–98.

Dimitrov, R. (2010) 'Inside Copenhagen: The State of Climate Governance', *Global Environmental Politics* 10(2): 18–24.

Drainville, A. (1994) 'International Political Economy in the Age of Open Marxism', *Review of International Political Economy* 1(1): 105–32.

——(2004) *Contesting Globalization: Space and Place in the World Economy*, Oxford and New York: Routledge.

——(2005) 'Beyond *Altermondialisme*: Anti-capitalist Dialectic of Presence', *Review of International Political Economy* 12(5): 884–908.

——(2011) 'Global Discipline and Dissent in the Longue Durée', *Globalizations* 8(4): 411–23.

——(2012) *A History of World Order and Resistance: The Making and Unmaking of Global Subjects*, London: Routledge.

Dryzek, J.S. (2012) 'Global Civil Society: The Progress of Post-Westphalian Politics', *Annual Review of Political Science* 15(1): 1–19.

Duffield, M.R. (2007) *Development, Security and Unending War: Governing the World of Peoples*, London: Polity.

Dufour, P. and Giraud, I. (2007) 'Globalization and Political Change in the Women's Movement: The Politics of Scale and Political Empowerment in the World March of Women', *Social Science Quarterly* 88(5): 1152–73.

Engler, M. (2005) 'The Last Porto Alegre: Discerning the State of the World Social Forum after Five Years', *Foreign Policy in Focus*, www.fpif.org/papers/0502alegre. html (accessed 26 July 2009).

Eschle, C. (2001) 'Globalising Civil Society? Social Movements and the Challenge of Global Politics from Below', in P. Hamel, H. Lustiger-Thaler, J. Nederveen Pieterse and S. Roseneil (eds) *Globalization and Social Movements*, Basingstoke: Palgrave, 61–85.

——(2005) 'Constructing "the Anti-globalisation Movement"', in C. Eschle and B. Maiguashca (eds) *Critical Theories, International Relations and 'the Anti-Globalisation Movement'*, New York: Routledge, 17–35.

Eschle, C. and Maiguashca, B. (eds) (2005) *Critical Theories, International Relations and 'the Anti-Globalisation Movement'*, New York: Routledge.

——(2007) 'Rethinking Globalised Resistance: Feminist Activism and Critical Theorising in International Relations', *British Journal of Politics and International Relations* 9: 284–301.

——(2010) *Making Feminist Sense of the Global Justice Movement*, Plymouth: Rowman and Littlefield.

Evans, P. (2008) 'Is an Alternative Globalization Possible?' *Politics & Society* 36(2): 271–305.

Falk, R. (1998) 'Global Civil Society: Perspectives, Initiatives, Movements', *Oxford Development Studies* 26(1): 99–111.

——(2005) 'The Changing Role of Global Civil Society', in G. Baker and D. Chandler (eds) *Global Civil Society: Contested Futures*, New York: Routledge, 69–84.

Farrands, C. and Worth, O. (2005) 'Critical Theory in Global Political Economy: Critique? Knowledge? Emancipation?' *Capital & Class* 85: 43–61.

Fisher, D. (2010) 'COP-15 in Copenhagen: How the Merging of Movements Left Civil Society Out in the Cold', *Global Environmental Politics* 10(2): 11–17.

Fisher, W.F. and Ponniah, T. (eds) (2003) *Another World is Possible: Popular Alternatives to Globalization at the World Social Forum*, London and New York: Zed Books.

——(2004) 'Under a Tree at Porto Alegre: Democracy in its Most Radical Sense', in J. Sen, A. Anand, A. Escobar and P. Waterman (eds) *World Social Forum: Challenging Empires*, New Delhi: The Viveka Foundation, 178–82.

Flyvbjerg, B. (2001) *Making Social Science Matter: Why Social Inquiry Fails and How it Can Succeed Again*, Cambridge: Cambridge University Press.

FNTG (2011) 'Funder Delegation to the World Social Forum Dakar Senegal', Funders Network on Transforming the Global Economy, February 6–11, 2011', March, www.fntg.org/test/fntg/docs/WSF2011Report.pdf (accessed 10 April 2012).

Fontana, B. (2006) 'Liberty and Domination: Civil Society in Gramsci', *Boundary 2* 33 (2): 51–74.

Ford, L.H. (2003) 'Challenging Global Environmental Governance: Social Movements Agency and Global Civil Society', *Global Environmental Politics* 3(2): 120–34.

Foucault, M. (1980) *Introduction: History of Sexuality*, Vol. 1, New York: Vintage Books.

——(1987) 'The Ethics of Care for the Self as a Practice of Freedom', interview conducted by Raul Fornett-Betancourt, Helmut Becker and Alfredo Gomez Müller, in J.W. Bernauer and D.M. Rasmussen (eds) *The Final Foucault*, MIT Press, 1–20.

Frankfort-Nachmias, C. and Nachmias, D. (1996) *Research Methods in the Social Sciences*, 5th edn, London: St Martin's Press.

Fukuyama, F. (1989) 'The End of History?' *The National Interest* 16: 3–18.

George, S. (2011) 'To the Evaluation Team', letter dated 30 April, www.nigd.org (accessed 24 May 2011).

Germain, R.D. and Kenny, M. (1998) 'Engaging Gramsci: International Relations Theory and the New Gramscians', *Review of International Studies* 24(1): 3–21.

——(eds) (2005) *The Idea of Global Civil Society: Politics and Ethics in a Globalizing Era*, Oxfordshire: Routledge.

Gill, S. (ed.) (1993) *Gramsci, Historical Materialism and International Relations*, Cambridge: Cambridge University Press.

——(1995) 'Theorizing the Interregnum: The Double Movement and Global Politics in the 1990s', in B. Hettne (ed.) *International Political Economy: Understanding Global Disorder*, London: Zed Books, 65–99.

——(1996) 'Globalization, Democratization, and the Politics of Indifference', in J.H. Mittelman (ed.) *Globalization: Critical Reflections*, Boulder: Lynne Rienner, 203–29.

——(1997a) 'Transformation and Innovation in the Study of World Order', in S. Gill and J.H. Mittelman (eds) *Innovation and Transformation in International Studies*, Cambridge: Cambridge University Press, 5–25.

——(1997b) 'Gramsci, Modernity and Globalization', *International Gramsci Society*, online article, January 2003, wwwitalnetndedu/gramsci/resources/online_articles/ articles/gill01shtml (accessed 23 November 2006).

——(1999) 'Structural Change in Multilateralism: The G7 Nexus and the Global Crisis', in M. Schechter (ed.) *Innovation in Multilateralism*, Tokyo: United Nations University, 113–63.

——(2000) 'Toward a Postmodern Prince? The Battle in Seattle as a Moment in the New Politics of Globalization', *Millennium* 29(1): 131–41.

——(2002a) 'Constitutionalizing Inequality and the Clash of Globalizations', *International Studies Review* 4(3): 47–65.

——(2002b) 'Globalisation, Market Civilisation and Disciplinary Neo-liberalism', in E. Hovden and E. Keene (eds) *The Globalisation of Liberalism*, Basingstoke: Palgrave.

——(2003) *Power and Resistance in the New World Order*, Basingstoke: Palgrave Macmillan.

——(2005) 'Theorizing the Interregnum: The Double Movement and Global Politics in the 1990s', in L. Amoore (ed.) *The Global Resistance Reader*, London: Routledge, 54–64.

——(2008) *Power and Resistance in the New World Order*, second edn, Basingstoke: Palgrave Macmillan.

——(ed.) (2012a) *Global Crises and the Crisis of Global Leadership*, Cambridge: Cambridge University Press.

——(2012b) 'Towards a Radical Concept of Praxis: Imperial "Common Sense" Versus the Post-modern Prince', *Millennium: Journal of International Studies* 40(3): 505–24.

Gill, S. and Mittelman, J. (eds) (1997) *Innovation and Transformation in International Studies*, Cambridge: Cambridge University Press.

Gills, B.K. (ed.) (2000) *Globalization and the Politics of Resistance*, Basingstoke: Palgrave Macmillan.

——(2001) 'Re-orienting the New (International) Political Economy', *New Political Economy* 6(2): 233–45.

——(2003) 'Globalization as Global History: Introducing a Dialectical Analysis', in M. A. Tétreault, R.A. Denemark, K.P. Thomas and K. Burch (eds) *Rethinking Global Political Economy: Emerging Issues, Unfolding Odysseys*, London: Routledge, 89–108.

——(2005) '"Empire" Versus "Cosmopolis": The Clash of Globalizations', *Globalizations* 2(1): 5–13.

Gills, B.K. and Gray, K. (2012) 'People Power in the Era of Global Crisis: Rebellion, Resistance and Liberation', *Third World Quarterly* 33(2): 205–24.

Glasius, M., Kaldor, M. and Anheier, H. (2005) *Global Civil Society 2005/6*, London: Sage.

Goodman, J. (2009) 'From Global Justice to Climate Justice? Justice Ecologism in an Era of Global Warming', *New Political Science* 31(4): 499–514.

Gramsci, A. (1971) *Selections from the Prison Notebooks of Antonio Gramsci*, trans. by Q. Hoare and G. Nowell Smith, New York: International Publishers; London: Lawrence and Wishart.

GRAP (2011) 'Thematic Social Forum Porto Alegre 2012', Discussion and Support Group for the WSF Process and Gaucho organizing committees, 22 September, www.forumsocialmundial.org.br/noticias_01.php?cd_news=3402&cd_language=2 (accessed 10 August 2012).

Group of Nineteen (2005) 'Porto Alegre Manifesto', *ZNet*, 20 February, www.zmag.org/sustainers/content/2005-02/20group_of_nineteen.cfm (accessed 6 November 2007).

Grzybowski, C. (2001) 'World Social Forum: Something New was Born in Porto Alegre', *Social Watch*, www.socialwatch.org/en/informesTematicos/1.html (accessed 21 July 2009).

——(2006) 'The World Social Forum: Reinventing Global Politics', *Global Governance* 12: 7–13.

Hall, J. and Trentmann, F. (eds) (2005) *Civil Society: A Reader in History, Theory, and Global Politics*, Basingstoke: Palgrave Macmillan.

Hall, S. (1988) *The Hard Road to Renewal*, London: Verso.

Hamel, P., Lustiger-Thaler, H., Nederveen Pieterse, J. and Roseneil, S. (eds) (2001) *Globalization and Social Movements*, Basingstoke: Palgrave.

Hardt, M. (2002) 'Today's Bandung?' *New Left Review* 14: 112–18.

Hardt, M. and Negri, A. (2000) *Empire*, Cambridge, MA: Harvard University Press.

——(2005) *Multitude*, London: Penguin Books.

Hardt, M. and Weeks, K. (eds) (2000) *The Jameson Reader*, Oxford: Blackwell.

Harvey, M., Ramlogan, R. and Randles, S. (eds) (2007) *Karl Polanyi: New Perspectives on the Place of the Economy in Society*, Manchester: Manchester University Press.

Hegel, G.W.F. (1952 [1821]) *The Philosophy of Right*, trans. by T.M. Knox, in W. Benton (ed.) *Encyclopaedia Britannica: Great Books of the Western World*, Vol. 46, Chicago: University of Chicago Press, 64: 75–80.

Helleiner, E. (1997) 'Braudelian Reflections on Economic Globalisation: The Historian as Pioneer', in S. Gill and J.H. Mittelman (eds) *Innovation and Transformation in International Studies*, Cambridge: Cambridge University Press, 90–105.

——(2001) 'Review: The Promise and Reality of Transnational Social Movements', *International Studies Review* 3(3): 129–33.

Hettne, B. (ed.) (1995) *International Political Economy: Understanding Global Disorder*, London: Zed Books.

Hoffman, M. (1987) 'Critical Theory and the Inter-paradigm Debate', *Millennium: Journal of International Studies* 16(2): 231–49.

Holab, R. (1992) *Antonio Gramsci: Beyond Marxism and Postmodernism*, London: Routledge.

Hollis, M. and Smith, S. (1990) *Explaining and Understanding International Relations*, Oxford: Clarendon Press.

Horkheimer, M. (1972) *Critical Theory*, trans. M. O'Connell *et al.*, New York: Herder and Herder.

Houtart, F. (2010) 'Après Copenhague, Cochabamba Comme Alternative? Note d'analyse mai 2010', Centre Tricontinental, www.cetri.be/IMG/pdf/Cochabamba1. pdf (accessed 10 August 2012).

Howell, J. and Lind, J. (2009) *Counter-Terrorism, Aid and Civil Society*, Basingstoke: Palgrave Macmillan.

Howell, J. and Pearce, J. (2002) *Civil Society and Development: A Critical Exploration*, Boulder: Lynne Rienner.

Hutchings, K. (2001) 'The Nature of Critique in Critical IR Theory', in R. Wyn Jones (ed.) *Critical Theory and World Politics*, Boulder: Lynne Rienner Publishers, 79–90.

——(2005) 'Global Civil Society: Thinking Politics and Progress', in G. Baker and D. Chandler (eds) *Global Civil Society: Contested Futures*, New York: Routledge, 130–48.

——(2011) 'Dialogue Between Whom? The Role of the West/non-west Distinction in Promoting Global Dialogue in IR', *Millennium: Journal of International Studies* 39 (3): 639–47.

IBASE (2005) 'World Social Forum: An X-ray of Participation in the 2005 Forum: Elements for Debate', Brazilian Institute of Social and Economic Analyses, www. ibase.org.br/userimages/relatorio_fsm2005_INGLES2.pdf (accessed 10 June 2010).

——(2009) 'World Social Forum Participant Survey Report', www.forumsocialmundial. org.br/dinamic.php?pagina=memoria_fsm_2009_en (accessed 23 April 2010).

Imbach, P. (2009) 'A New Start with the 2009 WSF: An Interview with Eric Toussaint', *International Viewpoint Online Magazine* IV410 (March), www.internationalviewpoint.org/spip.php?article1621 (accessed 23 April 2010).

Imig, D. and Tarrow, S. (eds) (2001) *Contentious Europeans: Protest and Politics in an Emerging Polity*, Maryland: Rowman & Littlefield.

IPS (2008) 'Interview with Boaventura de Sousa Santos', 22 January, www.openspaceforum.net/twiki/tiki-read_article.php?articleId=542 (accessed 10 August 2012).

Jameson, F. (1990) 'Cognitive Mapping', in C. Nelson and L. Grossberg (eds) *Marxism and the Interpretation of Culture*, University of Illinois Press.

Jasanoff, S. and Martello, M. (2004) *Earthly Politics*, Cambridge, MA: MIT Press.

Jessop, B. (2001) 'Bringing the State Back in (Yet Again): Reviews, Revisions, Rejections, and Redirections', *International Review of Sociology* 11(2): 149–73.

——(2005) 'Gramsci as a Spatial Theorist', *Critical Review of International Social and Political Philosophy* 8(4): 421–37.

Jessop, B. and Sum, N.-L. (2001) 'Pre-disciplinary and Post-disciplinary Perspectives', *New Political Economy* 6: 89–101.

——(2006) 'Towards a Cultural International Political Economy: Poststructuralism and the Italian School', in M. de Goede (ed.) *International Political Economy and Poststructural Politics*, London: Palgrave, 157–75.

Joseph, J. (2010) 'The Limits of Governmentality: Social Theory and the International', *European Journal of International Relations* 16(2): 223–46.

Jubilee South (2008) 'Submission to the WSF International Council Strategy Debate', 10 March, www.forumsocialmundial.org.br/noticias_textos.php?cd_news=499 (accessed 10 August 2012).

Juris, J.S. (2008a) *Networking Futures: The Movements against Corporate Globalization*, Duke University Press.

——(2008b) 'Spaces of Intentionality: Race, Class and Horizontality at the United States Social Forum', *Mobilization* 13(4): 353–71.

Kaldor, M. (1999) 'The Ideas of 1989: The Origins of the Concept of Global Civil Society', *International Organization* 9(2): 475–88.

——(2000) '"Civilising" Globalisation? The Implications of the "Battle in Seattle"', *Millennium: Journal of International Studies* 29(1): 105–14.

——(2003a) 'The Idea of Global Civil Society', *International Affairs* 79(3): 583–93.

——(2003b) *Global Civil Society: An Answer to War*, Cambridge: Polity.

——(2005a) 'The Idea of Global Civil Society', in G. Baker and D. Chandler (eds) *Global Civil Society: Contested Futures*, New York: Routledge, 103–13.

——(2005b) 'Commentary on Keane', *Journal of Civil Society* 1(1): 43–44.

——(2007) 'Reply to David Chandler', *Globalizations* 4(2): 299–300.

——(2011) 'Civil Society in 1989 and 2011', *Open Democracy*, www.opendemocracy. net (accessed 11 February 2011).

Kaldor, M., Anheier, H. and Glasius, M. (eds) (2004) *Global Civil Society 2004/5*, London: Sage.

Karumba, T. (2007) '7e Forum social mondial de Nairobi: Quatre jours pour défendre la voix des "plus faibles"', *Le Monde*, www.lemonde.fr/web/portfolio/0,12-0@2-3220,31-857888@51-857571,0.html (accessed 22 October 2007).

Kaviraj, S. and Khilnani, S. (eds) (2001) *Civil Society: History and Possibilities*, Cambridge: Cambridge University Press.

Keane, J. (2001) 'Global Civil Society?' in H. Anheier, M. Glasius and M. Kaldor (eds) *Global Civil Society 2001*, Oxford: Oxford University Press, 23–47.

——(2002) 'Cosmocracy: A Global System of Governance or Anarchy', *New Economy* 65–70.

——(2003) *Global Civil Society*, Cambridge: Cambridge University Press.

——(2005a) 'Eleven Theses on Markets and Civil Society', *Journal of Civil Society* 1 (1): 25–34.

——(2005b) 'Cosmocracy and Global Civil Society', in G. Baker and D. Chandler (eds) *Global Civil Society: Contested Futures*, New York: Routledge, 34–51.

Keck, M.E. and Sikkink, K. (1998) *Activists Beyond Borders: Advocacy Networks in International Politics*, Ithaca, NY: Cornell University Press.

Kenfield, I. (2010) 'Social Movements for System Change', *Climate Justice Now!*, 19 April, www.climate-justice-now.org/social-movements-for-system-change/ (accessed 10 August 2012).

Kennemore, A. and Weeks, G. (2011) 'Twenty-first Century Socialism? The Elusive Search for a Post-neoliberal Development Model', *Bulletin of Latin American Research* 30(3): 267–81.

Kenny, M. and Germain, R.D. (2005) 'The Idea(l) of Global Civil Society', in R.D. Germain and M. Kenny (eds) *The Idea of Global Civil Society: Politics and Ethics in a Globalizing Era*, Oxfordshire: Routledge, 1–15.

Keraghel, C. and Sen, J. (2004) 'Explorations in Open Space: The World Social Forum and Cultures of Politics', *International Social Science Journal* 56(4): 483–93.

Khilnani, S. (2001) 'The Development of Civil Society', in S. Kaviraj and S. Khilnani (eds) *Civil Society: History and Possibilities*, Cambridge: Cambridge University Press, 11–32.

Kiely, R. (2000) 'Globalization: From Domination to Resistance', *Third World Quarterly* 21(6): 1059–70.

——(2007) *The New Political Economy of Development: Globalization, Imperialism, Hegemony*, London: Palgrave.

Kim, D. (2011) 'At WSF Dakar, Ambassador Solon, Bolivians Outreach to Build Climate Justice Movement for COP17 Durban and Rio+20', *The Strategy Center*, 28 February, www.thestrategycenter.org/node/5490/%20%20%20%20 (accessed 10 August 2012).

Knafo, S. (2002) 'The Fetishizing Subject of Marx's Capital', *Capital and Class* 76: 183–213.

Lacher, H. (1999a) 'The Politics of the Market: Re-reading Karl Polanyi', *Global Society* 13(3): 313–26.

Laclau, E. (2005) *On Populist Reason*, London: Verso.

Laclau, E. and Mouffe, C. (1985) *Hegemony and Socialist Strategy*, London: Verso.

Laffey, M. (2004) 'The Red Herring of Economism: A Reply to Marieke de Goede', *Review of International Studies* 30: 459–68.

——(2010) 'Things Lost and Found: Richard Ashley and the Silences of Thinking Space', *Review of International Studies* 36: 989–1004.

Lander, E. (2010) 'Reflections on the Cochabamba Climate Summit', Transnational Institute, April, www.tni.org/article/reflections-cochabamba-climate-summit (accessed 10 August 2012).

Larmer, M., Dwyer, P. and Zeilig, L. (2009) 'Southern African Social Movements at the 2007 Nairobi World Social Forum', *Global Networks* 9(1): 41–62.

Lee, K. (1995) 'A Neo-Gramscian Approach to International Organisations: An Expanded Analysis of Current Reforms to UN Development Activities', in J. Macmillan and A. Linklater, *Boundaries in Question: New Directions in International Relations*, London: Pinter, 144–62.

Lewis, D. (2002) 'Civil Society in African Contexts: Reflections on the Usefulness of a Concept', *Development & Change* 33(4): 569–86.

Linklater, A. (1996) 'The Achievements of Critical Theory', in K. Booth, S. Smith and M. Zalewski (eds) *International Theory: Positivism and Beyond*, Cambridge: Cambridge University Press, 279–97.

Lipschutz, R.D. (1992) 'Reconstructing World Politics: The Emergence of Global Civil Society', *Millennium: Journal of International Studies* 21(3): 389–420.

——(2005a) 'Global Civil Society and Global Governmentality: Resistance, Reform or Resignation?' in G. Baker and D. Chandler (eds) *Global Civil Society: Contested Futures*, New York: Routledge, 171–85.

——(2005b) 'Power, Politics and Global Civil Society', *Millennium: Journal of International Studies* 33(3): 747–69.

——(2007) 'The Historical and Structural Origins of Global Civil Society', *Globalizations* 4(2): 304–8.

——(2008) 'Why Not Perfect Harmony? Commentary on Jan Aart Scholte's Article "Civil Society and the Legitimation of Global Governance"', *Journal of Civil Society* 4(1): 71–72.

McNally, D. (1993) 'E.P. Thompson: Class Struggle and Historical Materialism', *International Socialism Journal* 61, pubs.socialistreviewindex.org.uk/isj61/mcnally. htm#23 (accessed 21 Sept 2010).

McNally, M. (2009) 'Conclusions: The Enduring Attraction of Gramscian Analysis', in M. McNally and J.J. Schwarzmantel (eds) *Gramsci and Global Politics: Hegemony and Resistance*, London: Taylor and Francis, 187–99.

McNally, M. and Schwarzmantel, J.J. (eds) (2009) *Gramsci and Global Politics: Hegemony and Resistance*, London: Taylor and Francis.

Maiguashca, B. (2006) 'Rethinking Power from the Point of View of Resistance: The Politics of Gender', in M. de Goede (ed.) *International Political Economy and Poststructural Politics*, London: Palgrave, 238–54.

Marchand, M.H. (2000) 'Some Theoretical "Musings" About Gender and Resistance', in R. Teske and M.A. Tétreault (eds) *Feminist Approaches to Social Movements, Community and Power*, Columbia: University of South Carolina Press, 56–71.

——(2003) 'Challenging Globalisation: Toward a Feminist Understanding of Resistance', *Review of International Studies* 29: 145–60.

——(2005) 'Some Theoretical "Musings" About Gender and Resistance', in L. Amoore (ed.) *The Global Resistance Reader*, London: Routledge, 215–25.

Marchand, M.H. and Runyan, A.S. (2000) *Gender and Global Restructuring: Sightings, Sites and Resistances*, London: Routledge.

Martens, K. (2008) 'Is Incorporating Civil Society Further into the Structure of Global Governance Really the Way Forward? Commentary on Jan Aart Scholte's Article "Civil Society and the Legitimation of Global Governance"', *Journal of Civil Society* 4(1): 73–75.

Marx, K. (1967 [1867]) *Capital: A Critique of Political Economy, Volume 1: The Process of Capitalist Production*, New York: International Publishers.

——(1993) *Grundrisse*, London: Penguin Books.

——(1995) *Capital*, Oxford: Oxford University Press.

Melucci, A. (1980) 'The New Social Movements: A Theoretical Approach', *Social Science Information* 19: 199–226.

Mestrum, F. and Bacal, A. (2007) 'IC Berlin WSF 2009. News from the International Council of the WSF Berlin 29–31 May 2007—WSF 2009', *Network Institute for Global Democratization*, www.nigd.org/nan/nan-doc-store/05-2007/ic-berlin-wsf-2009 (accessed 8 June 2007).

Mittelman, J.H. (ed.) (1996) *Globalization: Critical Reflections*, Boulder: Lynne Rienner.

——(2004) *Whither Globalization? The Vortex of Knowledge and Ideology*, London: Routledge.

——(2005) 'What is a Critical Globalization Studies?' in R.P. Appelbaum and W.I. Robinson (eds) *Critical Globalization Studies*, New York: Routledge, 19–32.

Morales, W.Q. (2012) 'Social Movements and Revolutionary Change in Bolivia', in G. Prevost *et al.* (eds) *Social Movements and Leftist Governments in Latin America*, London: Zed, 49–87.

Morton, A.D. (2000) 'Mexico, Neoliberal Restructuring and the EZLN: A Neo-Gramscian Analysis', in B. Gills (ed.) *Globalization and the Politics of Resistance*, Basingstoke: Palgrave Macmillan, 255–79.

——(2003) 'Historicizing Gramsci: Situating Ideas in and Beyond their Context', *Review of International Political Economy* 10(1): 118–46.

——(2007a) *Unravelling Gramsci: Hegemony and Passive Revolution in the Global Political Economy*, London: Pluto.

——(2007b) 'Unquestioned Answers/Unanswered Questions in IPE: A Rejoinder to "Non-Marxist" Historical Materialism', *Politics* 27(2): 132–36.

Munck, R. (2002) 'Global Civil Society: Myths and Prospects', *Voluntas: International Journal of Voluntary and Nonprofit Organizations* 13(4): 349–61.

——(2006a) 'Globalization and Contestation: A Polanyian Problematic', *Globalizations* 3(2): 175–86.

——(2006b) 'Global Civil Society: Royal Road or Slippery Path', *Voluntas: International Journal of Voluntary and Nonprofit Organizations* 17: 325–32.

——(2007) *Globalization and Contestation: The New Great Counter-Movement*, Oxon: Routledge.

Murphy, C.N. (1994) *International Organization and Industrial Change: Global Governance since 1850*, Cambridge: Polity.

——(1998) 'Understanding IR: Understanding Gramsci', *Review of International Studies* 24: 417–25.

——(2000) 'Global Governance: Poorly Done and Poorly Understood', *International Affairs* 4: 789–803.

——(ed.) (2002) *Egalitarian Politics in the Age of Globalization*, London: Palgrave Macmillan.

Murphy, C.N. and Tooze, R. (eds) (1991) *The New International Political Economy*, Boulder: Lynne Rienner Publishers.

Nederveen Pieterse, J. (2001) *Development Theory: Deconstructions/ Reconstructions*, London: Sage.

Negrón-Gonzales, Jason (2010) 'Cochabamba Postscript: Lessons, Reflections, and the Road to Cancun', *Yes! Magazine*, 26 April, www.yesmagazine.org/blogs/a-peoples-climate-summit/cochabamba-postscript-lessons-reflections-and-the-road-to-cancun (accessed 10 August 2012).

Neufeld, M. (1994) 'Reflexivity and International Relations Theory', in C. Sjolander and W. Cox (eds) *Beyond Positivism: Critical Reflections on International Relations*, Boulder: Lynne Rienner, 11–37.

——(1995) *The Restructuring of International Relations Theory*, Cambridge: Cambridge University Press.

——(2001a) 'What's Critical About Critical International Relations Theory?' in R. Wyn Jones (ed.) *Critical Theory and World Politics*, Boulder: Lynne Rienner, 127–45.

——(2001b) 'Theorising Globalisation: Towards a Politics of Resistance. A Neo-Gramscian Response to Mathias Albert', *Global Society* 15(1): 93–106.

——(2002) 'Democratic Socialism in a Global(-izing) Context: Towards a Collective Research Programme', Trentu International Political Economy Centre Working Paper 02/04.

O'Brien, R., Goetz, A.M., Scholte, J.A. and Williams, M. (2000) *Contesting Global Governance: Multilateral Economic Institutions and Global Social Movements*, Cambridge: Cambridge University Press.

Olesen, T. (2005) 'World Politics and Social Movements: The Janus Face of the Global Democratic Structure', *Global Society* 19(2): 109–29.

Open Space Forum (2006) 'Signatories to the Bamako Appeal', *Open Space Forum*, www.openspaceforum.net/twiki/tiki-read_article.php?articleId=138 (accessed 8 November 2007).

Osterweil, M. (2004a) 'The Dynamics of Open Space: A Cultural-political Approach to Reinventing the Political', *International Social Science Journal* 56(4): 496–506.

——(2004b) 'De-centering the Forum: Is Another Critique of the Forum Possible?' in J. Sen, A. Anand, A. Escobar and P. Waterman (eds) *World Social Forum: Challenging Empires*, New Delhi: The Viveka Foundation, 183–90.

Parekh, B. (2004) 'Putting Civil Society in its Place', in M. Glasius, D. Lewis and H. Sechinelgin (eds) *Exploring Civil Society: Political and Cultural Contexts*, Routledge: London, 14–23.

Parmar, I. (2006) 'Anti-Americanism and Major Foundations', in B.O. Connor and M. Griffiths (eds) *The Rise of Anti-Americanism*, London: Routledge, 169–94.

Pasha, M. Kamal and Blaney, D.L. (1998) 'Elusive Paradise: The Promise and Peril of Global Civil Society', *Alternatives: Global, Local, Political* 23(4): 417–50.

Patomäki, H. (2007) 'The Role of "Critical" in the Theory and Practice of Global Civil Society', *Globalizations* 4(2): 312–17.

Patomäki, H. and Teivainen, T. (2004a) *A Possible World: Democratic Transformation of Global Institutions*, London: Zed.

——(2004b) 'The World Social Forum: An Open Space or a Movement of Movements?' *Theory, Culture & Society* 21(6): 145–54.

Patten, A. (2003) 'Hegel', in D. Boucher and P. Kelly (eds) *Political Thinkers: From Socrates to the Present*, New York: Oxford University Press, 383–403.

Payne, A. (2005) 'The Study of Governance in a Global Political Economy', in N. Phillips (ed.) *Globalizing International Political Economy*, Basingstoke: Palgrave Macmillan, 55–81.

Pearce, J. (1997) 'Civil Society, the Market, and Democracy in Latin America', *Democratization* 4(2): 57–83.

——(2004) 'Civil Society, the Market, and Democracy in Latin America', in P. Burnell and P. Calvert (eds) *Civil Society in Democratization*, Portland: Taylor & Francis, 90–116.

Pearse, R. (2010) 'Making a Market? Contestation and Climate Change', *Journal of Australian Political Economy* 66: 166–98.

Peet, R. (2007) *Geography of Power: The Making of Global Economic Policy*, London: Zed.

Peet, R., Robbins, P. and Watts, M. (eds) (2011) *Global Political Ecology*, London: Routledge.

People's Agreement (2010) 'People's Agreement', World People's Conference on Climate Change and the Rights of Mother Earth, 22 April, Cochabamba, Bolivia, pwccc.wordpress.com/support/ (available 26 February 2012).

Petras, J. and Veltmeyer, H. (2009) *What's Left in Latin America? Regime Change in New Times*, Burlington, VT: Ashgate.

Pianta, M., Silva, F. and Zola, D. (2004) 'Global Civil Society Events: Parallel Summits, Social Fora, Global Days of Action (update)', in H. Anheier, M. Glasius and M. Kaldor (eds) *Global Civil Society 2004/05*, London: Sage.

Pleyers, G. (2010) *Alter-Globalization: Becoming Actors in the Global Age*, Cambridge: Polity Press.

Polanyi, K. (2001) *The Great Transformation: The Political and Economic Origins of Our Time*, second edn, Boston: Beacon Press.

Ponniah, T. (2009) 'World Social Forum 2009: Time to Bring the WSF to the USA', *World Forum for Alternatives*, www.forumdesalternatives.org/EN/readarticle.php?article_id=5714 (accessed 22 July 2009).

Poster, M. (2001) 'Michel Foucault', in J. Krieger (ed.) *The Oxford Companion to the Politics of the World*, Oxford University Press, *Oxford Reference Online*, www.oxfordreference.com.proxy.lib.ul.ie/views/ENTRY.html?subview=Main&entry=t121.e0259 (accessed 20 October 2010).

Power, M. (2010) 'Geopolitics and "Development"', *Geopolitics* 15(3): 433–40.

Powless, B. (2010a) 'A Grassroots Agenda for Climate Change', Redeye Vancouver Cooperative Radio, interview, rabble.ca/podcasts/shows/redeye/2010/05/coming-grassroots-agenda-climate-change (accessed 10 August 2012).

——(2010b) 'Summit Difference', *New Internationalist* 433: 26–27.

Prevost, G., Oliva Campos, C. and Vanden, H.E. (eds) (2012) *Social Movements and Leftist Governments in Latin America*, London: Zed.

Prozorov, S. (2011) 'Critical Exchange on R.B.J. Walker's *After the Globe Before the World* (2010) Is World Politics a World Away?' *Contemporary Political Theory* 10 (2): 286–310.

Putnam, R. (2000) *Bowling Alone: The Collapse and Revival of American Community*, New York: Simon and Schuster.

Raina, V. (2008) 'Do Space and Actions have to be Contradictory? Towards an Inclusive WSF Strategy', *World Social Forum*, 22 February, www.forumsocialmundial.org.br/noticias_textos.php?cd_news=480 (accessed 10 August 2012).

Rayner, T. (2005) 'Refiguring the Multitude: From Exodus to the Production of Norms', *Radical Philosophy* 131: 28–38.

Redman, J. (2010) 'Cochabamba's Message: Let the People Speak', *Yes! Magazine*, 29 April, www.yesmagazine.org/blogs/a-peoples-climate-summit/cochabambas-message-let-the-people-speak (accessed 10 August 2012).

Reitan, R. (2007) *Global Activism*, Oxon: Routledge.

Rengger, N.J. (2001) 'Negative Dialectic? The Two Modes of Critical Theory in World Politics', in R. Wyn Jones (ed.) *Critical Theory and World Politics*, Boulder: Lynne Rienner, 91–110.

Research Unit for Political Economy (2003) 'The Economics and Politics of the World Social Forum', 35, www.rupe-india.org/index.html (accessed 1 November 2007).

Richter, I.K., Berking, S. and Müller-Schmid, R. (eds) (2006) *Building a Transnational Civil Society: Global Issues and Global Actors*, Palgrave Macmillan.

Robinson, F. (2003) 'Human Rights and the Global Politics of Resistance: Feminist Perspectives', *Review of International Studies* 29: 161–80.

Robinson, W.I. (1996) *Promoting Polyarchy: Globalization, US Intervention, and Hegemony*, Cambridge: Cambridge University Press.

——(2002) 'Latin America in an Age of Inequality: Confronting the New "utopia"', in C. N. Murphy (ed.) *Egalitarian Politics in the Age of Globalization*, Basingstoke: Palgrave.

——(2005) 'Gramsci and Globalisation: From Nation-state to Transnational Hegemony', *Critical Review of International Social and Political Philosophy* 8(4): 559–74.

Ruggie, J. (1993) 'Territoriality and Beyond: Problematizing Modernity in International Relations', *International Organization* 47(1): 139–74.

Rupert, M. (2000) *Ideologies of Globalisation: Contending Visions of a New World Order*, London: Routledge.

——(2003) 'Globalising Common Sense: A Marxian-Gramscian (Re-)vision of the Politics of Governance/Resistance', *Review of International Studies* 29: 181–98.

Rupert, M. and Solomon, M.S. (2006) *Globalization and International Political Economy: The Politics of Alternative Futures*, Oxford, UK: Rowman and Littlefield.

Sahabandhu, J. (2006) 'Portraying the person and the work of Francois Houtart', *Australian EJournal of Theology*, 8 October, dlibrary.acu.edu.au/research/theology/ejournal/aejt_8/houtart.htm (accessed 2 June 2007).

Sanbonmatsu, J. (2004) *The Postmodern Prince: Critical Theory, Left Strategy, and the Making of a New Political Subject*, New York: Monthly Review Press.

——(2009) 'The Crisis of the Global Left', *ZNet*, www.zcommunications.org/the-crisis-of-the-global-left-part-one-by-john-sanbonmatsu (accessed 6 July 2010).

Santos, B. de Sousa (2004) *The World Social Forum: A User's Manual*, Madison, www.ces.uc.pt/bss/documentos/fsm_eng.pdf (accessed 22 March 2007).

——(2006a) *The Rise of the Global Left: The World Social Forum and Beyond*, London: Zed Books.

——(2006b) 'Globalizations', *Theory, Culture, Society* 23: 393–99.

——(2007) 'The World Social Forum and the Global Left', paper prepared for the Politics and Society mini-conference, New York, 9 August, www.focusweb.org/node/1326 (accessed 10 August 2012).

——(2008) 'The World Social Forum and the Global Left', *Politics & Society* 36(2): 247–70.

Scholte, J.-A. (1993a) *International Relations of Social Change*, Buckingham: Open University Press.

——(1993b) 'From Power Politics to Social Change: An Alternative Focus for International Studies', *Review of International Studies* 19(1): 3–21.

——(2002) 'Civil Society and Democracy in Global Governance', *Global Governance* 8: 281–304.

——(2004) 'Civil Society and Democratically Accountable Global Governance', *Government and Opposition* 39(2): 211–33.

——(2007a) 'Civil Society and the Legitimation of Global Governance', *Centre for the Study of Globalisation and Regionalisation*, Working Paper No. 223/07, www2.warwick.ac.uk/fac/soc/csgr/research/workingpapers/2007/wp22307.pdf (accessed 30 July 2007).

——(2007b) 'Civil Society and the Legitimation of Global Governance', *Journal of Civil Society* 3(3): 305–26.

——(2008) 'Thoughts on Agency: A Response to Lipschutz and Martens', *Journal of Civil Society* 4(1): 77–79.

——(ed.) (2011) *Building Global Democracy? Civil Society and Accountable Global Governance*, Cambridge: Cambridge University Press.

Schouten, P. (2009) 'Theory Talk #37: Robert Cox on World Orders, Historical Change, and the Purpose of Theory in International Relations', *Theory Talks*, www.theory-talks.org/2010/03/theory-talk-37.html (accessed 10 August 2012).

Schuurman, F.J. (2000) 'Paradigms Lost, Paradigms Regained? Development Studies in the Twenty-first Century', *Third World Quarterly* 21(1): 7–20.

——(2009) 'Critical Development Theory: Moving Out of the Twilight Zone', *Third World Quarterly* 30(5): 831–48.

Scott, J.C. (1990) *Domination and the Arts of Resistance: Hidden Transcripts*, US: Yale University Press.

Sehm-Patomäki, K. and Ulvila, M. (2006) 'Political Parties and Global Democratisation: Lessons from the Past and Future Prospects', *Network Institute for Global Democratization*, Discussion Paper 1, www.nigd.org/nigd-publications/discussion-papers/?searchterm=sehm%20and%20ulvila%202006 (accessed 30 Jul 2007).

Sen, J. (2007) 'The World Social Forum as an Emergent Learning Process', *Futures* 39 (5): 505–22.

——(2009) 'On Open Space: Explorations Towards a Vocabulary of a More Open Politics', *Open Space Forum*, www.openspaceforum.net/twiki/tiki-index.php (accessed 28 July 2009).

——(2010) 'On Open Space: Explorations Towards a Vocabulary of a More Open Politics', *Antipode* 42(4): 994–1018.

Sen, J., Anand, A., Escobar, A. and Waterman, P. (eds) (2004) *World Social Forum: Challenging Empires*, New Delhi: The Viveka Foundation, www.choike.org/nuevo_eng/informes/1557.html (accessed 26 July 2007).

Sen, J. and Kumar, M. (with Bond, P. and Waterman, P.) (2007) *A Political Programme for the World Social Forum? Democracy, Substance and Debate in the Bamako Appeal and the Global Justice Movements. A Reader*, Indian Institute for Critical Action: Centre in Movement (CACIM) New Delhi, India and the University of KwaZulu-Natal Centre for Civil Society (CCS) Durban, South Africa, www.cacim.net/bareader/home.html (accessed 26 July 2007).

Shaw, M. (2003) 'The Global Transformation of the Social Sciences', *Global Civil Society Yearbook*, Centre for Civil Society, London School of Economics Online, www.lse.ac.uk/collections/CCS/ (accessed 13 August 2004).

Shields, S., Bruff, I. and Macartney, H. (eds) (2011) *Critical International Political Economy: Dialogue, Debate and Dissensus*, London: Palgrave.

Sjolander, C. and Cox, W. (eds) (1994) *Beyond Positivism: Critical Reflections on International Relations*, Boulder: Lynne Rienner.

Skidmore, D. (2001) 'Civil Society, Social Capital and Economic Development', *Global Society* 15(1): 53–72.

Sklair, L. (2002) *Globalization: Capitalism and its Alternatives*, Oxford: Oxford University Press.

Smismans, S. (2003) 'European Civil Society: Shaped by Discourses and Institutional Interests', *European Law Journal* 9(4): 482–504.

——(ed.) (2006) *Civil Society and Legitimate European Governance*, Northampton, MA: Edward Elgar.

Smith, H. (1996) 'The Silence of the Academics: International Social Theory, Historical Materialism and Political Values', *Review of International Studies* 22: 191–212.

Smith, J., Karides, M., Becker, M., Brunelle, D., Chase-Dunn, C., della Porta, D., Icaza Garza, R., Juris, J.S., Mosca, L., Reese, E., Smith, P.J. and Vazquez, R. (2008) *Global Democracy and the World Social Forums*, Boulder and London: Paradigm Publishers.

Smith, S. (1987) 'Paradigm Dominance in International Relations: The Development of International Relations as a Social Science', *Millennium Journal of International Studies* 16: 2.

Smith, S., Booth, K. and Zalewski, M. (eds) (1996) *International Theory: Positivism and Beyond*, Cambridge: Cambridge University Press.

Söderbaum, F. (2007) 'Regionalisation and Civil Society: The Case of Southern Africa', *New Political Economy* 12(3): 319–37.

Strange, S. (1995) 'Political Economy and International Relations', in K. Booth and S. Smith (eds) *International Relations Theory Today*, Polity: Cambridge, 154–75.

Sum, N.-L. (2009) 'Towards Gramscianizing Foucault: A Way of Developing Cultural Political Economy', IAS Research Cluster and CPERC, 'Foucault and Critical Realism Workshop 2: Marx, Gramsci and Foucault', Lancaster University, 27 July, www.lancs.ac.uk/cperc/docs/Foucault-CR2-Sum-short-ppt.pdf (accessed 20 October 2010).

Tarrow, S. (1998) *Power in Movement: Social Movements and Contentious Politics*, 2nd edn, New York: Cambridge University Press.

Taylor, R. (2002) 'Interpreting Global Civil Society', *Voluntas: International Journal of Voluntary and Nonprofit Organizations* 13(4): 339–47.

——(2004) *Creating a Better World: Interpreting Global Civil Society*, CT: Kumarian Press.

Teivainen, T. (2002) 'The World Social Forum and Global Democratisation: Learning from Porto Alegre', *Third World Quarterly* 23(4): 621–32.

——(2006) 'WSF 2009: Dilemmas of Decision-making on the Periodicity of the Forums', News and Notes, *Network Institute for Global Democratization*, www.nigd.org (accessed 9 June 2010).

——(2007) 'The Political and its Absence in the World Social Forum: Implications for Democracy', *Development Dialogue* 49: 69–79.

——(2012) 'Global Democratization without Hierarchy or Leadership? The World Social Forum in the Capitalist World', in S. Gills (ed.) *Global Crisis and the Crisis of Global Leadership*, Cambridge: Cambridge University Press.

Terrier, J. and Wagner, P. (2006) 'The Return of Civil Society and the Reopening of the Political Problématique', in P. Wagner (ed.) *The Languages of Civil Society*, New York: Berghahn Books, 223–34.

Thomas, G.D. (1998) 'Civil Society: Historical Uses versus Global Context', *International Politics* 35(2): 49–64.

Thomas, P. (2009) *The Gramscian Moment: Philosophy, Hegemony and Marxism*, Leiden: Brill.

Thompson, E.P. (1963) *The Making of the English Working Class*, London: Penguin.

——(1978) *The Poverty of Theory and Other Essays*, London: Merlin Press.

Thompson, P. (2003) 'Foundation and Empire: A Critique of Hardt and Negri', *Capital and Class* 83: 73–87.

Tocqueville, A. de (1945 [1835]) *Democracy in America*, New York: Vintage Books.

Townshend, J. (2002) 'Marx (1818–83)', in A. Edwards and J. Townshend (eds) *Interpreting Modern Political Philosophy: From Machiavelli to Marx*, Basingstoke: Palgrave, 198–218.

UN-NGLS (2009) 'World People's Conference on Climate Change and the Rights of Mother Earth', The United Nations Non-Governmental Liaison Service, www.un-ngls.org/spip.php?page=article_s&id_article=2394 (accessed 10 August 2012).

Urry, J. (2005) *Global Complexity*, Cambridge: Polity.

van Apeldoorn, B. (2000) 'Transnational Class Agency and European Governance: The Case of the European Round Table of Industrialists', *New Political Economy* 5(2): 157–81.

van der Pijl, K. (1984) *The Making of an Atlantic Ruling Class*, London: Verso.

——(1997) 'Transnational Class Formation', in S. Gill and J.H. Mittelman (eds) *Innovation and Transformation in International Studies*, Cambridge: Cambridge University Press, 115–38.

——(1998) *Transnational Classes and International Relations*, London: Routledge.

——(2001) 'Restoring the Radical Imagination in Political Economy', *New Political Economy* 6(3): 380–90.

——(2009) *A Survey of Global Political Economy*, ebook, www.sussex.ac.uk/ir/research/gpe/gpesurvey/ (accessed 21 September 2010).

Velitchkova, A., Smith, J. and Choi-Fitzpatrick, A. (2009) 'Windows on the Ninth World Social Forum in Belém', *Societies Without Borders* 4: 193–208.

Via Campesina (2010a) 'Social Movements for System Change', *Via Campesina*, 21 April, viacampesina.org/en/index.php/actions-and-events-mainmenu-26/-climate-change-and-agrofuels-mainmenu-75/880-social-movements-for-system-change (accessed 10 August 2012).

——(2010a) 'Invitation to the Assembly of Social Movements', *Via Campesina*, 23 March, www.viacampesina.org/en/index.php?view=article&catid=48%3A-climate-change-and-agrofuels&id=887%3Ainvitation-to-the-assembly-of-social-movements &option=com_content&Itemid=75 (accessed 21 February 2012).

Wagner, P. (ed.) (2006) *The Languages of Civil Society*, New York: Berghahn Books.

Wainwright, H. (2005) 'Civil Society, Democracy and Power: Global Connections', in H. Anheier, M. Glasius and M. Kaldor (eds) *Global Civil Society 2004/05*, London: Sage, 94–119.

Walker, R.B.J. (1988) *One World, Many Worlds: Struggles for a Just World Peace*, Boulder: Lynne Rienner Publications.

——(1993) *Inside/Outside: International Relations as Political Theory*, Newcastle upon Tyne: Cambridge University Press.

——(1994) 'Social Movements/World Politics', *Millennium: Journal of International Studies* 23(3): 669–700.

——(2005) 'Social Movements/World Politics', in L. Amoore (ed.) *The Global Resistance Reader*, London: Routledge, 136–49.

——(2010) *After the Globe, Before the World*, London: Routledge.

Wallerstein, I. (2004) 'The Dilemmas of Open Space: The Future of the WSF', *International Social Science Journal* 56(4): 629–37.

——(2007) 'The World Social Forum from Defense to Offense', *Agence Global*, 31 January, www.openspaceforum.net/twiki/tiki-read_article.php?articleId=328 (accessed 1 March 2007).

Warleigh, A. (2001) '"Europeanizing" Civil Society: NGOs as Agents of Political Socialization', *Journal of Common Market Studies* 39: 619–39.

Waterman, P. (2004a) 'The Global Justice and Solidarity Movement and the World Social Forum: A Backgounder', in J. Sen, A. Anand, A. Escobar and P. Waterman (eds) *The World Social Forum: Challenging Empires*, New Delhi: The Viveka Foundation, 55–66.

——(2004b) 'Globalization from the Middle? Reflections from a Margin', in J. Sen, A. Anand, A. Escobar and P. Waterman (eds) *The World Social Forum: Challenging Empires*, New Delhi: The Viveka Foundation, 87–94.

——(2006) 'The Bamako Appeal of Samir Amin: A Post-modern Janus?' CSGR Working Paper No. 212/06, University of Warwick, Centre for the Study of Globalisation and Regionalisation, www2.warwick.ac.uk/fac/soc/csgr/research/ workingpapers/2006/wp21206.pdf (accessed 10 August 2012).

——(2009) 'Labour at the 2009 Belém World Social Forum: Between an Ambiguous Past and an Uncertain Future', 24 January, blog.choike.org/eng/anlysis/188 (accessed 14 May 2010).

——(2010) 'Five, Six, Many New Internationalisms!' 6 April, blog.choike.org/eng/ peter-waterman/919 (accessed 20 February 2012).

Whitaker, F. (2003) 'Communication from the Brazilian Commission of Justice and Peace Regarding the World Social Forum', presented at The National Conference of the Bishops of Brazil 41st General Assembly, Itaicí, near Indaiatuba, São Paulo State, 30 April–9 May, www.franciscansisters.org/english/jpic/articles/ BishopsandWorldSocForum.htm (accessed 4 July 2007).

——(2004) 'World Social Forum: Origins and Aims', 20 June, www2.forumsocialmundial.org.br/dinamic.php?pagina=origem_fsm_ing (accessed 2 July 2007).

——(2007) 'Crossroads do Not Always Close Roads: Reflections in Continuity to Walden Bello', www.wsflibrary.org/index.php?title=Crossroads_do_not_always_close_roads&printable = yes (accessed 25 June 2007).

Whitaker, F., Santos, B. de Sousa and Cassen, B. (2006) 'The World Social Forum: Where do we Stand and Where are we Going?' in M. Glasius, M. Kaldor and H. Anheier (eds) *Global Civil Society 2005/6*, London: Sage.

Wilkinson, R. (2005) 'Managing Global Civil Society: The WTO's Engagement with NGOs', in R. Germain and M. Kenny (eds) *The Idea of Global Civil Society: Politics and Ethics in a Globalising Era*, London: Routledge, 156–74.

Wilkinson, R. and Hughes, S. (eds) (2002) *Global Governance: Critical Perspectives*, London: Routledge.

Williams, M. (2005) 'Globalization and Civil Society', in J. Ravenhill (ed.) *Global Political Economy*, Oxford: Oxford University Press, 344–69.

Williams, P. and Taylor, P. (2000) 'Neoliberalism and the Political Economy of the "New" South Africa', *New Political Economy* 5(1): 21–40.

WMW (2004) 'Women's Global Charter for Humanity', 10 December, World March of Women, www.marchemondiale.org/qui_nous_sommes/en/ (accessed 10 August 2012).

——(2007) 'The World March of Women and the World Social Forum: Evaluation of the Current Situation', World March of Women, September, www.marchemondiale. org/alliances_mondialisation/cmicfolder.2005-03-02.3713067089/cmicarticle.2007-11-13.2494214198/en (accessed 10 August 2012).

——(2008) 'Where Change is Needed: The World March of Women and the Debate About WSF's Future', February, www.forumsocialmundial.org.br/noticias_textos. php?cd_news=471 (accessed 13 August 2008).

——(2008a) 'Information on Alliances Policy: Document Prepared for the Debate on Alliances During the VII International Meeting, held in Galicia, in October 2008', www.marchemondiale.org/alliances_mondialisation/cmicfolder.2005-03-02.3713067089/alliances2008/en (accessed 10 August 2012).

World Council of Churches (2008) 'Views About the Future of the WSF', www.forumsocialmundial.org.br/noticias_textos.php?cd_news=494 (accessed 13 August 2008).

Worth, O. (2006) 'Accumulating the Critical Spirit: The Legacy of Rosa Luxemburg', paper presented at the British International Studies Annual Conference, 18–20 December.

——(2008) 'The Poverty and Potential of Gramscian Thought in International Relations', *International Politics* 45, 6(4): 633–49.

——(2011) 'Recasting Gramsci in International Politics', *Review of International Studies* 37(1): 373–92.

——(2012) 'Accumulating the Critical Spirit: Rosa Luxemburg and Critical IPE', *International Politics* 49(2): 136–53.

——(2013) *Resistance in the age of Austerity. Nationalism, the Failure of the Left and the Return of God*, London: Zed Books.

Worth, O. and Buckley, K. (2009) 'The World Social Forum: Post-modern Prince or Court Jester?' *Third World Quarterly* 30(4): 649–61.

——(2011) 'Is Another World Possible? Problems and Shortcomings of the World Social Forum', in L. Reydams (ed.) *The Global Activism Reader*, New York: Continuum.

Worth, O. and Kuhling, C. (2004) 'Counter-hegemony, Anti-globalisation and Culture in International Political Economy', *Capital & Class* 84: 31–42.

WPCCC (2010) 'World People's Conference on Climate Change and the Rights of Mother Earth: Building the People's Movement for Mother Earth', pwccc.wordpress.com (accessed 21 February 2012).

WSF (2002a) 'World Social Forum Charter of Principles', 8 June, www.forumsocialmundial.org.br/main.php?id_menu=4&cd_language=2 (accessed 25 July 2007).

——(2002b) 'International Council Document on the Barcelona Meeting', 22 August, www.forumsocialmundial.org.br/main.php?id_menu=4_2_2_4&cd_language=2 (accessed 10 August 2012).

——(2005a) 'Report on the World Social Forum International Council Meeting, Utrecht Holland from March 31st to April 2nd 2005', www.forumsocialmundial.org.br/main.php?id_menu=3_2_2&cd_language=2 (accessed 1 November 2007).

——(2005b) 'Report on the World Social Forum International Council Meeting in Barcelona, June 20–22, 2005', www.forumsocialmundial.org.br/main.php?id_menu=3_2_2& cd_language = 2 (accessed 5 November 2007).

——(2006a) 'World Social Forum Financial Strategy: Final Report and Recommendations', www.nigd.org/docs/WSFFinancialStrategyReportRecommendations (accessed 11 June 2008).

——(2006b) 'Brief Report of the World Social Forum IC Meeting in Parma Italy, October 10–12, 2006', World Social Forum Technical Office, www.forumsocialmundial.org.br/main.php?id_menu=3_2_2&cd_language=2 (accessed 11 June 2008).

——(2007) 'Frequently Asked Questions About the World Social Forum 2007', wsf2007.org/info/faq (accessed 22 October 2007).

——(2008a) 'Report on the WSF International Council Meeting, Abuja, Nigeria, March 31 to April 3, 2008', World Social Forum Technical Office, www.forumsocialmundial.org.br/main.php?id_menu=3_2_2&cd_language=2 (accessed 11 June 2010).

——(2008b) 'Guiding Principles for Holding WSF Events', openfsm.net/projects/organizingwsfevents/guiding-principles-en (accessed 26 July 2009).

——(2009) 'World Social Forum 2009: Converging of Networks to Face the Global Crisis', www.forumsocialmundial.org.br/noticias_01.php?cd_news=2556&cd_language=2 (accessed 21 July 2009).

——(2011) 'WSF International Council Meeting Report, Dakar, Senegal, February 12–13 2011', www.forumsocialmundial.org.br/download/IC%20Meeting%20Dakar%20Feb%202011%20EN.pdf (accessed 10 August 2012).

WSFDiscuss (2010) Online archive, openspaceforum.net/pipermail/worldsocialforum-discuss_openspaceforum.net/ (accessed 31 May 2010).

WSF OC (2007) 'Organizing Committee of WSF 2007 Narrative Report: People's Struggles, People's Alternatives', April, Nairobi, Kenya, wsf2007.net/wsf2007-evaluation-final-narrative-report-available-online (accessed 20 October 2008).

Wyn Jones, R. (ed.) (2001) *Critical Theory and World Politics*, Boulder: Lynne Rienner

Index

For Product Safety Concerns and Information please contact our EU
representative GPSR@taylorandfrancis.com
Taylor & Francis Verlag GmbH, Kaufingerstraße 24, 80331 München, Germany

9 781138 909403